# THE COMPLETE BOOK OF
# WOOD JOINERY

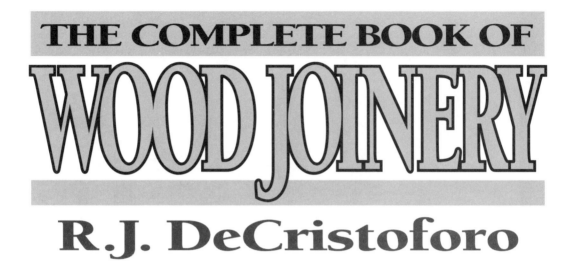

# THE COMPLETE BOOK OF
# WOOD JOINERY

## R.J. DeCristoforo

Sterling Publishing Co., Inc.
New York

10   9   8   7   6   5   4   3   2

Published by Sterling Publishing Company, Inc.
387 Park Avenue South, New York, N.Y. 10016
First published in 1992 by Meredith Books
Copyright © 1997 by R. J. DeCristoforo
Distributed in Canada by Sterling Publishing
% Canadian Manda Group, One Atlantic Avenue, Suite 105
Toronto, Ontario, Canada M6K 3E7
Distributed in Great Britain and Europe by Cassell PLC
Wellington House, 125 Strand, London WC2R 0BB, England
Distributed in Australia by Capricorn Link (Australia) Pty Ltd.
P.O. Box 6651, Baulkham Hills, Business Centre, NSW 2153, Australia
*Manufactured in the United States of America*

Sterling ISBN 0-8069-9950-0

# CONTENTS

## 1 FUNDAMENTALS OF WOOD JOINTS 1

Stresses • Joints Should Mesh • Measuring and Marking • Basic Measuring Tools • Markers • Hole Locations • Sharp Tools and Smooth Cuts • Power Sawing • Dowels • Splines • Buttons and Plugs • Wood Screws • Nails • Glue and Corner Blocks • Corner Blocks • Some Mechanical Fasteners • Hiding Edges • Round Projects From Flat Boards

## 2 BUTT JOINTS 51

Grain Direction • Reinforcement • Glue Blocks and Strips • Reinforcing Frame Butts • Hiding the Joint • Interlocks

## 3 DADOES AND GROOVES 59

Hiding the Joint • Reinforcement • Cutting with Hand Tools • Power Tool Work • Back-to-Back Dadoes • Stopped Dadoes • Corner Dadoes • Other Methods

## 4 RABBET JOINTS 71

Typical Applications • Forming with Hand Tools • Power Tool Work • Stopped Rabbets • Angled Rabbets

## 5 MITER JOINTS 83

Accuracy Is Critical • The Miter Box • Table Saw Work • Radial Arm Saw Cuts • Reinforcements *(Splines, Feathers, Dowels)* • Compound Miter Joints *(With Hand Tools, With Power Tools, With Splines, On a Radial Arm Saw)* • Special Miter Joints *(Tongue-and-Groove Miter, Housed Rabbet-Miter, True Rabbet-Miter, Locked Rabbet-Miter)*

## PLATE JOINERY

## MISCELLANEOUS JOINTS AND TREATMENTS

Drop Leaf Table Joint • Lock Corner Joint • Combination Dado Rabbet • The Waterfall Joint • Milled Drawer Joint • Door Joints • Cogged Joint • Round Corner Joints • Square Rail to Round Leg • Rounds to Flats • Two Special Slab Joints • Methods for Locking Joints

## SCULPTURED JOINTS

• Transition Pieces

## CHEST OR CASE CONSTRUCTIONS

## GLUING

General Considerations • Polyvinyl Resin Glue • Animal (Liquid Hide) Glue • Casein Glue • Plastic Resin Glue • Resorcinol Resin Glue • Aliphatic Resin Glue • Epoxy Cement • Urea Resin • Contact Cements

## CLAMPS AND CLAMP USE

Handscrews • Bar Clamps • Hinged Bar Clamps • Clamp Fixtures • C-Clamps • Three-Way Edging-Clamp • Band Clamps • Edge Clamp Fixtures • Miter Clamps • Spring Clamps • Universal Clamp • Improvising

# PREFACE

There is more to a piece of furniture, or any woodworking project, than meets the eye. What you see affects your sense of beauty, a factor that eludes definition. But what is not visible is tangible, bearing on the quality and permanence of the project and reflecting the dedication of the person who constructed it. All quality projects, regardless of their function or how the design affects the viewer, have one thing in common: connections that hold and last and that tell of careful craftsmanship.

Classic period pieces, many of which are still useful, not simply displayed in museums, are often revered as examples of a particular historical period and style, but they are valued antiques because they were assembled to resist the test of time, use, and abuse. They reflect not only admirable woodworking techniques but also the character of the manufacturer.

Joint-making is an art that involves practical knowledge and a strong intent. We might take a cue from the word "joiner," a term that was at one time a title indicating a highly skilled woodworker. It's possible that the term applied more to house construction than it did to furniture and cabinet-making, but the point is that it indicated the elite — the craftsman responsible for the visible interior carpentry that required tight, artistic connections.

Many furniture joints can't be seen so, unfortunately, both in commercial and custom work, this critical element of construction is often approached haphazardly. The most elaborate project made with the most exotic wood is of little value if it is poorly engineered. The best available glue will not substitute for uneducated joint selection or for inaccurate cuts. In terms of permanence and efficiency, construction ranks much higher than the materials.

An understanding of woodworking joints, their applications, and the cutting procedures involved, is often the difference between *superior, acceptable,* and *bad* work. But there is yet another factor — the intimacy between the worker and the wood.

Enjoyment and pride in working are opposite commercialism and any planned or unintended obsolescence. They have to do with the challenge *in the doing* that makes the final result an almost anticlimactic experience.

The choice of which joints to make and the degree of expertise with which you choose to execute them is a personal thing, regardless of available tools. Some people think that hand work can't match the precision of machine production. The thought has some validity, but only when applied to mechanical monsters that spew out hundreds of clones. Our main concern is with custom work by an individual producing one project that, like a work of art, can't be duplicated.

The craftsperson in industry has become less visible because of the need for mass production. There are engineers and designers and architects who do the creative work and the planning, and there are shop people who tend the machines that edge a board, form a mortise, or drill a hole. However, the fact that the tool must be set up to do a single thing uniformly and consistantly is to the advantage of the custom designer and worker. Production machines do not have talent and are completely disinterested in what they are programmed to do.

The individual, whether his or her interest is therapeutic or vocational, can use hand or power tools, or both. A quality project should not be discredited because it was done with power tools. It requires less time to rip or crosscut a board on a table saw or a radial arm saw than it does than it does to do the job with a hand saw, and it certainly consumes less energy. In the final analysis, if a hole is made correctly on a drill press or with a portable electric drill, it will be indistinguishable from a similar hole bored with a bit and brace.

Dovetails made with a portable router will be precise and uniform, but the job can also be done in competitive fashion by the dedicated craftsman working with a dovetail saw and chisels. The size and shape of the dovetails made with the router are determined by the finger template that is used with the power tool. The difference between template guidance and hand tool work is in flexibility of design. The average template is designed for uniformity in shape and size of tails and sockets. The custom worker doesn't have to follow such a pattern. He can, for example, design a joint with a large dovetail centered between two smaller ones or opt for several different size versions that are structurally correct and more pleasing esthetically than a line of machine-produced clones.

A person can be spoiled by machines by limiting himself to the cuts that can be made with a power tool, but this is a personal choice. It is not true that there are fewer craftsmen because there are more and more machines available — the machines are the servants, not the masters.

Actually, a power tool is merely an extension of a hand tool. It has built-in components that help increase accuracy and consistency, but the user must still set up the tool and guide the work. Errors are possible whether work is done with hand or power tools.

School shops today have more sophisticated machinery than the average homeowner or often, even the professional worker might dream of owning, but this should not result in fewer or inferior craftsmen — not if the instructor can relate the mysticism of a tree to projects made from its wood. Wood is alive in more than the biologic sense. Being intimate with the material is as important as using tools correctly. The ceramicist feels the clay with his fingers and establishes a close bond. A woodworker should touch the wood, feel its pattern, and relate to it. Intimacy is more feasible when working with hand tools, but it's really a moot point. Wood responds whether it is worked with hand or power tools. The modern woodworker establishes a balance between hand and power tool use.

Old-timers made many of their tools and no doubt this created a special atmosphere, a camaraderie that carried over to the job being done. But the fact that we buy our tools today doesn't mean that we can't have the same workshop climate. It's all in the mind and attitude.

In joint design, making a fetish of complicated connections is a fault. A good principle is to choose the least elaborate joint that is suitable for the assembly. There is little point is being more complicated than necessary when, for example, installing storage shelves against studs in a garage. The built-in shelves made with shop-grade plywood don't call for the joints that should go with a walnut grandfather's clock. Always, the material and the intent set the stage.

By way of example, I can relate the story of a kitchen table and chairs project I undertook when the furniture was needed now and not intended as heirloom pieces. Knotty pine was the material, the fanciest joint was a rabbet, and the bonding agents were glue and nails. The chairs remained squeak-free for an impressivly long period of time, but then, what could not be seen became vocal. The project was successful, however. It delivered what was needed and expected — but no more. The moral is, be true to the purpose. If I had presented the project as an example of super craftsmanship, it would have been fraudulent.

It's important to be honest. No one can be criticized for the quickie job if that is what is needed and wanted. After all, a heavy plank sitting on cement-block legs does make a suitable, if temporary, bench for a patio. Fraud occurs when the project is visually pleasing, but functionally and structurally deficient.

Folks who buy or make custom-designed and executed pieces are seeking more than a storage unit or something to sit on. They are truly interested in quality work and materials, especially when the two go hand-in-hand with function. They know that high construction standards usually go together with original and exclusive designs.

In all situations, the craftsman should keep in mind the answers to two questions: How long should this project last? Should I envision it as an heirloom?

Although it is not the purpose of this book to teach the use of tools, it is necessary, to show tools being used to make various cuts. Whenever you use tools, powered or not, you are in danger of being hurt. Be aware of this, maintain respect for the tool, and accept that it can't think for you. Never be overconfident. Statistics show that professionals, more so than amateurs, suffer injuries because of carelessness or disregard of basic safety rules.

When you encounter an unusual procedure or a technique you haven't tried before, do a dry run first. That is, go through the operation with the power *off*. Thus, you preview the course of action and judge the safe way to use your body and hands.

Showing a method with a photograph or drawing often makes it necessary, for clarity, to illustrate the procedure without the safety guards that would ordinarily be used. We *do not* recommend that you work this way. *Always* use safety guards. Being careful is wiser than being sorry. Tools that can cut wood can cut you. And finally, remember two woodworking adages — *Measure twice, cut once* and *Think twice before cutting.*

# FUNDAMENTALS OF WOOD JOINTS

Stresses • Joints Should Mesh • Measuring and Marking • Basic Measuring Tools • Markers • Hole Locations • Sharp Tools and Smooth Cuts • Power Sawing • Dowels • Splines • Buttons and Plugs • Wood Screws • Nails • Glue and Corner Blocks • Corner Blocks • Some Mechanical Fasteners • Hiding Edges • Round Projects from Flat Boards

There are two important factors when choosing a wood joint — appearance and strength. Appearance decisions can go to opposite extremes. You can design to conceal the joint, or you can intentionally expose it as a design element or because it reveals quality construction. Examples of the latter connections are dovetails, fingerlaps (or box joints), and mortise-tenons that are husked or pegged. Often, dowels are allowed to project from a surface, or screw holes are covered with wooden buttons (**Fig. 1-1**) instead of plain plugs that can be sanded flush for maximum concealment.

**1-1 Projecting dowels and prominent wood buttons are compatible with the heavy appearance of the chair frame.**

1

**1-2 Side panels composed of rails, stiles, and recessed inserts contribute to the hand-carved appearance of the mini-chest.**

Quite often the design of the project dictates the appearance of joints even though this may not be the basic intent. Compare the sides of the mini-chest shown in **Figure 1-2** with a similar project made with sides of plain plywood. Here, the side assembly consists of rails, stiles, and raised solid wood panels. Various joints are involved. For example, the panel edges fit grooves that are formed in the vertical frame pieces (*stiles*) and the horizontal ones (*rails*). The rails have a tenon at

each end that also mates with the grooves in the stiles. To emphasize the carved or three dimensional design, the inside edges of the rails and stiles are chamfered to introduce additional planes.

The casual observer will be affected by the visual impact of the design, but the experienced worker will know that the joints and the method of assembly were actually part of the builder's creative process. The final result was envisioned before sawing began.

The strength factor is easy to understand and accept. It applies to simple and complex projects and to all joints. Fortunately, there is such a variety of possible connections that the designer can make the optimum choice in relation to the project and its purpose. Movable shelves in a cabinet or closet, or dividers in a chest or drawer justify a less demanding approach than, say, the strong union that should exist between the front of a drawer and its sides, or all the joints in a chair.

It's said, justifiably, that if you can construct a strong, durable chair, you can build just about anything. The design of the chair, whether like the rocker shown in **Figure 1-3** or a more straightforward piece like a dining chair, doesn't matter. While most pieces of furniture are assembled so the components stay together while supporting contents, chairs must be engineered to stay rigid under constant use, and abuse, by users of various sizes and weights.

The design of a rocking chair usually dictates that components be assembled with what are essentially dowel joints. The *dowels* will be an integral part of, for example, a leg where it connects to the seat and the rocker. Other chairs, especially those with a conventional leg-rail assembly, can be assembled with routine dowel joints or mortise-tenon joints.

**1-3 Chairs, especially rockers, rank high among projects that require strong, durable joints.**

In any case, with all projects, while the *design* of the joint might be arbitrary, the *execution* is not. Quality work must prevail. Accepting that joints are projects within a project places anyone on the road to enviable craftsmanship.

## STRESSES

In addition to internal stresses caused by changes in moisture content that occur in any piece of wood, and which we will discuss from time to time, there are the more obvious physical stresses on joints and glue lines. **Figure 1-4** shows the most common forces that tend to separate connections and offers examples of modifications and additions that will parry negative factors.

A first step in the design of any project is to preview its function and to judge what forces will contribute to potential failure at any point. A mental picture might do for some, but it's better to prepare a sketch, no matter how rough. Use arrows to indicate the direction of stresses on each joint: point up critical areas.

An example —- The major stress on a trestle design (**Fig. 1-5A**) like you might use for a sawhorse occurs when the project is used as legs for a temporary scaffold. Even though the connection between the top of the legs and the beam can be reinforced with bolts or lag screws, there is always the tendency for the legs to splay outward. The danger of failure increases with use. A simple brace (**Fig. 1-5B**) placed across the legs is a major contribution toward a sounder, more durable project.

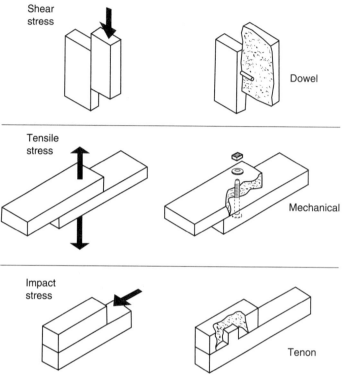

**1-4 Some of the stresses that joints and glue lines must resist.**

In this example the builder decided to "limit" his contribution. While the nailed-on brace is a simple solution, the half dovetail design shown in **Figure 1-5C** does a superior job because it furnishes an interlock that holds parts together. The extra effort reveals

**1-5 Trestle joints. The design at (C) will provide most stability and durability because of the interlocking feature.**

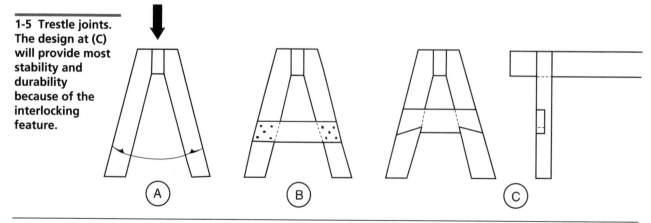

that the worker anticipated a possible failure point and that he took pride in his work even though it was a prosaic sawhorse.

To a great extent, the trestle idea applies to tables and benches. The connection between leg and top is least likely to fail when the leg is vertical (**Fig. 1-6A**). If the leg is slanted in any direction (**Fig. 1-6B**), the stress on the joint increases, and it's likely that the legs will eventually loosen, especially if the project is a bench or a low table that people are apt to sit on.

To guard against failure, many constructions in this area employ a substructure composed of rails and stretchers (**Fig. 1-6C**). Often, only rails are used, but it would be preferable to provide four of them so a top view of the leg-rail assembly would show a closed frame. Regardless of design, it's best to consider the substructure as an individual project that will stand rigidly and permanently on its own. View the top as a platform, not as a reinforcement. Usually, especially when the top is solid lumber, the attachment allows a degree of movement to guard against splits and cracks that can be caused by internal stresses.

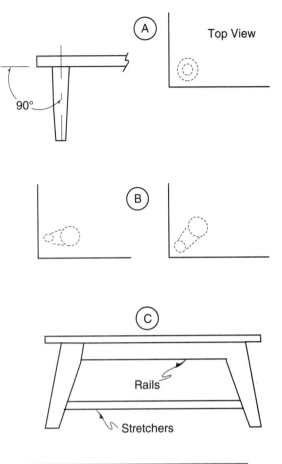

**1-6  Rails and stretchers that provide strength and durability are standard components of many table and bench assemblies.**

**1-7  The arrows indicate the major stresses that a drawer must withstand.**

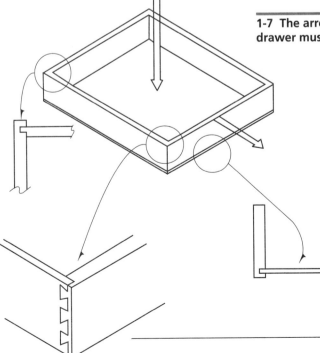

A drawer is punished most where the drawer front joins the sides (**Fig. 1-7**). There is a tendency for the parts to separate each time the drawer is pulled out. The heavier the contents of the drawer, the greater the stress. That's why the dovetail is commonly used at those points. The sockets and tails form an interlock that will hold the parts together even if the glue should fail.

A reasonable substitute for the dovetail is shown in **Figure 1-8**. The

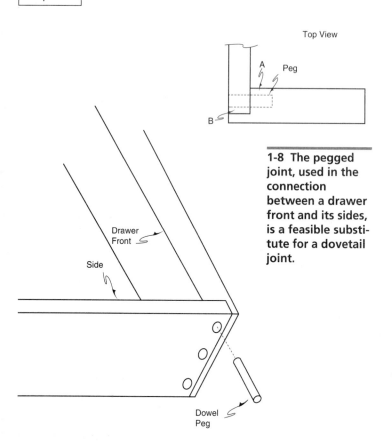

Top View

A

Peg

B

**1-8 The pegged joint, used in the connection between a drawer front and its sides, is a feasible substitute for a dovetail joint.**

Drawer Front

Side

Dowel Peg

whose contents weigh only ounces, as with stamps or pencils or napkins?" Obviously, the stresses will be minimal when compared to a shop drawer that will hold tools.

The answer is twofold. The drawer itself must withstand hundreds of openings and closings and, again, the design can reveal the dedication and pride of the builder. The correct reaction to the material being used is also a consideration. We don't react as negatively when simple joints, reinforced with mechanical fasteners, are used with shop grade plywood as we would if similar methods were used with walnut or Honduras mahogany.

## JOINTS SHOULD MESH

Joint planes that do not make maximum contact will not result in strong bonds. No amount or type of glue or wood dough can compensate for a sloppy fit. The contact areas of even a butt joint should be seriously viewed before final assembly. If you hold the parts together against some backlighting and see slivers of light coming through, accept that one or both of the components require additional attention.

Conversely, joint surfaces that do not mesh nicely without excessive clamp force or blows from a mallet can cause serious problems. A dowel that fits too tightly, especially if it is not designed to allow for the escape of air and excess glue, can cause splitting. It's not strange for excess glue, unable to escape as it should, to find passages through the pores of the wood and emerge on a surface where it forms a glaze that causes blemishes in the finish. An oversize tenon or tail in a dovetail joint also subjects the mating part to unnecessary strain, which merely adds to the stresses the area must withstand.

Joint components that come together as they should facilitate assembly procedures. It's frustrating and discouraging to coat parts

drawer front is rabbeted to receive the sides, and short dowels are added as illustrated. View the joint without glue and it is obvious that the dowels fight the stresses that occur when the drawer is pulled out. The diameter of the dowels should not be so great that wood surrounding them at points "A" and "B" (**Fig. 1-8**) will be too slight for strength.

Drawer bottoms are also likely to fail since they must support contents. Inserting them in grooves cut in the sides and front — not necessarily the back — is a common way to add strength. The back of the drawer also takes punishment since drawer contents often slide to the rear. Since the back also contributes to the rigidity of the project as a whole, the back-to-sides connection is as critical as any. This is often just a butt joint but designing to let the back into dadoes cut in the sides is a stronger method.

The question is often asked, "Why use the more complicated joints on a drawer with glue and then discover they will not mate nicely even under clamp pressure. The answer is to work carefully and accurately when cutting and to do a dry run before final assembly. That is, assemble components without glue and with only hand pressure so you can check the fit before you take the final step.

## MEASURING AND MARKING

Acceptable tolerances in woodworking may not be as critical as the standards in a machine shop, yet the importance of accuracy when cutting and fitting joint pieces should not be viewed casually. It will not be a disaster if all the shelves in a bookcase are 1/16-inch longer or shorter than they should be, but if the lengths vary, there will be trouble at assembly time. The sides of the project will have slight waves when you pull parts together. Some shelves will be weaker than others, and there will be occasional gaps.

It's a good idea not to tolerate inaccuracy. An oversize or off-center hole will make a poor dowel joint. An "obese" tenon can cause the mortised part to split, while one that is undersize just won't do its job. Being accurate starts with measuring and marking carefully. There are a host of tools that will help, but they are useless if they are not used with precision. Measuring and checking more than once is a good approach.

## BASIC MEASURING TOOLS

Flexible *push-pull rules* (**Fig. 1-9**), often called *steel tapes* or *flex tapes*, are justifiably popular because they are easy to use, store, and carry. Some, like the one shown, have a built-in device that locks the tape at any extended

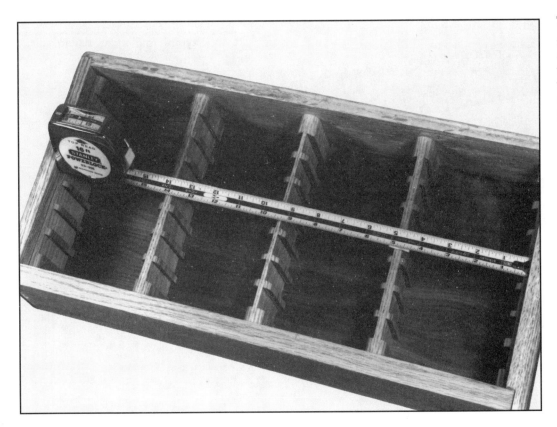

**1-9 A flexible steel tape with a built-in lock that will hold the blade at any extended position.**

position. Common graduations are in six-teenths and eighths of an inch, but tapes are also available in metric and in inch-metric measures so conversions can be made while working.

Lengths vary from 3 feet to 100 feet, blade widths from 1/4-inch to 1 inch. A tape used in a wood shop should be at least 8 feet, since that is the longest dimension of a stan-dard plywood panel. A width of 1/2-inch or 3/4-inch is good, since it will provide neces-sary stiffness when the blade is extended.

Choosing a unit that has a recessing or swiveling tip is a personal decision. You can make mistakes with either one. Be sure a recessing tip is kept clean, so it will move smoothly when used to check inside or out-side dimensions. Be sure to move a swivel tip aside when checking an inside distance, so that you will not add the thickness of the tip to the dimension.

The folding wood rule (**Fig. 1-10**), or *zigzag rule*, as it is often called because of the way it folds, has always been popular with carpenters and cabinetmakers. The most common length is 6 feet, but rules are also available in 8 foot lengths. Like flex tapes, folding rules may be marked in inches, met-rics, or metric-inches. An advantage of the folding rule is that several of the blades can project at a right angle from the others which makes it easy to reach inside a project for a measurement. Also, since metal joints lock the blades, the units serve as pretty rigid mea-suring devices no matter how many are extended.

Some folding rules have one or two built-in brass slides so the rule is convenient to use for inside measuring (**Figs. 1-11** and **1-12**). The slides are removable so they can be used as short bench rules or for depth measurements.

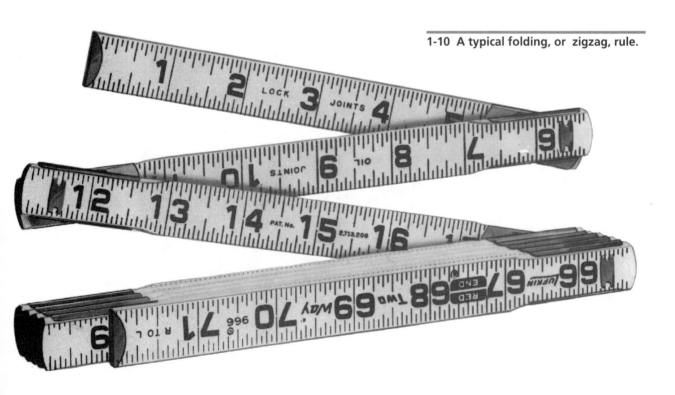

**1-10 A typical folding, or zigzag, rule.**

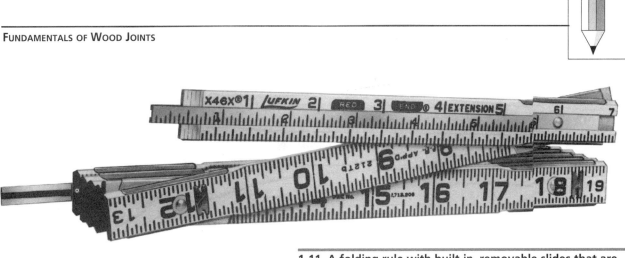

1-11  A folding rule with built-in, removable slides that are actually small measuring devices.

1-12  A folding rule with a built-in slide can be used to take inside measurements.

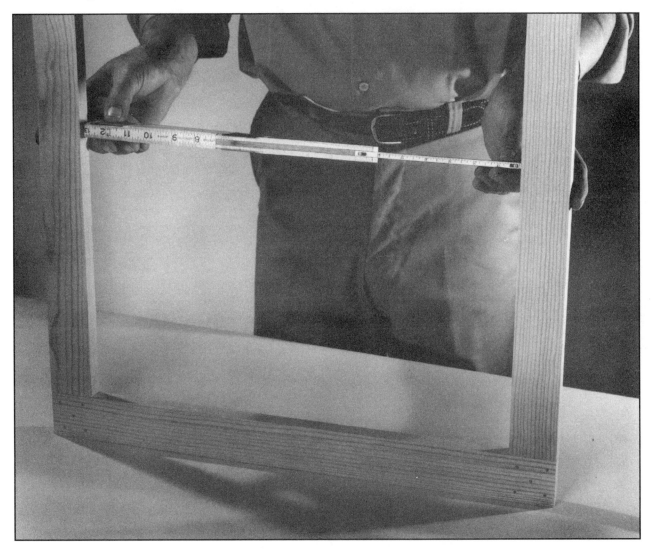

A *marking gauge*, like the one shown in **Figure 1-13**, is an important part of any woodworker's tool kit. Some are made with fixed points. Others, like the example, have removable pins that can be easily sharpened or replaced with a strip of pencil lead. The latter type is recommended since there are times when you will want to choose between marking with a steel point or a pencil point.

A common mistake when using a marking gauge is demonstrated in **Figure 1-14**. Holding the pin vertically makes it easy to snag the point. It also increases drag which can result in a rough, inaccurate line. Correct usage is shown in **Figure 1-15**. Place the beam flat on the work so the pin or lead will travel smoothly as you move the gauge. This method also allows a clear view of the point. Always pull the gauge *away* from the point. Moving in the opposite direction will cause the point to dig in.

The beam is marked so the head of the gauge can be set to a specific dimension, but checking with a second rule before marking the work is a good idea. Testing the setting on a piece of scrap is also wise. Since the head of the gauge rides the edge of the work when marking a line parallel to an edge (**Fig. 1-16**), the layout line will not be accurate unless the work-edge is smooth and straight.

**1-13 This type of marking gauge can be used with steel or pencil lead points.**

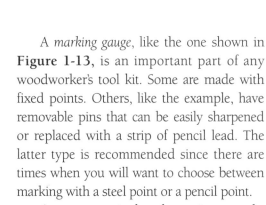

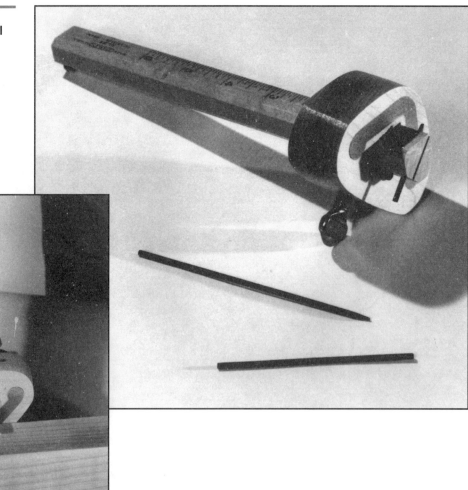

**1-14 The wrong way to use a marking gauge. The point, especially a steel one, will surely snag.**

*Squares* are important layout tools and especially useful when it's necessary to mark at right angles to a line or an edge. The ALL-IN-ONE® concept is a variation of the conventional combination square (**Fig. 1-17**). The head is designed so it can be used for drawing small circles, or as a protractor, or for checking screw gauges. Like many other squares, it has a built-in scriber and a vial so the head may be used as a level. The removable blade has equally spaced holes so that, by using a scriber

in one hole and a pencil in another, it can be used to mark arcs or circles. Like other squares, it is used as shown in **Figure 1-18** to draw lines at right angles to an edge. Be sure the blade is locked securely and that the head is held snugly against the edge of the work as you move the pencil.

Other types of squares, which will be shown in use later, are the *combination square*, whose head permits drawing lines at 45 degrees as well as 90 degrees, and the *try*

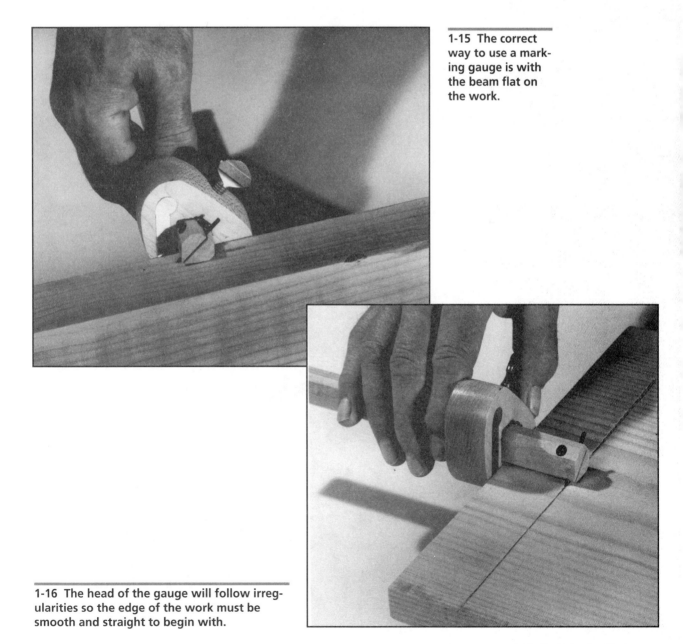

1-15 The correct way to use a marking gauge is with the beam flat on the work.

1-16 The head of the gauge will follow irregularities so the edge of the work must be smooth and straight to begin with.

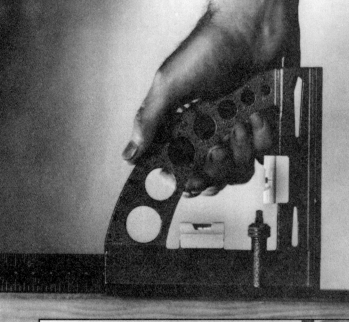

1-17 This type of square is used for more than drawing lines or checking edges. One of the extra features is the tapered slots that are used to check screw gauges.

1-18 Keep the head of the square firmly against the work. Rotating the pencil as it is moved will prevent it from developing a flat point.

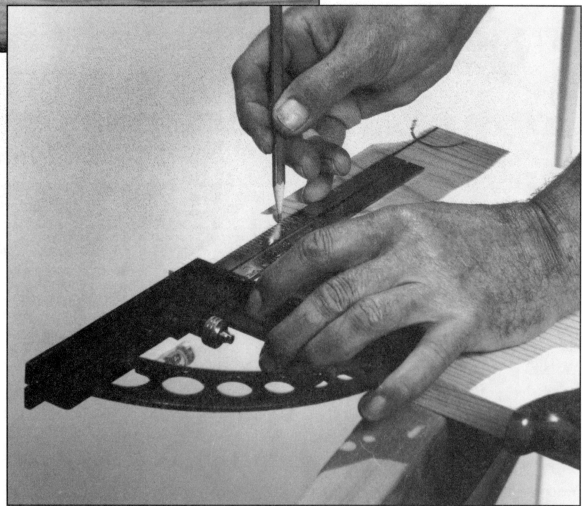

*square*, which has a fixed head. Some try squares have a handle that ends in a 45 degree angle where it meets the blade. These are called *miter squares* since they allow marking and checking 45 degree angles.

Steel squares are most often thought of in relation to house building and rough carpentry, but they are very useful layout and checking tools in a woodworking shop. The longer blades allow marking longer lines than are possible with 12-inch squares (**Fig. 1-19**). Long blades are also an asset when checking assemblies (**Fig. 1-20**), a step to take before, during, and after parts are joined. The joints must not only be sound but should also be accurate enough so mating components form the correct angle.

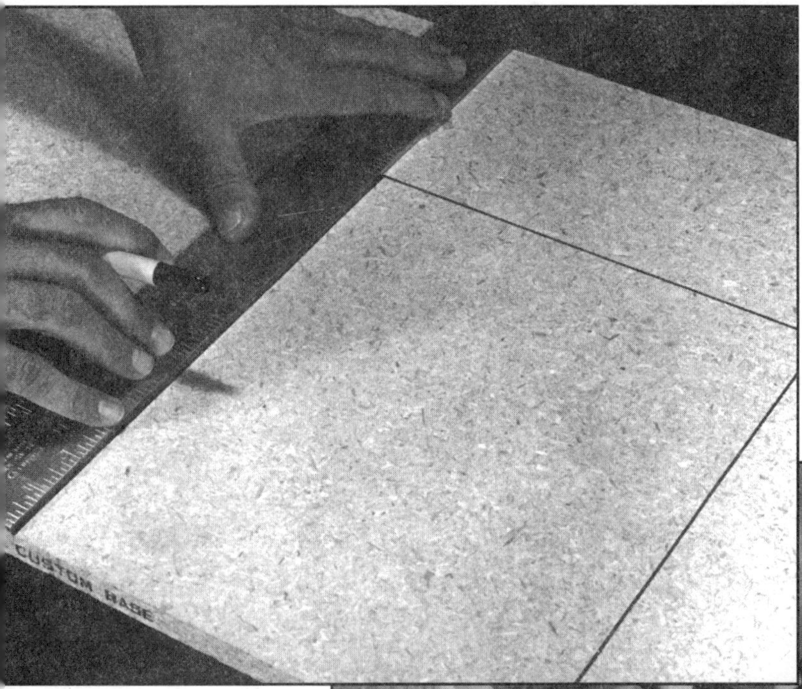

**1-19 A steel square is handy for layout jobs like marking a long line at right angles to an edge.**

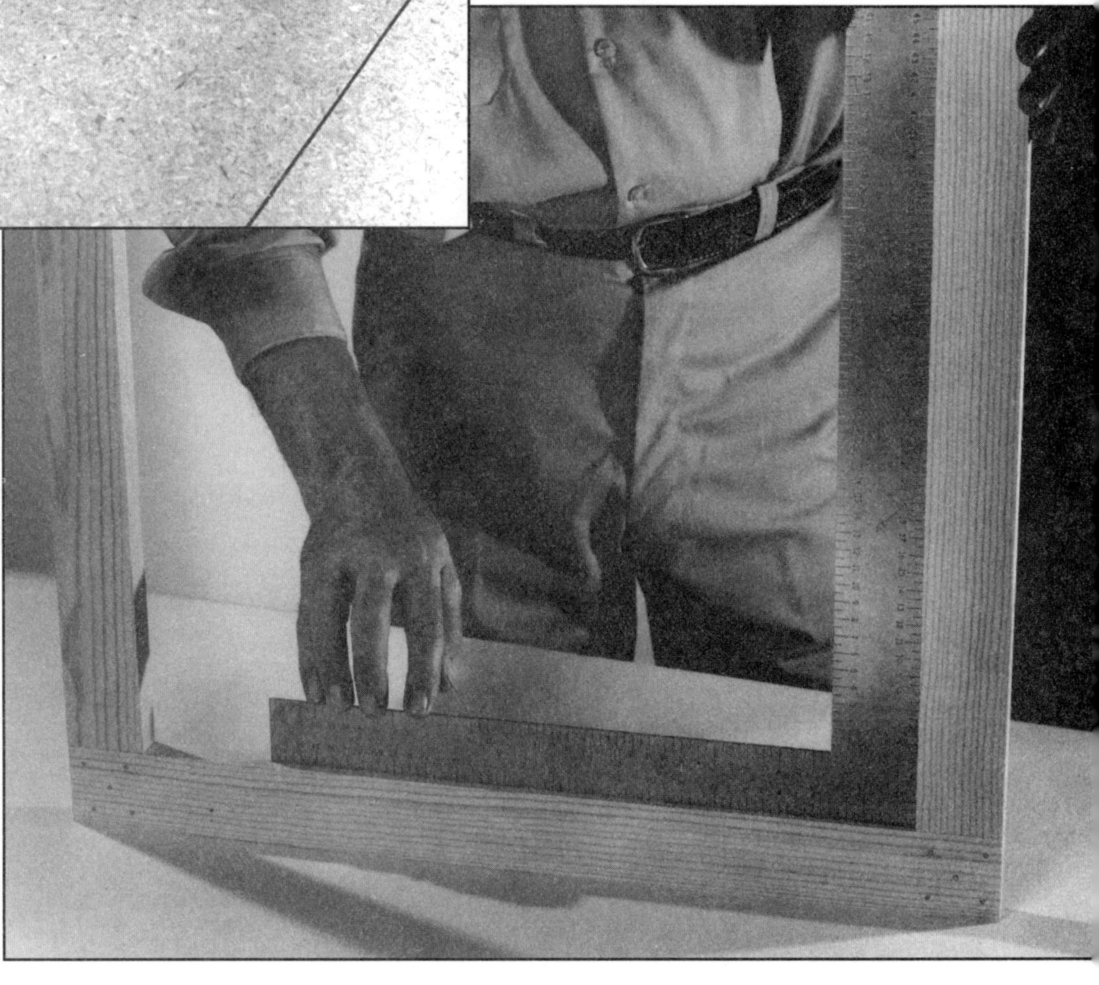

**1-20 Large squares are also good for checking squareness of assemblies.**

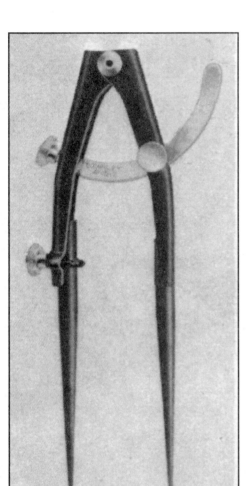

that can be used to strike arcs, form circles, or to step off equal spaces are called *dividers* or *compasses*. The difference between the two is that dividers have two metal points and are considered metal working tools, and compasses employ a pencil as one point and so can be used to mark wood or paper. The example shown in **Figure 1-21** is a *wing divider* that is equipped with two metal points. However, one point is removable so it's possible, as demonstrated in **Figure 1-22**, to substitute an ordinary pencil for the steel point. In essence, the tool is both a divider and a compass.

Good measuring and marking tools contribute to accuracy but the best are useless if lines and dimension points are not drawn carefully. Too often, the measuring device is placed flat on the work and the mark made by moving a pencil to and fro

**1-22 A conventional pencil may be used instead of the steel point.**

Most steel squares are called *rafter squares, carpenter's squares,* or *flat squares*. While all can be useful in layout and checking work, the *homeowner's square* is especially useful for in-the-shop woodworking. The tool is stamped with information that includes decimal equivalents, a metric conversion table, wood-screw gauges, drill-bit sizes, and other data. Since it is made of aluminum, it is not literally a "steel" square.

Handy layout tools

(**Fig. 1-23**). The mark is more a blob than a sharp, clean indication. A more accurate method, especially when the graduations on the rule are grooved, is to hold the instrument on edge as shown in **Figure 1-24**. Sliding the pencil down the grooved line results in just a small dot on the work. This is a feasible procedure with any rule that has incised lines since they act as guide-grooves for the marker. Flex tapes can't be used this way. In any event, guide marks should not be larger than a dot made with a sharp, hard pencil. There are heavy dots and broad lines visible in many illustrations in this book, but they were deliberately emphasized for photo purposes.

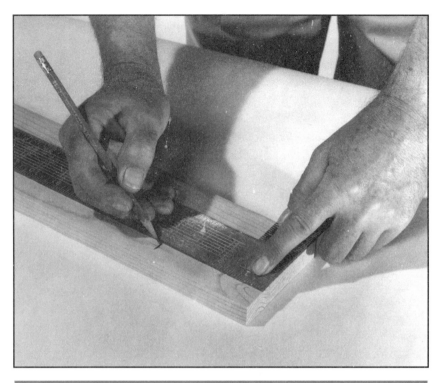

1-23 Scratching a dimension mark with the rule placed flat does not contribute to accuracy.

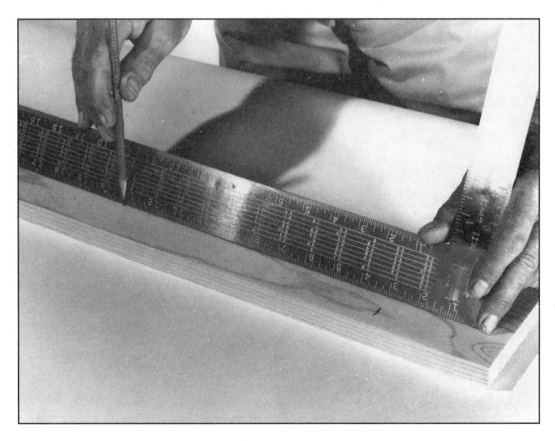

1-24 A better procedure is to use the rule on edge and a sharp, hard pencil so the dimension mark is a small dot.

## MARKERS

Items used for marking lines and points are as important as any tool. The carpenter's pencil, which has a rectangular body and a broad lead, is okay as long as a lot of the lead is exposed and brought to a chisel point by sharpening and then honing on fine sandpaper. The No. 2 lead pencil, common for writing, may also be used, but it wears quickly and requires frequent sharpening to produce clear, sharp lines. Pencils with No. 4H or 5H lead will hold points longer and produce finer lines. In any case, when using conventional pencils to draw long lines, it's wise to rotate the pencil as you move it. This avoids creating a flat point that would result in a broad line.

Marking cut-lines with a sharp knife (**Fig.**

1-25) has several advantages. The line will be fine and the knife will sever surface fibers so a smoother cut results when sawing is done.

Often, when it's necessary to mark a line on long or wide material, dimension points are established at each end of the stock. Then, a straightedge to guide the marker is spanned across the points. This is okay if done carefully, but it does pose the possibility of human error. A more accurate method is to mark by placing a square against one edge of the stock (**Fig. 1-26**). If the stock is too wide for the blade of the square, use the tool on opposite edges and then connect the lines by using a straightedge. It will be evident, after placing the straightedge, whether or not the initial line markings are in line.

Adjustable squares are good gauges to use when marking a line parallel to an edge (**Fig. 1-27**). Both the square and the marker

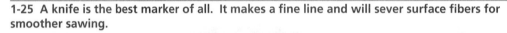

**1-25  A knife is the best marker of all.  It makes a fine line and will sever surface fibers for smoother sawing.**

1-26  Try squares have fixed heads.  Always use a square when drawing a line at right angles to an edge.

1-27  Using a square to draw a line parallel to an edge.  Keep pencil and square moving smoothly.

must be moved steadily and the work-edge must be smooth and straight. If it isn't, the marker will just duplicate inaccuracies.

## HOLE LOCATIONS

Pinpoint locations for holes by drawing intersecting lines. Then, form an indent where the lines intersect by using an *awl* as shown in **Figure 1-28**. The indent forms a seat for the bit that will be used to drill the hole. Hold the awl at a slight angle when placing it so there is a clear view of its point and the intersection. Tilt the tool to vertical position before pressing down to form the indent.

A good way to be accurate when drilling is to provide a marked guide block like the one being used in **Figure 1-29**. The marks on the guide are aligned with the intersecting lines on the work so the drill will be accurately placed. The guide also ensures that the

drilled hole will be perpendicular to the work surface.

A small hole, say, 1/16 or 1/8-inch, through the guide allows it to be used for various hole sizes. The first drilling supplies a pilot hole that is enlarged to the size required for the work.

## SHARP TOOLS AND SMOOTH CUTS

Good tool handling, sharp tools, and the right tool all contribute to smooth cuts that make joint lines less visible. Producing a fine or a coarse cut depends on the number and the style of the teeth on a saw blade. Generally, the more teeth per inch, the smoother the cut. The teeth on most saw blades are "set," which means that alternate teeth are bent in opposite directions. This is necessary to provide freedom in the cut so the blade won't

**1-28 Use an awl to form an indent at the intersection of lines that have been drawn for a hole location.**

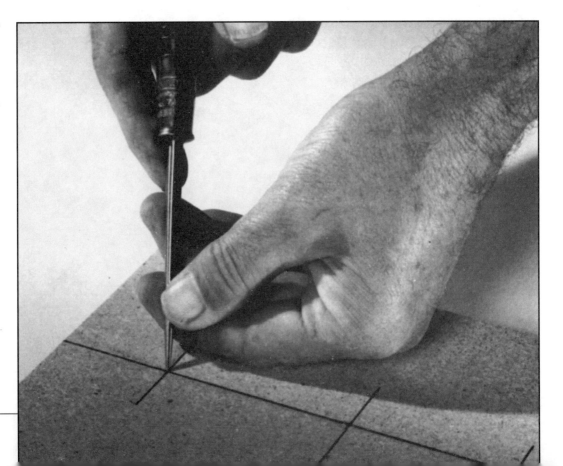

**1-29** A simple guide block provides accuracy when drilling holes. It also ensures that the hole will be perpendicular.

bind. The width of the cut — the *kerf* — equals the gauge of the blade plus the amount of set, as sketched in **Figure 1-30**. Smoother cuts result when the set is minimal or when the blade is taper ground. The latter design provides for blade clearance because the gauge of the blade gradually reduces from the

teeth to the free area. Most such blades are called *planers* and produce the smoothest cuts available with a saw.

There is a distinction between saws used for preliminary sizing cuts and those that are best for the finesse sawing that is required for good joints. The sample cuts shown in

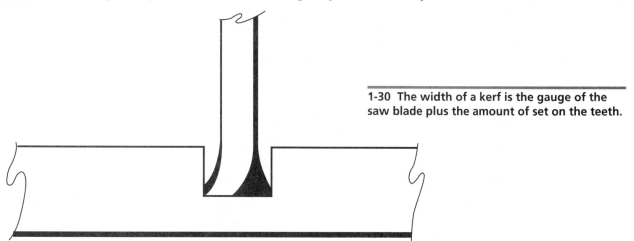

**1-30** The width of a kerf is the gauge of the saw blade plus the amount of set on the teeth.

**Figure 1-31** demonstrate the difference in texture and edge feathering that are the result of sawing with different blades. Both cuts were made on a table saw; the one on the right with a combination blade, the other with a high-quality, carbide-tipped planer.

*Crosscut saws* are designed for sawing across the grain of the wood. The teeth on hand crosscut saws run from 7 to 12 per inch. The more teeth, the smoother the cut. Crosscut saws work best when there is an angle of about 45 degrees between the teeth and the surface of the work (**Fig. 1-32**). Long, smooth strokes are in order. Rushing will ask the teeth to do more than they were designed for and will only result in tearing and splintering. Always saw to a marked line and maintain a 90-degree angle between the side of the blade and the work surface. An L-shaped guide like the one shown in **Figure 1-33** will minimize the possibility of human error. When clamped as shown, it will guide the saw and ensure that the cut edge will be square to adjacent surfaces.

**1-31** Both cuts were carefully made, but the one on the left was made with a carbide-tipped planer blade, the one on the right with a standard combination blade.

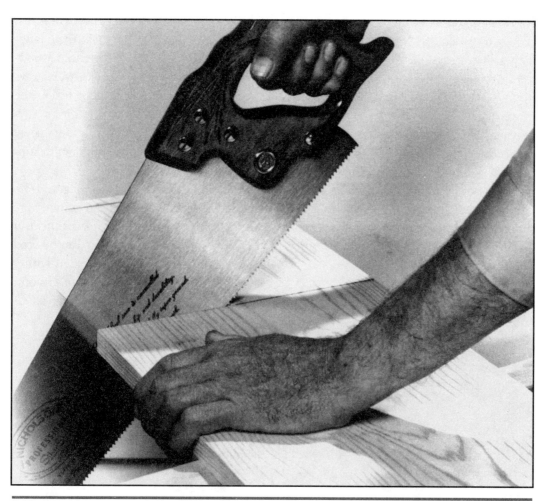

**1-32** Crosscut saws are designed specifically for sawing across the grain of the wood. They have more and smaller teeth per inch than a ripsaw.

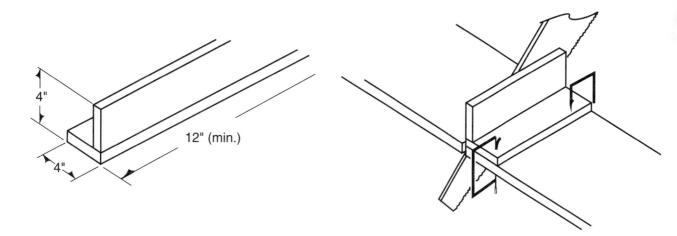

**1-33** Guides like this, which you can make, are a step in the direction of better, more accurate sawing.

*Ripsaws*, designed for cutting with the grain of the wood, have fewer and larger teeth than crosscut saws. This is so because the teeth work like tiny chisels. Saw dust from a rip saw is much coarser than that produced by a crosscut saw. Ripping goes more smoothly when the angle between teeth and work surface is about 60 degrees (**Fig 1-34**). The photo makes another point. When ripping, the kerf often tends to close. Keeping it open with a strip of wood will prevent the blade from binding. The normal angle between blade and work should be reduced when sawing thin stock.

Both types of saws will cut with or across the grain, but that does not make them interchangeable. Often, the experienced woodworker who must make a choice will always choose the crosscut saw since it makes the smoothest cuts. He will also select it for sawing plywood but will use it at a more acute angle since it will result in minimum disruption of surface fibers.

*Backsaws*, like the example in **Figure 1-35**, are used when smooth cuts and accuracy are critical, which automatically places them in the joint-forming category. They can be used freehand but are usually combined with a *miter box* that can be purchased or custom-made in the shop. Chapter 5 offers a plan for making one.

**1-34** Ripsaws, which have larger and fewer teeth per inch than crosscut saws, do the best job when sawing with the grain. Do not use them for sawing plywood in any direction. The wood strip keeps the kerf open so the blade won't bind.

**1-35** Stanley's new backsaw has a special tooth design that allows it to cut faster than conventional saws.

**1-36 The dovetail saw resembles the backsaw but is slighter and has smaller teeth.**

*Dovetail saws*, like the one in use in **Figure 1-36**, are light tools with a thin blade and many small teeth. It's an ideal saw for the slanted cuts that are required for dovetail sockets and tails but should not be limited to that application. It's an excellent tool to use for tenons, dadoes, rabbets, and similar joint forms.

Both the backsaw and the dovetail saw have a heavy spine that runs along the top edge. Its purpose is to stiffen the comparative-

ly thin-gauge blades and so eliminate any buckling or twisting action when sawing.

All sawing operations can be improved by employing guides and jigs that minimize the possibility of human error. There will be many to consider as we study various types of joints but, by way of example, here are a duo that are used with hand saws and that are in the category of *bench hooks*.

**Figure 1-37** details a basic design for bench hooks. The project is gripped in a

**1-37 Bench hooks help to hold work securely while sawing is going on.**

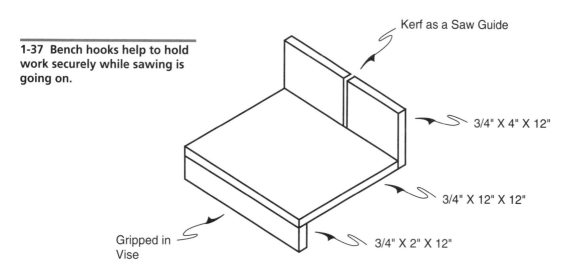

Kerf as a Saw Guide

3/4" X 4" X 12"

3/4" X 12" X 12"

Gripped in Vise

3/4" X 2" X 12"

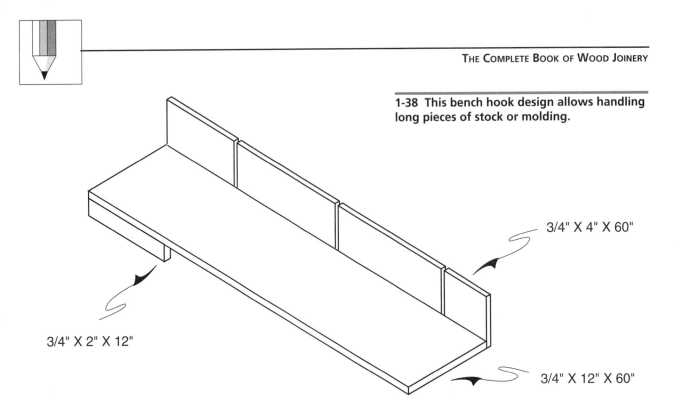

**1-38** This bench hook design allows handling long pieces of stock or molding.

3/4" X 4" X 60"

3/4" X 2" X 12"

3/4" X 12" X 60"

bench vise and serves as a guide for crosscutting boards of various widths. The dimensions are not critical since the unit can be larger or even smaller than the drawing suggests. The important element is the kerf in the vertical member. It should be cut with the saw that will be used, and it must be perpendicular to the base and at right angles to the edge and surface of the upright.

A variation of the crosscut guide is offered in **Figure 1-38**. This is a larger unit and has several kerf-guides so the user can opt for the best work position.

## POWER SAWING

Cutting techniques with power tools differ from those with hand work, but the basic considerations do not. Good work setups and careful handling are always in order. Notice in **Figure 1-39**, which shows a dadoing operation on a table saw, how the location of the cut is determined through the use of *stop rods* and how the work will be held securely during the cutting because of the accessory hold-down on the miter gauge. The example setup is typical of

good procedures to use when multiple, similar pieces are required.

**Figure 1-40** illustrates a crosscutting operation on a radial arm saw. Here, the free hand, which can't be seen in the photo, holds the work securely against the fence. The cutline marked on the work is there so the operator will know right off if cutting is accurate. When the guide line is drawn with a square, as it should be, and the saw is not following it, it will be evident that the machine requires some adjustment.

## DOWELS

Commercial dowels that are commonly used in joints are birch or maple or hickory pegs that are chamfered at each end and grooved spirally or longitudinally so glue and air can move when joint parts are brought together (**Fig. 1-41**). Joint pegs can be made from dowel rod that is available in three- or four-foot lengths, but they may not be as precise in diameter as the preformed pegs made for the purpose. When pegs are made from dowel rod, it is necessary to provide the

1-39 Stop rods situate the work for the cut, in this case, a dado. The hold-down accessory on the miter gauge keeps the work secure during the cut.

1-40 A line on the work will reveal the accuracy of the cut.

# Dowel Pegs

Spiral Groove

Straight Groove

Made from regular dowels

| Typical Sizes | |
|---|---|
| Diameter | Length |
| 1/4" | 1 1/2" |
| 3/8" | 1 1/2" – 1 3/4" – 2" |
| 7/16" | 2" |
| 1/2" | |

# General Rules

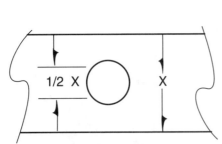

1/2 X    X

Diameter of peg equals 1/2 thickness of stock (max.)

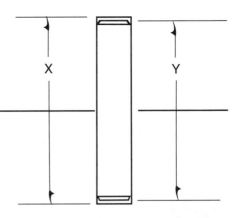

X    Y

Peg is 1/ 32" to 1/16"shorter than total hole depth

1-41  Basic facts about dowel pegs.

essential chamfering and grooving. Form the grooves with a small V-chisel, or, in a unique method, form glue-catching indents by squeezing the pegs with pliers that have serrated jaws (**Fig. 1-42**).

Holes for dowels must be drilled and aligned correctly in order for mating parts to join as they should. *Dowel centers* can help, especially on the type of frame joint shown in **Figure 1-43**. The correct size dowel centers

are inserted in holes drilled in one piece. The parts are then pressed together so the points on the dowel centers mark the hole locations on the mating part.

Professional shops use a drill press or a horizontal boring machine to form holes for dowels. Special jigs or fixtures are added to ensure accuracy. Many of these, as will be shown later, can be homemade for use in any vocational or avocational woodshop.

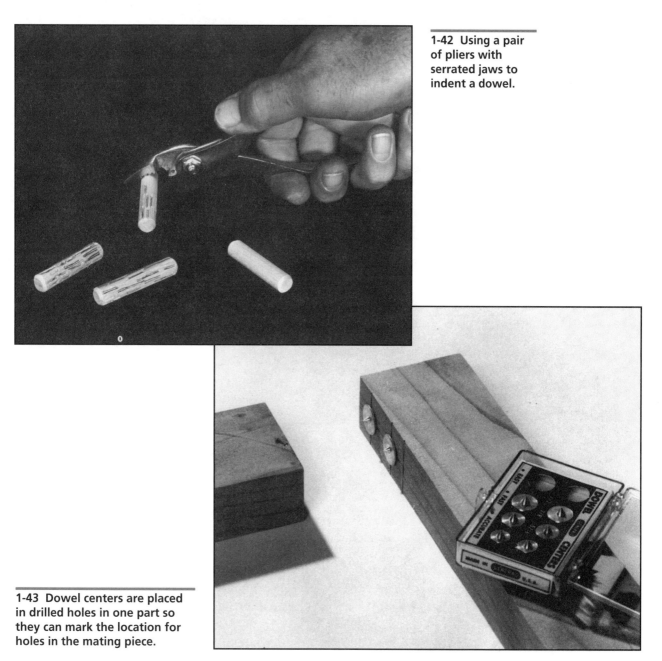

**1-42 Using a pair of pliers with serrated jaws to indent a dowel.**

**1-43 Dowel centers are placed in drilled holes in one part so they can mark the location for holes in the mating piece.**

**1-44 A typical hand brace.**

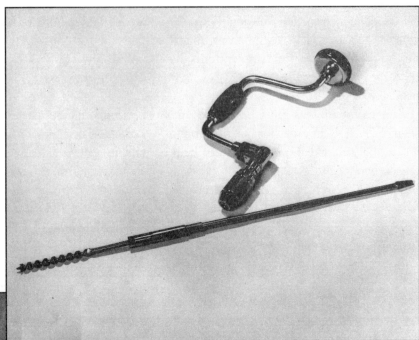

**1-45 A bit gauge makes it possible to bore any number of holes to the same depth.**

Holes that must be made by hand are often done with a *brace* (**Fig. 1-44**). A common set of screw-tipped bits that are used with the brace includes sizes from 1/4-inch to 1-inch with incremental increases of 1/16-inch. A complete set allows forming any size hole that is required in joint constructions.

Providing a mechanical means of gauging hole-depth is a necessary part of hole drilling. A power tool, like the drill press, has built-in adjustable stops that can be set to limit quill extension. Similar devices are available for hand tools. For a brace, there is an accessory called a *bit gauge* (**Fig. 1-45**). The device locks to the shank of the bit and is adjusted so the bit can drill only to a specific depth.

Working by hand calls for considerable care to keep the bit perpendicular to the work surface. However, there are special accessories called *doweling jigs* that can be used with a brace or even a portable electric drill (**Fig. 1-46**). The example in the photo comes with a set of sleeve guides to accommodate various bit diameters. The tool is designed so it can be quickly clamped in position, and it is

**1-46 A typical doweling jig. Many other types are available.**

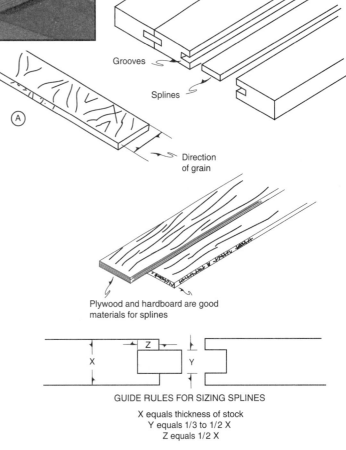

Grooves

Splines

(A)

Direction of grain

Plywood and hardboard are good materials for splines

GUIDE RULES FOR SIZING SPLINES

X equals thickness of stock
Y equals 1/3 to 1/2 X
Z equals 1/2 X

**1-47 Nomenclature of splines.**

calibrated so it can be centered on various thicknesses of stock.

The moisture content of a dowel should not be more than five percent. A "wet" dowel will not absorb glue as it should and will shrink as it dries, thus causing a poor joint and potential failure. Store dowels in a dry, warm place. One technique that ensures a reasonable moisture content is to place the dowels in a warm oven for a short time before using them.

A pair of dowels is recommended for any joint as a guard against stresses that might cause components to pivot about a single one. There will be additional information regarding dowel applications in other chapters.

## SPLINES

Splines are strips of material that are used in joints to add strength and to hold parts in alignment during assembly (**Fig. 1-47**). Applications range from edge-to-edge joints to miters; but always, the important consideration when the spline is made from lumber is

that the grain of the spline must run across the small dimension (**Fig. 1-47A**). This is easy to appreciate if you consider that wood is easier to split *with* the grain than it is to crack it *across* the grain. When a spline is made and used as shown in the illustration, its

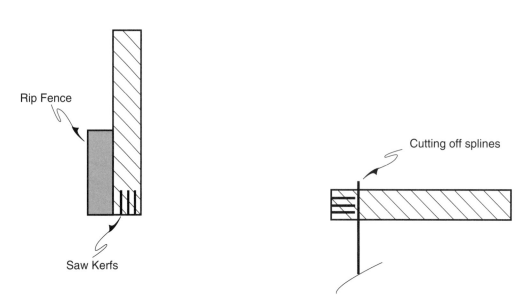

Depth of saw kerfs to equal width of splines

**1-48  One way to produce short splines.**

strength is at right angles to the joint line. This does not apply if plywood or a material like hardboard is used for spline material. Plywood has layers of crossing grain, and hardboard has no grain.

Short splines can easily be made by running kerfs through the end of a board and then slicing off the pieces as shown in **Figure** **1-48**. Long splines are best made from plywood or hardboard. Both materials are available in various thicknesses so choosing what is needed in relation to the thickness of the parts being joined is not difficult.

A different spline concept is shown in **Figure 1-49**. The cross-shaped spline behaves as a joiner between components, but also

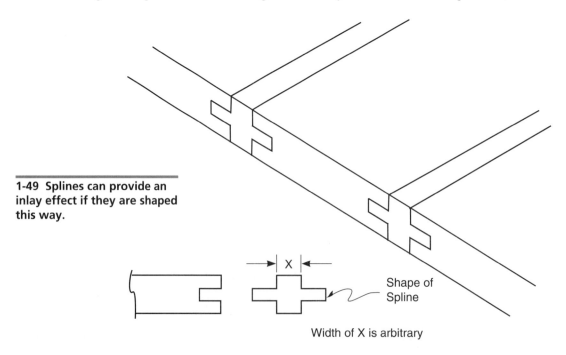

**1-49  Splines can provide an inlay effect if they are shaped this way.**

Width of X is arbitrary

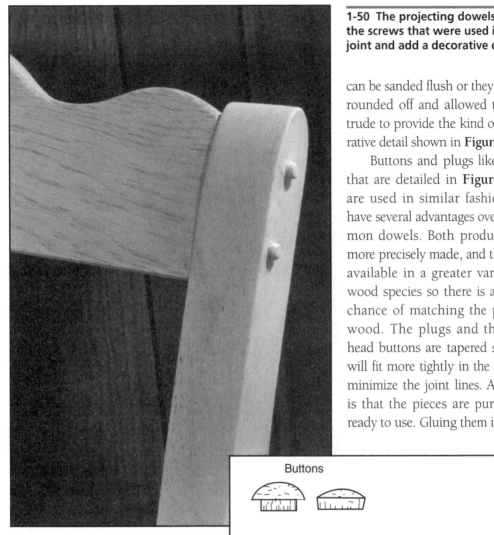

**1-50 The projecting dowels hide the screws that were used in the joint and add a decorative detail.**

can be sanded flush or they can be rounded off and allowed to protrude to provide the kind of decorative detail shown in **Figure 1-50**.

Buttons and plugs like those that are detailed in **Figure 1-51** are used in similar fashion but have several advantages over common dowels. Both products are more precisely made, and they are available in a greater variety of wood species so there is a better chance of matching the project wood. The plugs and the oval head buttons are tapered so they will fit more tightly in the hole to minimize the joint lines. An asset is that the pieces are purchased ready to use. Gluing them in place

provides a design element especially if the splines are made of a contrasting material. A following chapter will provide information about how such splines are made and the various ways they can be used.

## BUTTONS AND PLUGS

Dowels are often used to fill holes through which mechanical fasteners, like screws, are driven. The dowels

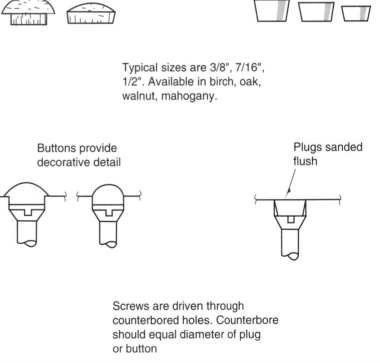

Buttons

Plugs

Typical sizes are 3/8", 7/16", 1/2". Available in birch, oak, walnut, mahogany.

Buttons provide decorative detail

Plugs sanded flush

Screws are driven through counterbored holes. Counterbore should equal diameter of plug or button

**1-51 Some of the ways in which plugs and buttons can be used.**

**1-52 One type of plug cutter.**

and maybe a little sanding when plugs are used are the only chores.

Many craftsmen prefer to make plugs and the idea has advantages. First, plugs can be cut from the same wood used for the project, thus achieving a closer match than is available any other way. Second, by using a *plug cutter* like the one shown in **Figure 1-52**, cuts can be made through the surface of the wood or down through end-grain. This allows achieving a grain direction on the plug that will conform with adjacent surfaces on the project.

The best way to use the cutter is in a drill press (**Fig. 1-53**). Bore as deep as the cutter will allow so the top end of the cylinder will be rounded off. The plugs can be removed from the parent stock by snapping them off with a screwdriver (**Fig. 1-54**) or by separating them with a saw cut on a table saw

**1-53 The plug cutter forms short cylinders that have a rounded end.**

**1-54 The plugs are removed by snapping them off with a screwdriver.**

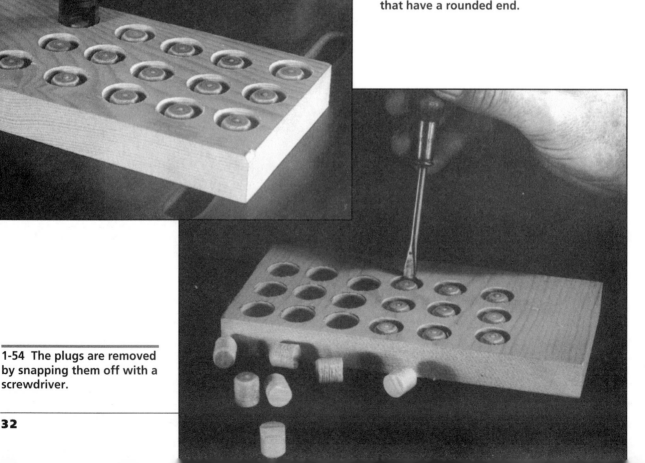

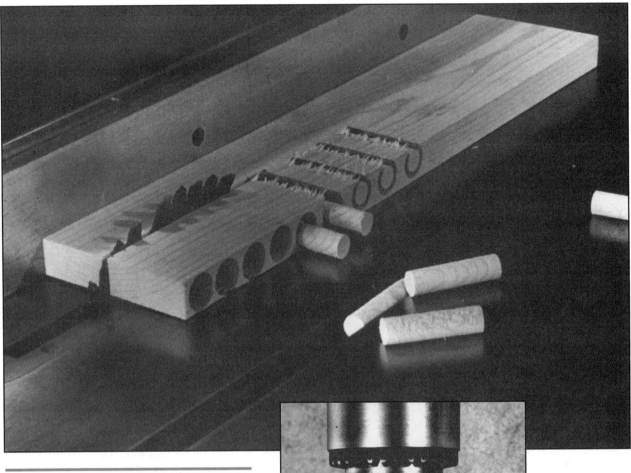

**1-55 A saw cut can also be used to separate plugs or dowels from the parent stock.**

(**Fig. 1-55**). An advantage of working the latter way is that the bottom of the plugs will be flat. Breaking them off with a screwdriver doesn't ensure this.

Another type of plug cutter, definitely for drill press application, is shown in **Figure 1-56**. This type of cutter has greater depth of cut so it can penetrate 3/4-inch stock (**Fig. 1-57**) or be used as shown in **Figure 1-58** to produce dowel pegs. Another use for the cutter, that will be described later, is forming an integral dowel on the end of a stretcher or rail to serve as a round tenon.

There are a variety of plug cutters on the market. Be sure to read instructions that come with them so you will be aware of the driver and the speed that is recommended by the manufacturer.

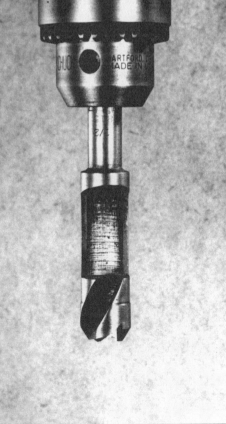

**1-56 This type of plug cutter can be used to produce short plugs or dowel pegs up to about 2-inches long.**

**1-57** With the long plug cutter, cuts can be made through 3/4-inch stock.

**1-58** Using the long plug cutter to form dowel pegs. Note that cutting is done parallel to the wood grain.

## WOOD SCREWS

Many pieces of quality furniture will have screws in some assembly areas if only to secure reinforcements or backs of cabinets. Actually, screws used judiciously add strength to many joint designs and, of course, they are needed for attaching hardware items like hinges and drawer pulls. The common screws, shown in **Figure 1-59**, are *flathead*, *roundhead*, and *ovalhead*.

The flathead screw, unless it will be concealed with a plug, is driven flush with the wood surface. The roundhead screw may also be driven in a counterbored hole so a plug can be used to conceal it, but it is often left exposed. The ovalhead requires a partial countersink. Ideally, the length of a screw should be about 1/8-inch less than the combined thickness of the parts being fastened. It's not always possible to obey the rule so, in practice, the screw-length that is practical for the connection is chosen.

In order for a screw to hold with maximum strength, the hole for it should be drilled as shown in **Figure 1-60**. A lead hole that is too small makes it difficult to drive the screw, especially in dense wood. If it is too large, the screw won't grip. If the body hole is oversize, the attached part will not be secure, and if it is too small, the screw can cause splits, especially if the stock is thin or the screw is near an edge (**Fig. 1-61**). The depth of the body hole may match the thickness of the part being fastened. Ideally, the depth of the lead hole should be about half the length of the screw's threaded area.

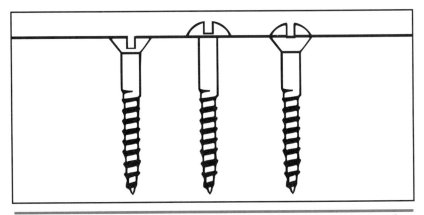

**1-59 Three common screw head designs are flathead, roundhead, and ovalhead.**

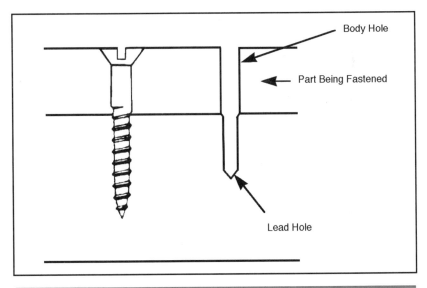

Body Hole

Part Being Fastened

Lead Hole

**1-60 Screw holes must be drilled correctly for the screw to hold with maximum strength. Correct cavities also make it easier to drive the screw.**

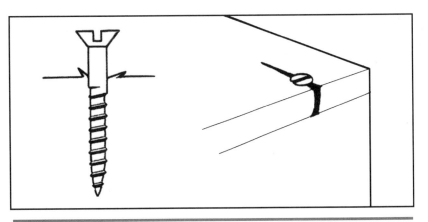

**1-61 A shank hole that is too small can cause splits, especially on thin stock and close to edges.**

| SIZES OF DRILL POINTS TO USE WHEN DRILLING HOLES FOR WOOD SCREWS | | | |
|---|---|---|---|
| SIZE OF SCREW (No) | BODY DIAMETER OF SCREW (Inches) | BODY HOLE (Inches) | LEAD HOLE (Inches) |
| 0 | 1/16 | 1/16 | |
| 1 | 5/64 | 5/64 | |
| 2 | 3/32 | 3/32 | 1/16 |
| 3 | 3/32 | 7/64 | 5/64 |
| 4 | 7/64 | 1/8 | 5/64 |
| 5 | 1/8 | 1/8 | 3/32 |
| 6 | 9/64 | 9/64 | 7/64 |
| 7 | 5/32 | 5/32 | 1/8 |
| 8 | 11/64 | 11/64 | 1/8 |

| SIZES OF TWIST DRILLS TO USE WHEN FORMING SCREW HOLES | | | |
|---|---|---|---|
| NUMBER SIZE OF SCREW | SIZE OF SCREW (Inches) | BODY HOLE | LEAD HOLE |
| 0 | .060 | 53 | |
| 1 | .073 | 49 | |
| 2 | .086 | 44 | 56* |
| 3 | .099 | 40 | 52* |
| 4 | .112 | 33 | 51* |
| 5 | .125 | 1/8 | 49* |
| 6 | .138 | 28 | 47 |
| 7 | .151 | 24 | 46 |
| 8 | .164 | 19 | 42 |
| 9 | .177 | 15 | 41 |
| 10 | .190 | 10 | 38 |
| 11 | .203 | 5 | 37 |
| 12 | .216 | 7/32 | 36 |
| 14 | .242 | D | 31 |
| 16 | .268 | 1 | 28 |
| 18 | .294 | 19/64 | 23 |
| *may be necessary in hardwoods only | | | |

**1-62 Correct sizes of drilling tools to use when forming holes for screws.**

Correct sizes of drilling tools to use are listed in **Figure 1-62**. The only time to ignore this information is when the screw is small and thin and the stock is soft. In such cases you can usually install the screw correctly by forming a starting hole with an awl.

Ordinarily you have to go through several drilling procedures to establish a correct cavity for a screw, but there are modern tools that make the job easier and even more accurate.

The SCREW-MATE® (**Fig. 1-63**) will form the lead and body holes and also a countersink. SCREW-SINK® tools will form lead and body holes plus a counterbore (**Fig. 1-64**). Both tools are available in sizes to accommodate screws from No. 6 X 3/4-inch up to No. 12 X 2-inch.

Counterbores are needed to accommodate plugs that hide screws, but they also make it possible to attach thick or wide stock with short screws (**Fig. 1-65**). For example, attaching a 3/4-inch thick slab to a 2-1/2-inch wide rail would ordinarily require a screw more than 3 inches long. By driving the screw through a counterbore of particular depth, the screw-length can be reduced by as much as 50 percent.

Screws driven at an angle will seat correctly if a counterbore is provided so there will be a flat area for the screwhead (**Fig. 1-66**). If the counterbore can't be accomplished with a conventional drilling tool, the job can be done with a small, sharp chisel.

Countersinks are available for forming full seats for flathead screws or partial ones for ovalhead screws (**Fig. 1-67**). A full-depth countersink is required if the wood is hard. A full cut is not required on softwoods since driving the screw will pull it down flush. In effect, driving the screw completes the countersink.

*Washers* (**Fig. 1-68**) are often used with exposed screws for two reasons. They prevent the screwhead from biting into the wood, and they increase strength by providing a metal surface for the screw to bear against. Flat washers are used with roundhead screws. Countersink types, whether depressed or raised, are used with either flathead or ovalhead screws.

When driving screws into counterbored holes, use a driver whose width is less than the diameter of the hole to prevent damaged edges (**Fig. 1-69**). When placing plugs, use a minimum amount of glue. Wipe off excess glue immediately with a damp cloth. If the plug will be flush, sand it after being sure the glue is dry (**Fig. 1-70**).

Screws that are installed correctly will hold as they should, but, when necessary, extra precautions like those shown in **Figure 1-71** can be taken to be sure the screw won't loosen. In one method, a small hole is drilled through the screwhead at an angle of about 45 degrees and then a brad is driven through

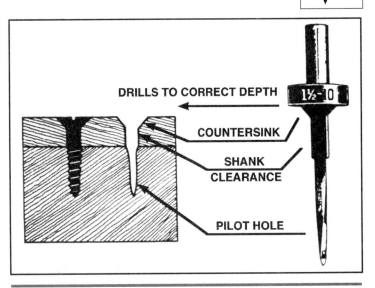

**1-63 SCREW-MATE® bits produce correct screw-hole configurations in a single operation.**

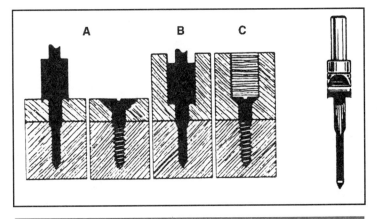

**1-64 SCREW-SINK® bits will form counterbores as well as the holes required for screws.**

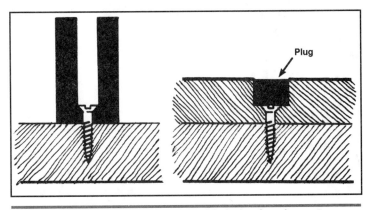

**1-65 Counterboring is done to provide holes for plugs. Deep counterbores allow attaching wide pieces with short screws.**

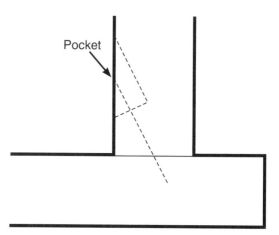

1-66  Holes provided for screws that will be driven at an angle should have pockets so the screw head will seat correctly.

Pocket

1-67  Forming a countersink for a flathead screw.  The arrow points to a seated screw.

1-68  Washers will prevent screws from biting into the wood and they increase the bearing surface of the screw head.

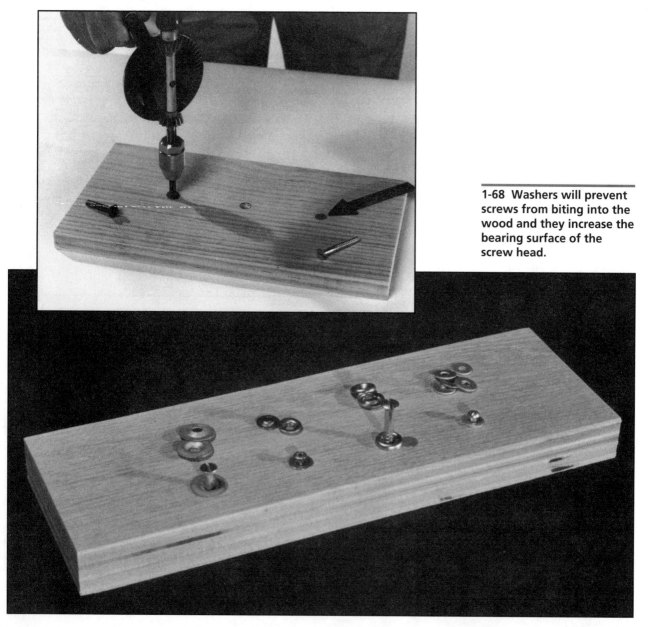

the hole into the wood. In the second method, a staple that fits the slot in the screw is employed.

Steel screws work okay with most woods except oak. The combination of acid in the oak and the steel will often cause staining. Use brass screws instead. These are softer than steel and can be marred or even broken when forced. Coating them with wax helps — an idea that can be used with any stubborn screw.

Sometimes, even when holes have been prepared correctly, a screw will be difficult to drive, especially if the wood is very dense. A problem solver, when there are many screws to drive, is to make a *tapping screw* by filing off half the diameter of the screw's threaded area. The tapping screw is used first to form threads in the hole, a result that makes it much easier to install the permanent screw.

**1-69 The width of the screwdriver's tip must not be greater than the diameter of a screw head or counterbore.**

**1-70 Wait for the glue to dry before sanding plugs flush. The arrow points to a tight fitting, sanded plug.**

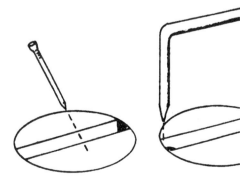

**1-71 Two techniques that can be used to lock a screw.**

## NAILS

Nails are often used to reinforce joints, especially on rough work, utility projects, and cabinets that do not call for the connections found in quality furniture. Even on superior work they are used to secure cabinet backs or to keep glue blocks in place.

*Common* and *box* nails, shown in **Figure 1-72**, are similar. Box nails have slimmer shanks than common nails and are a better choice for in-the-shop work, especially if wood for the project has a tendency to split. Both have broad heads to provide good bearing surface and can be used when an exposed nail head is not objectionable. A standard rule is to avoid driving nails on a common centerline. A staggered pattern is less likely to cause splits (**Fig. 1-73**).

*Wire brads* and *finishing nails* (**Fig. 1-74**) are not uncommon on interior trim and cabinetwork and even on furniture where they might be used to secure moldings. Generally, nails of this type are used when the intent is to conceal the fastener. The nails are driven only to the point where the head remains exposed. Then, a *nail set* is used to sink the head about 1/8-inch below the surface of the wood (**Fig. 1-75**). Filling the indent with wood dough conceals the fastener.

There are many sizes of nails sets and it is important to choose one whose point is not larger than the nail head. Self-centering nail sets, like the one being used in **Figure 1-76**, are commonly used to start screw holes for

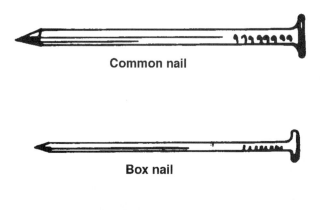

**Common nail**

**Box nail**

1-72 Common and box nails are similar but the box nail has a slimmer shank.

1-73 A staggered nail pattern provides maximum strength and is less likely to cause splitting.

| WIRE BRADS | LENGTH IN INCHES | GAUGE |
|---|---|---|
| | 3/16 | 20 to 30 |
| | 1/4 | 19 to 24 |
| | 3/8 | 18 to 24 |
| | 1/2 | 14 to 23 |
| | 5/8 | 13 to 22 |
| | 3/4 | 13 to 21 |
| | 7/8 | 13 to 20 |

1-74 Wire brads and finishing nails are designed to be set below the surface of the wood.

| FINISHING NAILS | SIZE (d) | LENGTH IN INCHES | GAUGE | APPROXIMATE NUMBER PER POUND |
|---|---|---|---|---|
| | 2 | 1 | 16-1/2 | 1350 |
| | 3 | 1-1/4 | 15-1/2 | 880 |
| | 4 | 1-1/2 | 15 | 630 |
| | 6 | 2 | 13 | 290 |
| | 8 | 2-1/2 | 12-1/2 | 196 |
| | 10 | 3 | 11-1/2 | 125 |

hinges, but they also serve to set finishing nails. The case of the tool sits over the nail head; tapping the plunger with a hammer does the setting. Using them eliminates the possibility of damaging the wood.

Decorative *wrought iron nails* (**Fig. 1-77**) are nice to use when their exposed heads add a decorative detail to the project. Many times, they do not serve a structural purpose. That is, the design of the joint supplies necessary strength; the nails are added for appearance.

When the wood has a tendency to split, or when nails must be driven close to edges or ends, it's good practice to provide a small pilot hole before driving the nail. Often, the nail itself with its head snipped off can be used in a drill, just like a bit. It won't work like a twist drill, but it will serve to form a pilot hole. The hole should not be more than about half the length of the nail.

1-75 Nails are set with special tools. Be sure to use the right size for the nail head.

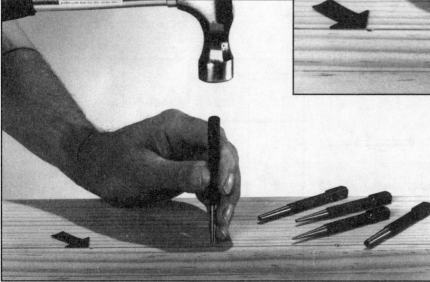

1-76 Self-centering nail sets are available in various sizes. The arrow indicates a nail that has already been set.

1-77 Wrought iron nails can be used for structural purposes and to add design elements to a project.

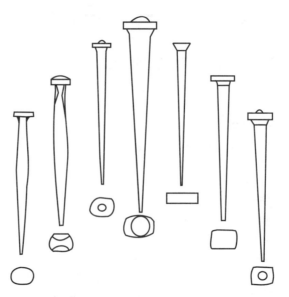

## GLUE AND CORNER BLOCKS

Check the hidden areas of many cabinets and furniture projects and you will discover that glue blocks have been added to supply additional strength. Even when intricate and interlocking joinery is part of the concept, a glue block is added to increase rigidity and to ensure a more durable project (**Fig. 1-78**).

*Glue blocks*, sometimes called *rub blocks*, can be square or triangular (**Fig. 1-79**). They are always installed with generous applications of glue. A good procedure is to coat the block and then put it in place with a sliding action so there will be good contact with mating surfaces. Adding a nail or a screw will provide additional security.

Often, especially when projects are made of thin plywood, glue blocks play a more structural role. As shown in **Figure 1-80**, they actually serve as components of a structural frame.

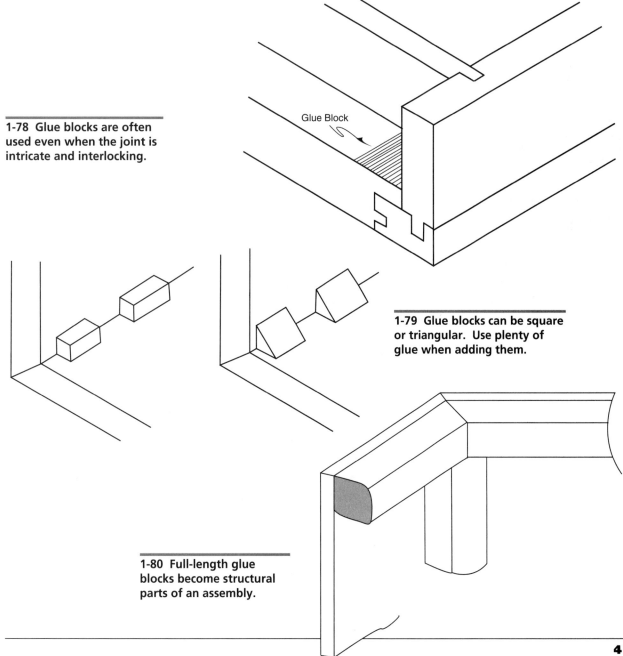

**1-78** Glue blocks are often used even when the joint is intricate and interlocking.

Glue Block

**1-79** Glue blocks can be square or triangular. Use plenty of glue when adding them.

**1-80** Full-length glue blocks become structural parts of an assembly.

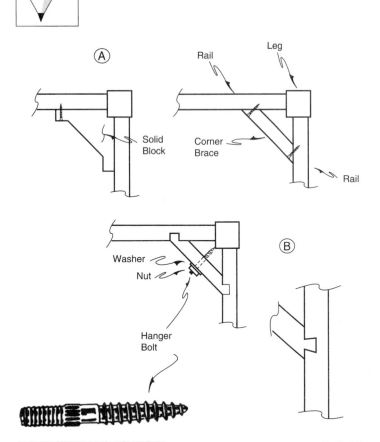

## CORNER BLOCKS

*Corner blocks* add considerable strength where, for example, legs and rails of tables and chairs connect. They usually have a triangular configuration and are attached with glue and screws. **Figure 1-81A** shows a corner block that is shaped to provide shoulders so screws can be more easily installed. The same illustration shows a *corner brace*, which is often used in place of a block. It does not, however, supply the reinforcement of a full block.

Workers who really care, and manufacturers of quality units, will often design corner reinforcements like those shown in **Figure 1-81B**. This degree of attention requires time and effort, but it is one hallmark of craftsmanship. The *hanger bolt* that is shown is a standard item, one that can be tightened at any time should components loosen.

**1-81 Corner blocks and braces add considerable strength to leg and rail assemblies.**

**1-82 Nuts and bolts can be used on rough assemblies and on knock down projects.**

## SOME MECHANICAL FASTENERS

Nuts and bolts don't play a large role in furniture assemblies, but they can be useful for heavy, utility-type constructions because they supply more strength than nails or screws (**Fig. 1-82**). They are a good choice for outdoor projects since they allow disassembly for storage. Bolts do not thread into the wood, but pass through full-size shank holes. A good choice for wood assemblies is a *carriage bolt*. These fasteners have oval or round heads that are not unattractive, and they have a square shoulder under the head that bites into the wood and so prevents the bolt from turning when the nut is tightened.

*Lag screws* may be viewed as a combination wood screw and bolt. They are heavy-duty fasteners that are available in many lengths and diameters and with either square or hexagonal heads. Most times they are used in heavy constructions, but occasionally they can serve to add strength to furniture projects. The example assembly in **Figure 1-83** shows a lag screw used to reinforce what would otherwise be a weak connection — end grain on the stretcher to surface grain on the rail. The lag screw isn't pretty but it was later hidden with a wooden rosette.

*Tee-Nuts* (**Fig. 1-84**) are used to provide metal threads in wood so components can be held together with machine screws. They can also be used for knock-down assemblies. The units are installed in holes that suit the outside diameter of the barrel. The prongs on the flange sink into the wood when the Tee-Nut is pressed into place. They can be surface-mounted, or flush-mounted if a counterbore is provided to accommodate the flange.

*Threaded inserts,* like the one shown in **Figure 1-85**, are used in similar fashion but can be installed in blind or through holes. Installation calls for a hole that is the same size as the body diameter of the insert. Since

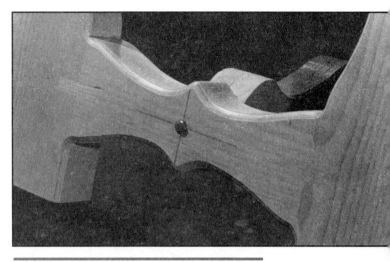

**1-83 A lag screw was used to strengthen this joint. Later, a wooden rosette concealed it.**

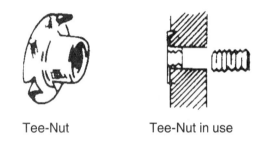

Tee-Nut                    Tee-Nut in use

**1-84 Tee-Nuts are used to supply metal threads in wood. The prongs on the flange dig into the wood to secure the unit.**

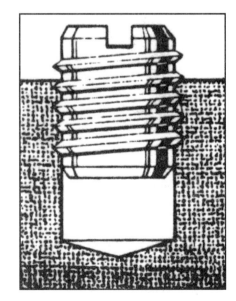

**1-85 Threaded inserts form their own threads when they are driven into the wood with a screwdriver.**

the threads on the units are "knife threads" that cut into wood, the inserts can be driven home with an ordinary screwdriver.

Both Tee-Nuts and threaded inserts are available in various sizes and can be used with standard machine screws or bolts.

There are many types of ready-made metal fasteners or reinforcement products that are practical for strengthening furniture connections. The one shown in **Figure 1-86** is

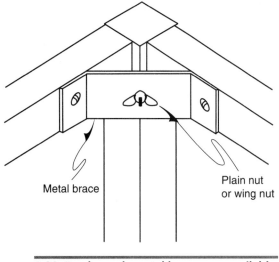

1-86 Ready-made metal braces are available for use in place of custom made corner blocks.

a suitable substitute for a handmade corner block or brace. Some of these are made with right angle end flanges that fit into kerfs cut into rails.

The *chair brace* shown in **Figure 1-87** is usually thought of as a repair piece to stiffen wobbly assemblies, but there is no reason why it can't be used on new work.

*Corner braces* and *mending plates* (**Figs. 1-88** and **1-89**) are typical of available hardware that is specially designed to strengthen simple joints or to reinforce old ones. They can

1-87 A chair brace, often used for repair work, can also be used on new constructions.

1-88 Corner irons are available in many sizes and in different materials like steel and brass.

1-89 Mending plates also come in different sizes and materials.

1-90 The three-surface corner brace is a relatively new piece of reinforcement hardware.

be used on end-to-end joints or on frame components that are just butted together. Either type can be surface-mounted or set flush with wood surfaces by providing a mortise.

A relatively new product in reinforcement hardware is the three-surface corner brace shown in **Figure 1-90**. The unit is steel, one piece, and made so it will fit inside corners perfectly.

## HIDING EDGES

Hiding edges applies mostly to projects made of plywood or to assemblies of various materials that will be covered with a wood veneer or plastic laminate (**Fig. 1-91**). While the joints in the project have to be strong, they do

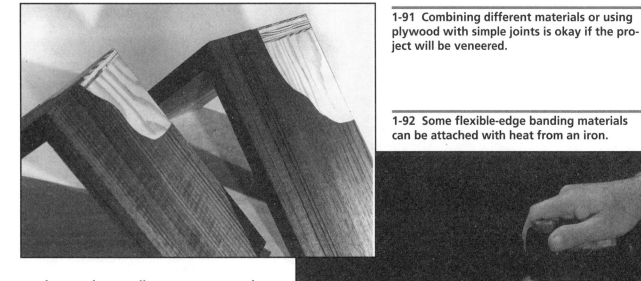

**1-91 Combining different materials or using plywood with simple joints is okay if the project will be veneered.**

**1-92 Some flexible-edge banding materials can be attached with heat from an iron.**

so grain direction will conform with surface grain of the panel on only two edges. Many craftsman manufacture their own veneer tapes by working along the lines shown in **Figure 1-93**. The cut is made to separate the surface veneer from the body of the plywood. A second cut removes the strip which is then applied to the panel's edge with contact

not have to be visually attractive since they will be covered anyway. Lumber and plywood can be combined; joints can be rabbets or dadoes reinforced with glue and screws or nails. If uncovered the project would not be an example of prime workmanship, but if it is strong enough for its purpose, it will be successful and the cover up will not reveal what joints were used.

Plywood edges can be covered with flexible bands of veneer that are made for the purpose. Some are self-adhesive; others require application with contact cement. Some have an adhesive coating that is activated with an ordinary household pressing iron (**Fig. 1-92**).

One of the problems with commercial edgings is that the grain runs longitudinally,

**1-93 Cutting strips of surface veneer produces edge banding with a grain direction that will flow with the grain pattern of the panel.**

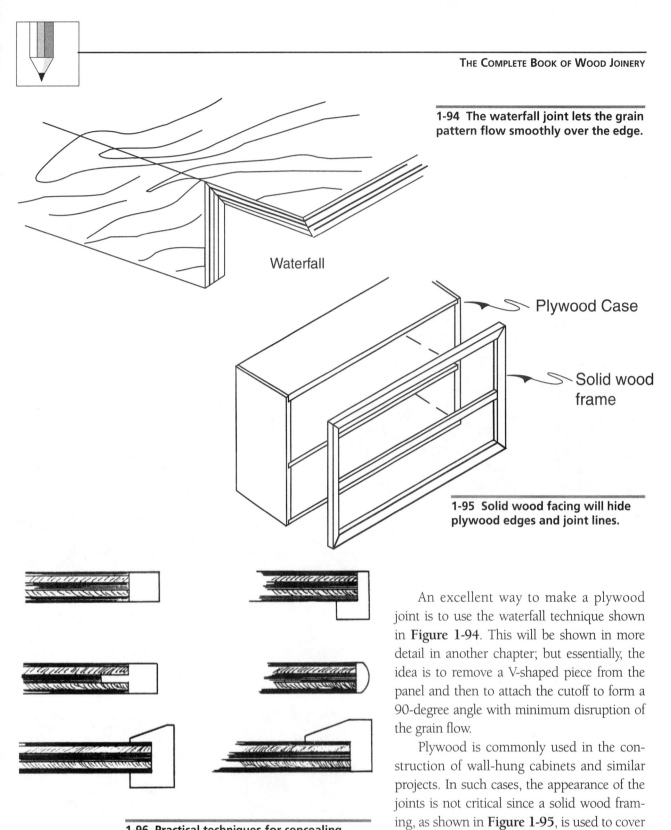

**1-94 The waterfall joint lets the grain pattern flow smoothly over the edge.**

Waterfall

Plywood Case

Solid wood frame

**1-95 Solid wood facing will hide plywood edges and joint lines.**

**1-96 Practical techniques for concealing plywood edges.**

An excellent way to make a plywood joint is to use the waterfall technique shown in **Figure 1-94**. This will be shown in more detail in another chapter; but essentially, the idea is to remove a V-shaped piece from the panel and then to attach the cutoff to form a 90-degree angle with minimum disruption of the grain flow.

Plywood is commonly used in the construction of wall-hung cabinets and similar projects. In such cases, the appearance of the joints is not critical since a solid wood framing, as shown in **Figure 1-95**, is used to cover the edges of the frame and the joint lines.

Some ideas for hiding edges when plywood is used as a slab for table tops or chests are offered in **Figure 1-96**. Note that some of the designs provide a lip or bulk the edge so the slab will have a heavier appearance.

cement. Note that the grain direction on the edge of the sample panel follows the line of the surface grain.

# ROUND PROJECTS FROM FLAT BOARDS

When X-number of segments are bevel-cut at a particular angle, the parts can be assembled to form a circle. This leads to the construction of the barrel-type furniture shown in **Figure 1-97**. The cuts required are simple bevels, but accuracy is critical because of the number of joints involved. A slight error on, say, each of 24 pieces amounts to disaster at assembly time.

Segments can be cut consecutively from parent stock as shown in **Figure 1-98A** and assembled as shown in **Figure 1-98B.** The narrower the segments and the more of them there are, the closer the assembly will come to being a true circle (**Fig. 1-98C**).

The arithmetic that is required to plan projects is detailed in **Figure 1-99**. It is important to understand that the cut-angle for the joints is one half the included angle of the segments. Since segment joinery is important in many areas of woodworking, we will explore the techniques in more detail in a special chapter.

**1-97 Typical of the round projects that can be made by using the bevel cutting technique.**

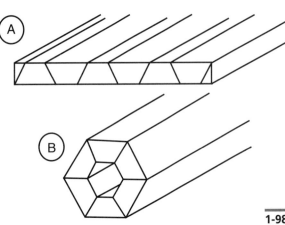

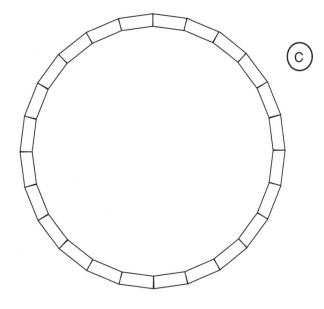

**1-98** The greater the number of beveled segments and the narrower they are, the closer the project gets to a true circle.

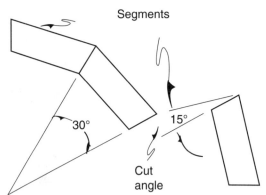

Use this formula to determine
the cut angle on each segment:

1. Decide on number of segments.
2. Divide 360 (number of degrees in
   a circle) by the number of
   segments.
3. Divide the answer by two.

**EXAMPLE** (for 24 segments)

$$\frac{360}{24} = 15$$

$15 \div 2 = 7\frac{1}{2}$ (the cut angle)

**1-99** The formula that is used when
producing beveled segments.

# 2

# BUTT JOINTS

---

Grain Direction • Reinforcement • Glue Blocks and Strips • Reinforcing Frame Butts • Hiding the Joint • Interlocks

---

Simple butt joints are classified as the weakest of wood joints and are often shunned because they leave end-grain exposed. The examples in **Figure 2-1** show that the joint supplies minimum contact area and that often the connection is end-grain to surface-grain, a design that doesn't contribute much to joint strength. However, despite criticism, butt joints are found in many furniture projects. A butt joint that is long-grain to long-grain has adequate strength. However, when end-grain is involved in the joint, the joint is weak because open pores don't offer much effective glue surface, and therefore, reinforcements are necessary to compensate for the joint weakness.

In appearance though, the joint actually leaves little to be

desired, since merely butting parts together results in the least amount of visible joint line. Even the cross-miter, which conceals end-grain, has a longer joint line than a butt joint

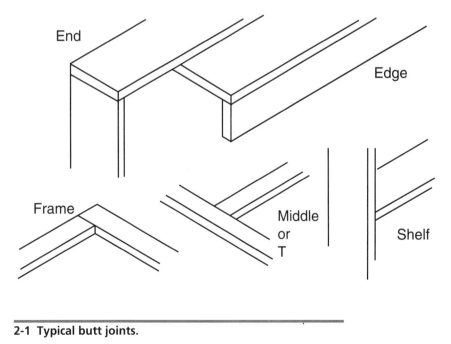

**2-1 Typical butt joints.**

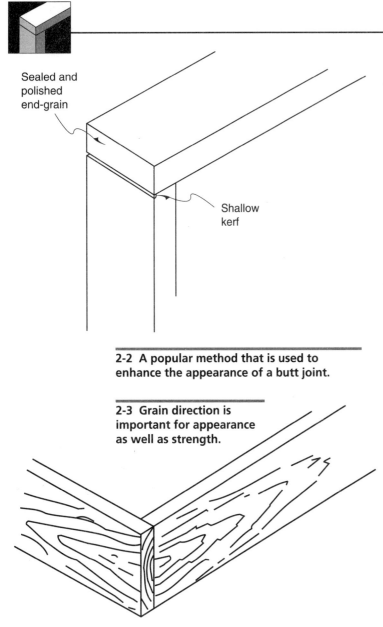

Sealed and polished end-grain

Shallow kerf

**2-2  A popular method that is used to enhance the appearance of a butt joint.**

**2-3  Grain direction is important for appearance as well as strength.**

when it is viewed from an end. An end view of a butt joint, compared with, for example, a dado or rabbet, leaves no doubt about which joint looks better.

Many craftsmen and manufacturers will treat an end butt as shown in **Figure 2-2**. The technique will be successful only if the end-grain is sanded and sealed enough so it can be stained and polished for a slick appearance. The shallow kerf serves as a decorative detail. The depth of the kerf is slight, so it doesn't drastically reduce contact area. The end-grain of close-grain wood like maple or birch won't be difficult to treat in the manner described, but open-grain wood like oak needs more careful attention.

## GRAIN DIRECTION

The grain direction of mating parts of all joints has a bearing on strength and appearance, but it is especially true with connections like the end butt. Dimensional changes along the length of a board, that is, *with* the grain, aren't critical enough to cause problems. Changes in the width of a board, that is, *across* the grain, can actually be measured. That's one reason why the grain direction of parts joined in an end butt should be planned as shown in **Figure 2-3**. Theoretically, any change that occurs will be similar in both pieces. If a change happens in only one piece, the joint will be weakened and splitting might occur.

Take special precautions when coating end-grain with glue. A common procedure is to dilute a small amount of glue and use it as a sizing. Check the amount the wood soaks up and apply a second coat if necessary before using full-strength glue for the final assembly.

## REINFORCEMENT

Reinforcements, as well as glue, will, of course, increase the strength of any butt joint. The most common reinforcement techniques involve nails, screws, or dowels (**Fig. 2-4**).

Nails driven at an angle will hold much better than those hammered straight in. If it is likely that the wood might split, drill a pilot hole for the nails, at least through the part being fastened.

Screws don't grip as well in end-grain as they do in cross-grain. Choose a longer screw than you would ordinarily use and try working with a smaller lead hole than is technically correct. **Figure 2-5** demonstrates one way to eliminate the weakness of screw threads in end-grain. When the joint is designed as shown, the screws will penetrate the cross-grain of the dowel, and this increases their holding power considerably.

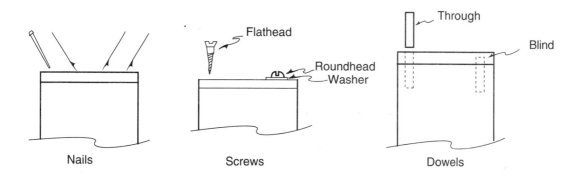

Nails      Screws      Dowels

**2-4 Butt joints can be reinforced by using any of these methods. Nails will hold best when they are driven at a slight angle.**

Dowels should be used when the appearance of nails or screws is not acceptable. As suggested in **Figure 2-4**, the dowels may be through or blind. The holes for through dowels are easier to do. Alignment will be exact if the parts are clamped together so the hole can be drilled through both pieces. The parts are separated after drilling to clean away wood chips before the application of glue and final assembly.

*Flat corner irons* can be used to add strength (**Fig. 2-6**). The hardware is often thought of as mending material for use on utility or rough projects where the appearance is not important. But they can be used effectively on showpieces, like a well-executed open case, painted white, and with corner irons finished in matte black. The hardware supplies strength and contributes to appear-

**2-5 Screws driven into end-grain will hold securely if a dowel is installed in this manner.**

ance. As the illustration shows, the irons may be surface-mounted or set flush in a mortise.

One of the disadvantages of the butt joint is its weakness under lateral stress. *Gusset plates* will counter failure if the purpose of the

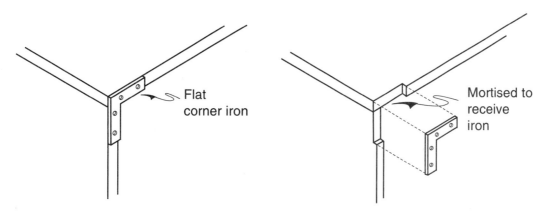

Flat corner iron

Mortised to receive iron

**2-6 Flat corner irons supply considerable strength, and they can also serve as decorative details.**

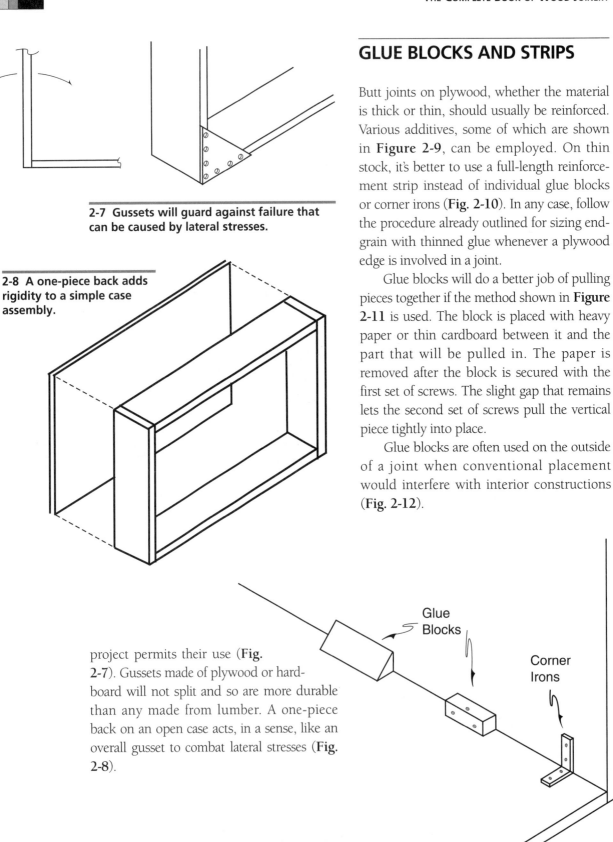

**2-7 Gussets will guard against failure that can be caused by lateral stresses.**

**2-8 A one-piece back adds rigidity to a simple case assembly.**

## GLUE BLOCKS AND STRIPS

Butt joints on plywood, whether the material is thick or thin, should usually be reinforced. Various additives, some of which are shown in **Figure 2-9**, can be employed. On thin stock, it's better to use a full-length reinforcement strip instead of individual glue blocks or corner irons (**Fig. 2-10**). In any case, follow the procedure already outlined for sizing end-grain with thinned glue whenever a plywood edge is involved in a joint.

Glue blocks will do a better job of pulling pieces together if the method shown in **Figure 2-11** is used. The block is placed with heavy paper or thin cardboard between it and the part that will be pulled in. The paper is removed after the block is secured with the first set of screws. The slight gap that remains lets the second set of screws pull the vertical piece tightly into place.

Glue blocks are often used on the outside of a joint when conventional placement would interfere with interior constructions (**Fig. 2-12**).

Glue Blocks

Corner Irons

project permits their use (**Fig. 2-7**). Gussets made of plywood or hardboard will not split and so are more durable than any made from lumber. A one-piece back on an open case acts, in a sense, like an overall gusset to combat lateral stresses (**Fig. 2-8**).

**2-9 Conventional corner blocks or corner irons can be used on any material.**

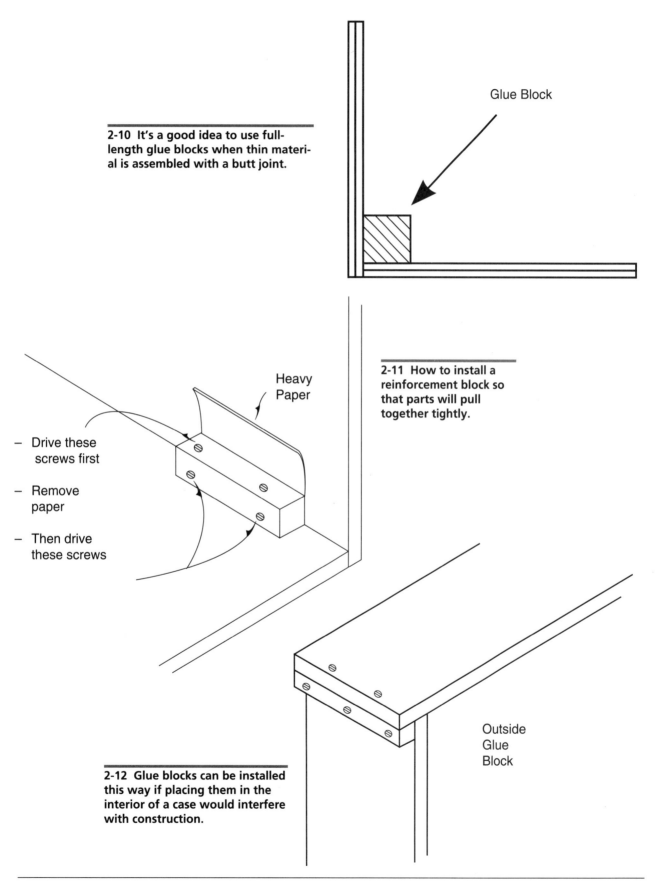

**2-10** It's a good idea to use full-length glue blocks when thin material is assembled with a butt joint.

Glue Block

Heavy Paper

**2-11** How to install a reinforcement block so that parts will pull together tightly.

– Drive these screws first

– Remove paper

– Then drive these screws

Outside Glue Block

**2-12** Glue blocks can be installed this way if placing them in the interior of a case would interfere with construction.

Butt shelf-joints are very weak unless *cleats*, which behave like glue blocks, are added to provide support (**Fig. 2-13**). The cleat can be fastened to both the shelf and the side, or to just the side if the shelf must be removable. Butt shelf-joints may be reinforced with any of the methods that were illustrated for end butts (**Fig. 2-14**).

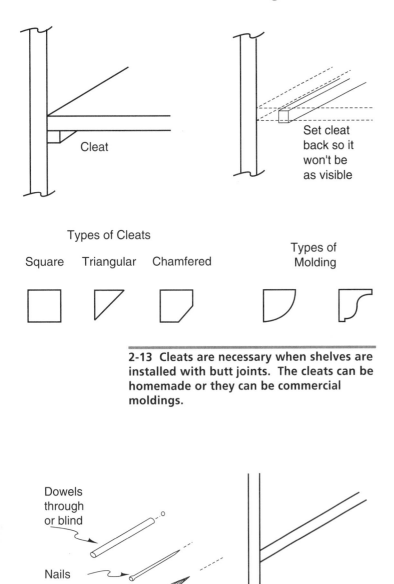

**2-13 Cleats are necessary when shelves are installed with butt joints. The cleats can be homemade or they can be commercial moldings.**

**2-14 Dowels, nails, or screws can be used to reinforce shelf butts.**

## REINFORCING FRAME BUTTS

Frame butts are reinforced by applying the methods that are shown in **Figure 2-15**. Corrugated nails are available in different sizes so a choice can be made in relation to the thickness of the parts being joined. The parts must be clamped firmly together while the nails are driven. It's best to hold them at a slight angle and to use them on both sides of the joint.

Both the through dowel and the dowel placed at an angle should be drilled for and installed while the frame parts are together under clamp pressure.

Frame butts are often used to assemble the skeleton that is required for the fabrication of hollow core panels (**Fig. 2-16**).

Reinforcement methods for middle, or T, butts are shown in **Figure 2-17**. The design — and this applies to all types of joints and their variations — depends on what the project will be used for and the general quality of the construction.

## HIDING THE JOINT

Two basic methods for concealing a butt joint using covers that can be purchased or homemade are shown in **Figure 2-18**. Method (**A**) employs a square block with one chamfered edge; method (**B**) uses a strip that is rabbeted to fit the corner. Additions like this are attached with glue and brads or finishing nails that are set and then hidden with wood dough. There are many types of commercial moldings that are suitable for the purpose.

This type of detail can contribute to the appearance of the project, but the extra pieces should not be viewed as structural members, even though they might add some reinforcement. The strength of the union must be in the joint itself.

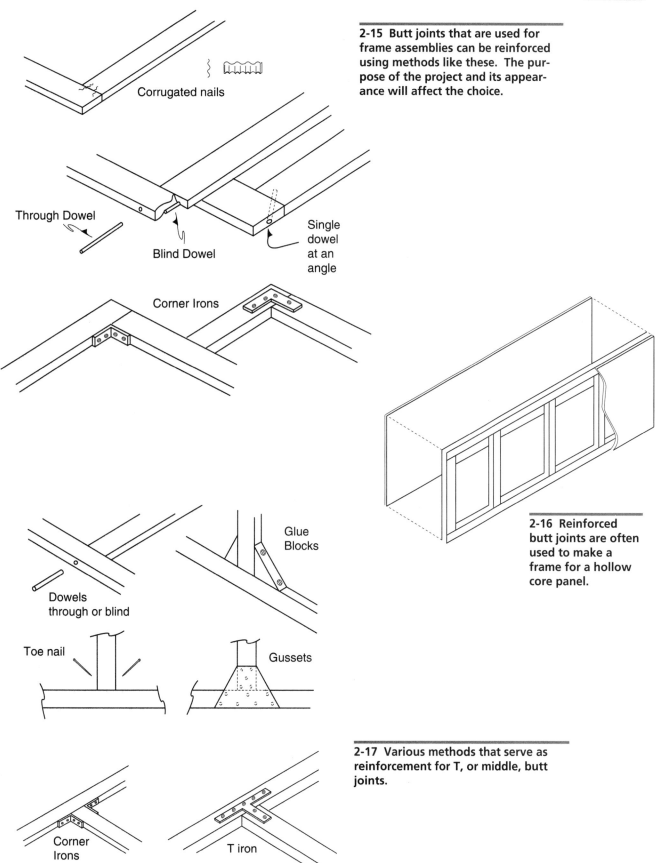

Corrugated nails

Through Dowel

Blind Dowel

Single dowel at an angle

Corner Irons

Glue Blocks

Dowels through or blind

Toe nail

Gussets

Corner Irons

T iron

**2-15** Butt joints that are used for frame assemblies can be reinforced using methods like these. The purpose of the project and its appearance will affect the choice.

**2-16** Reinforced butt joints are often used to make a frame for a hollow core panel.

**2-17** Various methods that serve as reinforcement for T, or middle, butt joints.

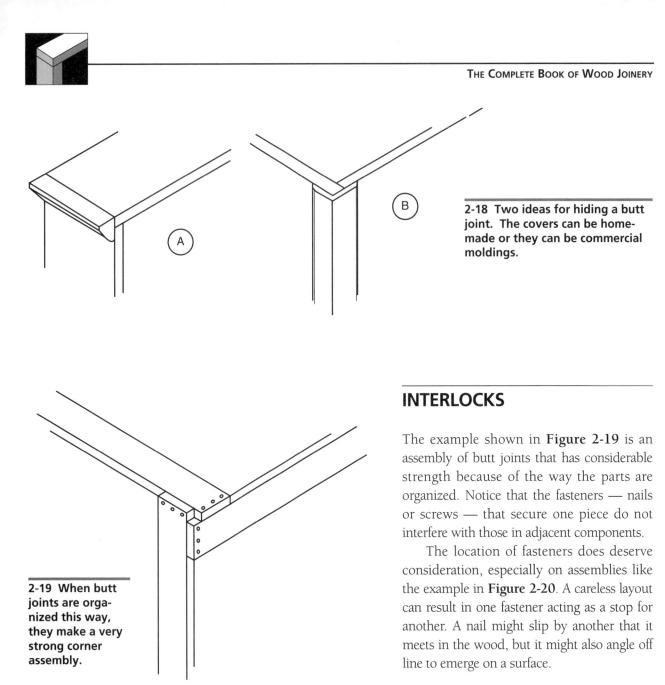

**2-18 Two ideas for hiding a butt joint. The covers can be home-made or they can be commercial moldings.**

**2-19 When butt joints are organized this way, they make a very strong corner assembly.**

## INTERLOCKS

The example shown in **Figure 2-19** is an assembly of butt joints that has considerable strength because of the way the parts are organized. Notice that the fasteners — nails or screws — that secure one piece do not interfere with those in adjacent components.

The location of fasteners does deserve consideration, especially on assemblies like the example in **Figure 2-20**. A careless layout can result in one fastener acting as a stop for another. A nail might slip by another that it meets in the wood, but it might also angle off line to emerge on a surface.

Leg

Rails

**2-20 Fasteners in adjacent pieces should be located so they don't interfere with each other. The length, as well as the location of the fastener, is a factor.**

# 3

# DADOES AND GROOVES

Hiding the Joint • Reinforcement • Cutting with Hand Tools • Power Tool Work • Back-to-Back Dadoes • Stopped Dadoes • Corner Dadoes • Other Methods

**D**adoes and grooves are U-shaped cuts that are formed in one part to receive the butt end of another component. The terms are often used interchangeably even though, technically, a *dado* is made *across* the grain and a *groove* is made *with* the grain (**Fig. 3-1**). Many times, the act of forming a groove is called *ploughing*. The width of the cut matches the thickness of the insert; the depth of the cut is usually about one-half the thickness of the stock. Cut-depth can be less but making it too deep will cause a weakness in the area.

The width of the cut should permit the insert to fit smoothly into place (**Fig. 3-2**). Having to force the insert into place will

create stresses in the area and will interfere with assembly procedures. When the groove or dado does not allow an easy assembly, take the time to make an adjustment. If the cut is

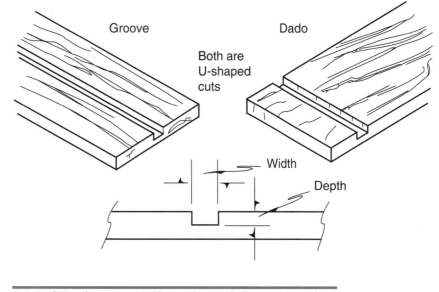

**3-1 U-shaped cuts *across* the grain are dadoes. When they are cut *with* the grain, they are called grooves.**

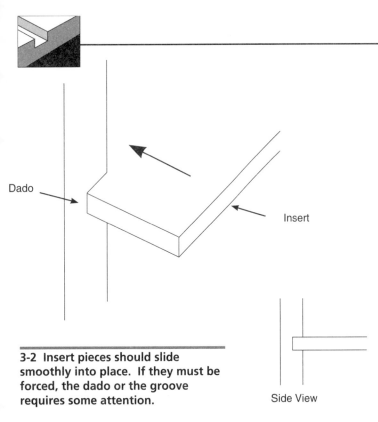

Dado

Insert

Side View

**3-2 Insert pieces should slide smoothly into place. If they must be forced, the dado or the groove requires some attention.**

too narrow, wrap a sheet of fine sandpaper around a suitable block of wood and use it as shown in **Figure 3-3**. There is not much that can be done about a cut that is too wide unless a shim can be used to fill the gap.

A major advantage of the joint is obvious when it is compared to a butt joint. Contact area is increased so there is more surface for glue and the shape of the joint includes a supporting ledge. The value of the ledge is obvious when, for example, the insert will be a shelf. A disadvantage is the visible joint lines (**Fig. 3-4**).

**3-3 This is one way to make an adjustment when the dado is too narrow. Use very fine sandpaper.**

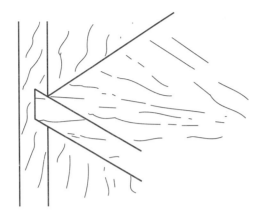

**3-4  A major objection to the dado is its appearance when it is left exposed.**

## HIDING THE JOINT

There are practical techniques to use when you need the strength of the dado joint but wish to conceal its unattractive appearance. The objection is automatically eliminated if a case, for example, is designed with a front frame (or *faceplate trim* ) as shown in **Figure 3-5**.

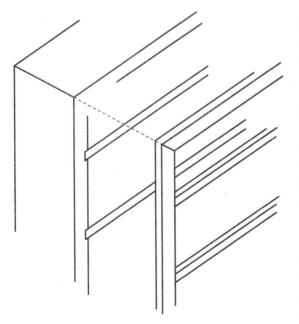

**3-5  A front frame, or faceplate trim  as it is often called, hides the joints effectively.**

When trim is not used, the joint lines can be obscured by using shelves that are wider than the sides of the case so they project at the front as shown in **Figure 3-6**. This does not eliminate the joint lines but makes them less visible because the eye is attracted to the shelf instead. Note that the corners or the edge of the insert can be treated in various ways to add a detail. Strips of wood, moldings, edge banding — all can be used to cover edges that show dado lines.

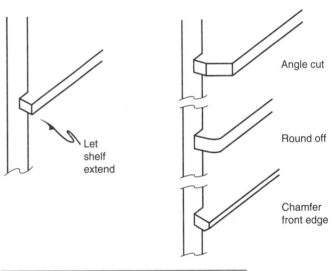

**3-6  Using shelves that are wider than the sides of the case serves to draw the eye away from the joint lines.**

An alternate method, one that is commonly used, is to form *stopped dadoes*. As shown in **Figure 3-7**, the U-cut does not run completely across the board, so there are no visible joint lines. The inserts can be cut narrower than the sides, as in (**A**), or they can be notched, as in (**B**).

The technique requires some handiwork with chisels if the dado is to be square where it is stopped. If cutting is done with a power tool, the handiwork can be eliminated by accepting the arc that remains at the end of the cut when it is formed with a dadoing tool. The insert, for conformity, can be shaped as shown in **Figure 3-8A** or **3-8B**.

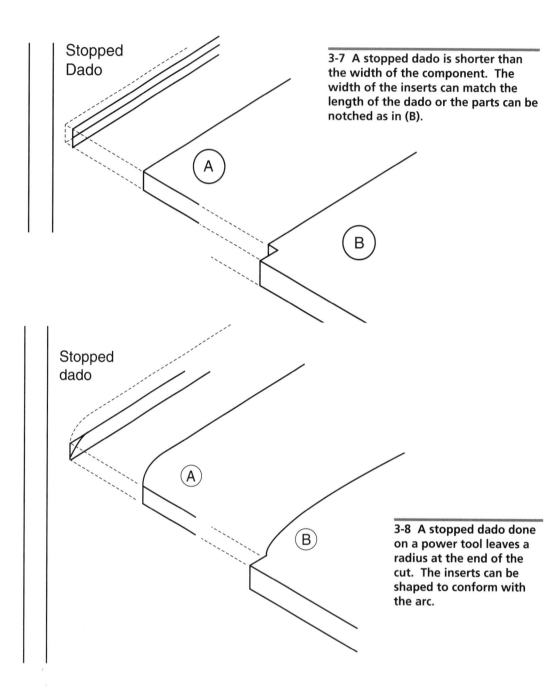

Stopped Dado

3-7 A stopped dado is shorter than the width of the component. The width of the inserts can match the length of the dado or the parts can be notched as in (B).

A

B

Stopped dado

A

B

3-8 A stopped dado done on a power tool leaves a radius at the end of the cut. The inserts can be shaped to conform with the arc.

## REINFORCEMENT

Quite often, especially when the components are solid lumber, the inserts are not secured in the groove. This allows possible dimensional changes that might occur because of variations in moisture content to occur without damage. If reinforcements are added they can be the same as those used with a butt joint (**Fig. 3-9**). Nails or screws can be used unobtrusively if they are installed as shown in **Fig. 3-9A**.

Loose shelves do not add at all to the rigidity of a project. If they are installed carelessly, the joints in the case itself become more critical since the unit will have to stand on its own.

**3-9 Fasteners that can be used to reinforce a dado joint. Nails or screws will be secrets if they are driven as shown in detail (A).**

## CUTTING WITH HAND TOOLS

When cutting with hand tools, first make a careful layout with a square, marking lines across the stock and down both edges. A good procedure is to mark one line with a square and then to place the insert piece on the line so it can be used as a guide for marking the second line. The two lines will tell how wide the dado must be.

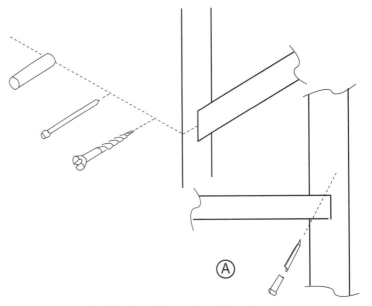

Make the shoulder cuts first by using a backsaw as shown in **Figure 3-10**. The strip of wood that is clamped to the saw acts as a depth gauge and ensures that the cuts will be to the same depth throughout their length. The wood strip also helps to keep the saw perpendicular as sawing is done. Remove the waste by using a chisel, working mostly from

**3-10 Shoulder cuts made with a backsaw will be more accurate and of uniform depth if control is established with a strip of wood clamped to the saw.**

**3-11 Clean away the waste between the shoulder cuts with a chisel of suitable width.**

the end to the center and removing thinner shavings the closer you get to the bottom of the groove (**Fig. 3-11**).

Another way to remove the waste is to work with a *router plane,* but do not set its blade to the full depth of the groove right off (**Fig. 3-12**). It's better to make a few shallow cuts rather than a single deep one. Often, the bulk of the waste is removed with a chisel and the router plane is used to complete the job.

Stopped cuts can be formed by hand using the router plane but it's best to start with a square or rectangular cavity as indicated by the arrow in **Figure 3-13**. The cavity can be formed entirely with chisels or by first boring blind holes to remove the bulk of the waste and then cleaning out remaining waste with a chisel. The final steps are done in routine fashion — shoulder cuts with a backsaw followed by waste removal with the router plane or with chisels.

**3-12 A router plane can be used to clean out the waste, but do the job in stages. Deep cuts, where the tool must be forced, lead to rough work and inaccuracies.**

**3-13 Forming a square cavity first with chisels is the way to start forming a stopped dado with hand tools.**

**3-14** Forming a dado on a table saw. A miter gauge hold-down keeps the work secure, while stop rods gauge the location of the cut. The cutting tool used here is a dado assembly.

**3-15** Dadoing on a radial arm saw. Here too, the cutting tool is a dado assembly.

## POWER TOOL WORK

U-shaped cuts can be made quickly and precisely on a table saw (**Fig. 3-14**) or on a radial arm saw (**Fig. 3-15**). The cuts being demonstrated, since they are across the grain, are *dadoes*. **Figure 3-16** shows *grooves* being formed on a radial arm saw. Normally, the head of the machine is turned 90 degrees counterclockwise and the workpiece is moved from right to left, which means *against* the cutter's direction of rotation — a standard, and critical, procedure. The distance of the cutter from the fence determines the edge distance of the groove. On a table saw, the setup is the same as you would use for ripping. The fence is set to gauge the distance from the edge of the stock to the cut.

Quick and accurate work is possible because of special tools that are used in place of the saw blade. A common one, known as a *dado assembly,* consists of two *outside* blades and a number of *chippers* that are placed between the blades. The blades, used alone, make a cut that is 1/4-inch wide. Chippers, of appropriate width, are placed between the blades to increase the width of the dado or groove. Often, since there is some variation in

**3-16** Grooving is accomplished on a radial arm saw by situating the cutter so it is parallel to the fence. Work is always fed *against* the cutter's direction of rotation.

stock thicknesses, paper washers are used along with the chippers to bring the cut-width to a precise dimension.

Adjustable dadoing tools have attracted a wide woodworking audience since they are infinitely adjustable from zero to their widest setting. Thus, by some means that is peculiar

**3-17 An adjustable dadoing tool. Turning the hub adjusts the cutting blades for a specific cut width.**

**3-18 A twin-blade, adjustable dadoing tool. The collar is used to adjust width of cut. (Sears Roebuck photo)**

to the accessory, settings are easily organized to match exactly the thickness of any stock within its capacity. Examples of adjustable dadoing tools are shown in **Figures 3-17** and **3-18**.

Dadoing tools remove a lot of material so feed speed, how fast the work is moved, should be moderate, only enough to allow the cutters to work as they should. Forcing the cut will only result in burn marks on the work and the tool. When a very deep dado is needed, several passes, with a depth adjustment after each, will make the job easier to do and will result in smoother, more accurate work. Always make a test cut in scrap stock before working on the project material.

## BACK-TO-BACK DADOES

Many projects require back-to-back dadoes. An example would be a bookcase with an intermediate partition. The work can be done with careful layout, but a better technique is to supply a jig that will automatically align the cuts. Example jigs that can be used on a table saw are shown in **Figures 3-19** and **3-20**. One jig is secured with clamps; the alternate jig is secured with bolts. After the cut is made on one side of the stock, the work is flipped over and the opposite dado is formed. The location of the guide determines the spacing between cuts. It's important to situate the guide correctly so that the dadoes will be at right angles to the edge of the work.

## STOPPED DADOES

Stopped dadoes can be done on a radial arm saw as shown in **Figure 3-21**. The cut can be made to a line on the work, but controlling the length of the cut is done best by using a clamp on the arm of the machine. The purpose of the clamp is to limit the distance the

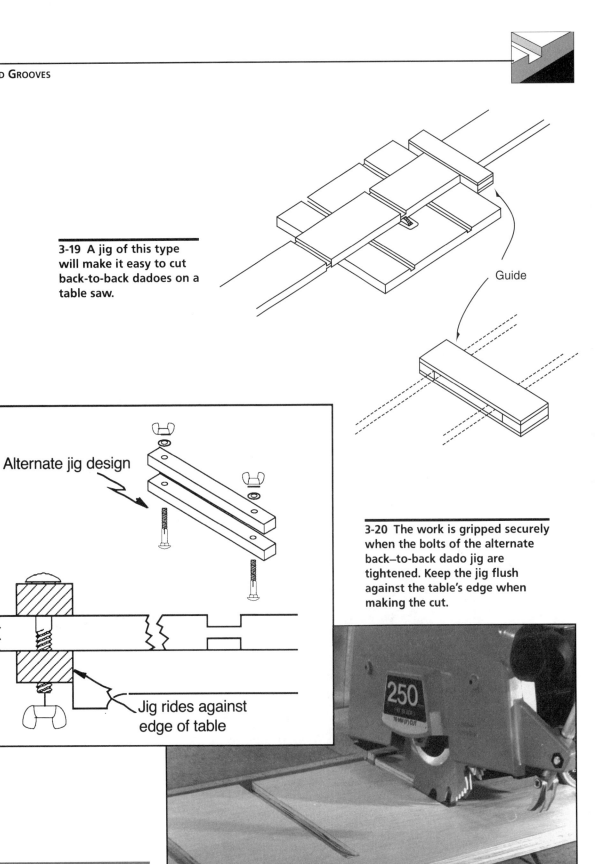

3-19 A jig of this type will make it easy to cut back-to-back dadoes on a table saw.

Guide

Alternate jig design

Jig rides against edge of table

3-20 The work is gripped securely when the bolts of the alternate back–to-back dado jig are tightened. Keep the jig flush against the table's edge when making the cut.

3-21 Stopped dadoes can be accomplished on a radial arm saw by cutting to a line on the work, or by using a clamp on the machine's arm to limit how far the cutting tool can be brought forward.

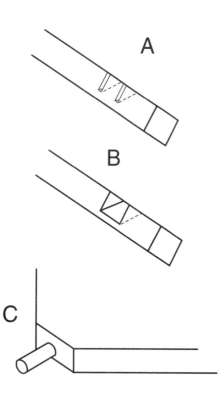

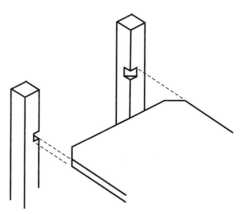

**3-22 Corner dadoes will provide good support for a table shelf or shelves in open case projects.**

cutting tool can be brought forward. The best way to work on a table saw is to clamp a length of wood at the back of the saw to serve as a stop. The length of the cut will equal the distance from the edge of the stop to the front edge of the cutter.

**3-23 The method to use when cutting corner dadoes on a radial arm saw. The support block has a V-groove along its length.**

## CORNER DADOES

The corner dado is a U-shaped cut made across a corner of a furniture component. An example of where it can be used effectively is the installation of a lower shelf on a table project (**Fig. 3-22**). The form is accomplished with hand tools by first making the shoulder cuts (**A**) and then cleaning out the waste with a chisel (**B**). The corners of the insert piece are shaped to fit the dado cut. Adding a dowel (**C**) will make the joint more secure.

Corner dadoes can be cut on power tools by using a method like the one demonstrated in **Figure 3-23**. The control block, which has a V-cut down its center, supports the work and holds it in correct position for the cut.

## OTHER METHODS

Dado sets are the tools to use when many similar cuts are required, but if the project calls for just one or two, the work can be accomplished with minimum fuss by making repeat passes with a regular saw blade (**Fig. 3-24**). Mark the dado outline on the work and then make as many passes as are needed to remove the waste. It's a good idea to make the shoulder cuts first and then cut between them with slightly overlapping passes.

with the tool or are available at extra cost, are also usable. The guides lock to the base of the router and have a fence to ride against the edge of the work. The distance from the fence to the cutter determines the edge distance of the cut.

The router bit should be the straight shank type like the one shown in **Figure 3-26**. Since these are available in various diameters, it's likely that one can be selected to suit the width of the cut required. If not, widening the cut can be accomplished by making a

**3-24** Dadoes or grooves can be formed by making repeat passes with a regular saw blade. Make the shoulder cuts first, then clean out between them with slightly overlapping cuts.

**3-25** A portable router, guided by a straightedge, will produce smooth, accurate grooves or dadoes. The router is moved from left to right.

Portable *routers* will produce smooth, accurate dadoes and grooves when a straightedge guide is provided (**Fig. 3-25**). A straight piece of wood that is tack-nailed or clamped to the work will serve as well as any commercial accessory. *Edge guides*, which might be supplied

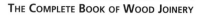

Router bits may also be used in a drill press if a special chuck that will withstand the side thrust is substituted for the standard 3-jaw chuck (**Fig. 3-27**). Use the machine's highest speed and move the workpiece from left to right. The direction of rotation of the cutter will tend to keep the work snug against the fence as the pass is made. Edge distance is controlled by the position of the fence, if the drill press has one, or by a straight strip of wood that is clamped in place. If the cut is a deep one, accomplish it by making repeat passes, lowering the cutter a bit after each one. Use the stop rod on the machine to control the maximum depth of the cut.

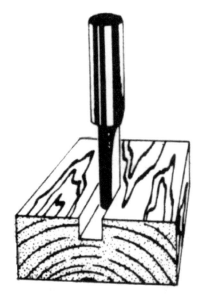

**3-26 Straight shank bits are used in a portable router to produce U-shapes.**

**3-27 Router bits may also be used in a drill press. It's necessary to substitute a special router chuck for the standard 3-jaw unit.**

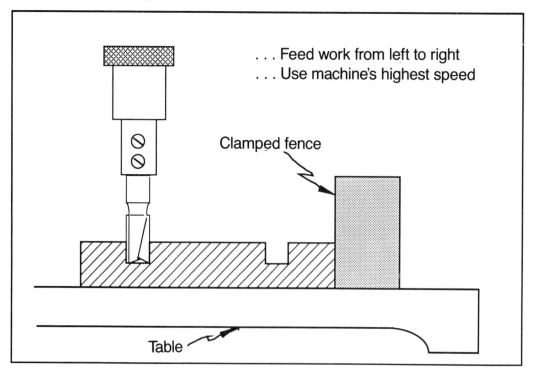

. . . Feed work from left to right
. . . Use machine's highest speed

Clamped fence

Table

# 4

# RABBET JOINTS

---

Typical Applications • Forming with Hand Tools • Power Tool Work •
Stopped Rabbets • Angled Rabbets

---

**T**he L-shaped cut that is required to form a rabbet joint is made in one of the pieces to be joined. It is always formed along the edge or on the end of stock and is called a "rabbet" regardless of whether it it is made *with* or *across* the grain (**Fig. 4-1**). The width of the cut usually matches the thickness of the insert. The depth of the cut may be one-half to two-thirds the thickness of the part in which it is made.

A good technique that will result in clean, smooth surfaces at the joint line is shown in **Figure 4-2**. The rabbet is cut a bit wider than necessary, so that after the parts are joined and the glue is dry, the excess can be sanded off so the

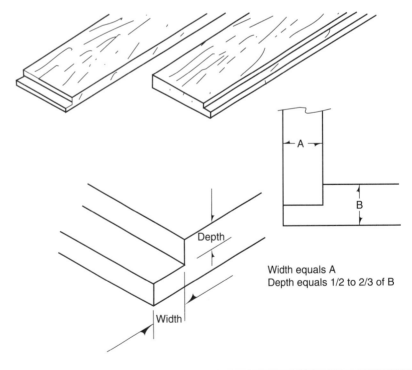

Width equals A
Depth equals 1/2 to 2/3 of B

**4-1 L-shaped cuts made *with* or *across* the grain are called rabbets — whether they are on the end or along the edge of stock.**

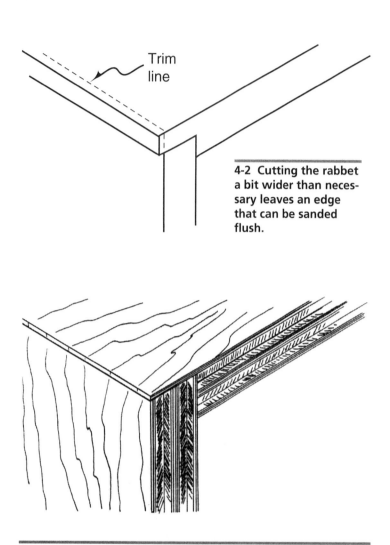

Trim line

**4-2 Cutting the rabbet a bit wider than necessary leaves an edge that can be sanded flush.**

**4-3 Very deep rabbets are often done on plywood joints to minimize unattractive edges. This leaves a weak area at the shoulder of the rabbet so reinforcements should be introduced when possible.**

## TYPICAL APPLICATIONS

Rabbet joints are commonly found in case and box constructions. Usually, it's best to form the L-shape in side members so the partial end-grain that is exposed will be less visible. Much depends on the purpose of the project; whether, for example, it will be wall-hung or freestanding. Decide which components will have the rabbet cut in relation to how the project will be seen.

Many cases and cabinets that have back panels will have rabbet cuts along the back edges of the case members so the panel can be inset (**Fig. 4-4**). Cut the rabbets a bit deeper than the thickness of the panel. When the project is wall-hung, it's better to form the rabbets 1/4-inch to 1/2-inch deeper than necessary so the back edges of the cabinet can be trimmed to conform to any irregularities that might be on the wall. One possibility is that the wall might be a bit out of plumb.

A rabbet is often used as the front-to-side joint in drawers. The side of the drawer can be flush or the rabbet can be deep enough so the front of the drawer will have a lip (**Fig. 4-5**). This is not a very strong joint if the only bond is glue. However, nails, screws, or dowel pegs driven through the side into the edge of the drawer-front can be included to compensate.

Rabbeted pieces are frequently used to conceal joints (butt joints, rabbets, even miters) in a project, or they might be added to adorn a corner (**Fig. 4-6**). When the motive is adornment, the additional parts can be treated in the various ways suggested in **Figure 4-7**. Components of this nature, when they are slight, do not add much strength and should not be viewed as structural elements. However, if they have substantial cross-sections, they can serve as panel framing and can even extend below a case to serve as legs.

Rabbet cuts formed in legs can perform

edge will be perfectly flush with the adjacent surface.

Sometimes, especially when the project material is plywood, the rabbet is deep enough so only the surface veneer remains (**Fig. 4-3**). This helps to conceal unattractive plywood edges but results in a weak area at the base of the shoulder. When the joint is designed this way, the case as a whole must be very strong. When possible, glue blocks or other reinforcements should be added to increase strength.

**4-4 Back panels on cabinets and chests should be installed in rabbets, so they will be flush or set back a bit from back edges.**

Cut rabbet deeper than thickness of back panel

Back Panel

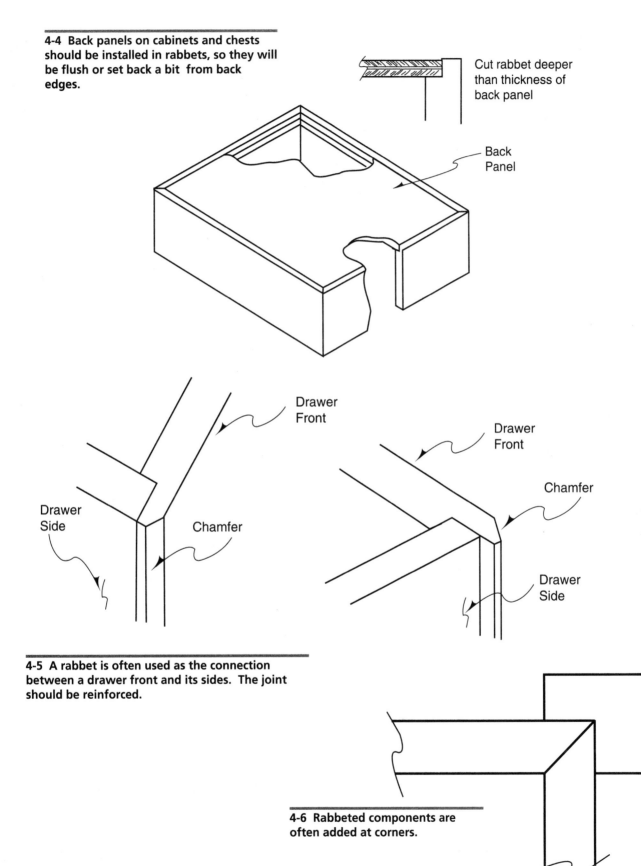

Drawer Front

Drawer Side

Chamfer

Drawer Front

Chamfer

Drawer Side

**4-5 A rabbet is often used as the connection between a drawer front and its sides. The joint should be reinforced.**

**4-6 Rabbeted components are often added at corners.**

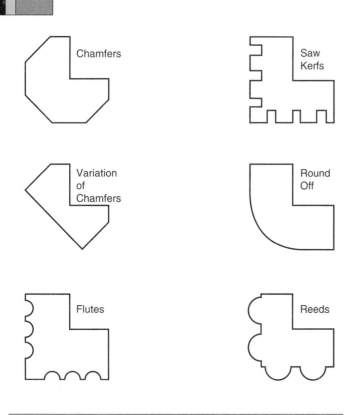

Chamfers

Saw
Kerfs

Variation
of
Chamfers

Round
Off

Flutes

Reeds

**4-7  Some of the ways that rabbeted corner pieces can be treated to make them more decorative.**

the full length of the leg. But rabbet cuts, like dadoes, can be stopped. We'll discuss that aspect of the joint a bit later.

## FORMING WITH HAND TOOLS

Rabbets, especially short ones, can be formed efficiently with a backsaw by making the two cuts that are illustrated in **Figure 4-9**. Use the insert piece first as a gauge to mark the width of the cut, adding, if you wish, the slight projection that was suggested in **Figure 4-2**. Use a square to extend the guide line down both edges and across the end of the stock. Use a backsaw to make the shoulder cut employing the same type of clamped-on guide that was described in Chapter 3 for dado work. Then make a second cut to remove the waste. Accuracy will depend on how carefully the sawing is done. Some workers will choose the optional method of removing the waste with a chisel. What method to use is a moot point; the result is what counts.

Long rabbets, whether they are with or across the grain, are easy to form with a *rabbet plane* (**Fig. 4-10**). This is a special hand tool that is equipped with a fence to control the width of the cut and with a stop that is adjustable for cut-depth. The plane will do its job precisely, but some preliminary practice on scrap stock is advisable. Be sure to operate so the tool's fence is snug against the work

as seats for rails (**Fig. 4-8**). When the rabbet cut is a bit deeper than the thickness of the rail, it will provide the shoulder indicated by detail (**A**) in the same illustration. This is a good way to design such assemblies, regardless of the joint that is used, since any separation that might occur in time will not be as visible as it would be if the parts were installed flush. Rabbet cuts formed in legs as seats for rails will not be attractive if they run

**4-8 Rabbets are often used as seats for other components. A set-back (A) is a good idea.**

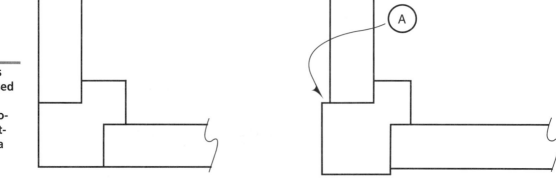

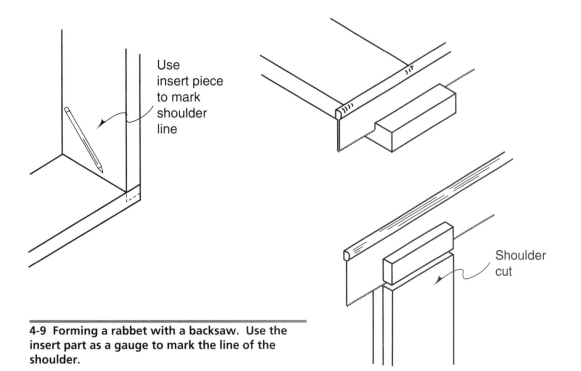

Use insert piece to mark shoulder line

Shoulder cut

**4-9 Forming a rabbet with a backsaw.** Use the insert part as a gauge to mark the line of the shoulder.

throughout the pass. Adjust the projection of the blade so you have to make several passes to achieve full depth of cut. Several light cuts are always better than a single deep one. Make passes *with* the grain whenever possible just as you would with a conventional plane.

Another feature of the plane is a *spur* that severs surface fibers in front of the cutter when work is done across the grain. Be sure to set the spur correctly by following the instructions that come with the tool. Splintering and feathering will occur if the spur is not set correctly.

**4-10 Using a rabbet plane.** Keep the tool's fence snug against the work throughout the pass.

## POWER TOOL WORK

Rabbets can be cut on a table saw by using a two-pass technique, which is similar to the procedure described for doing the job with a backsaw. Make the shoulder cut with the work flat on the table and with the rip fence used as a gauge (**Fig. 4-11**). It's okay to use the rip fence like this on job of this nature

since no cutoff is involved. Do be sure that alignment is correct. The rip fence must be parallel to the blade.

The width of the rabbet is the distance from the *outside* of the blade to the fence; its depth is the amount of saw blade projection. The waste is removed by making a second pass with the stock on edge. The saw-blade projection is adjusted to conform to the width

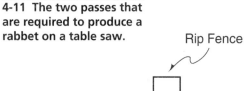

**4-11 The two passes that are required to produce a rabbet on a table saw.**

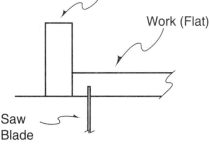

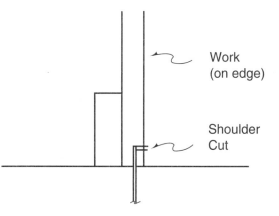

of the cut; the fence is set to control its depth. Always use a tenon jig when making cuts like this on narrow stock. Never make the second pass so that the waste will be captured between the blade and the fence; a kickback will surely result.

A dadoing tool can be used to form rabbets in a single pass as shown in **Figure 4-12**. The work can also be done with the stock riding against the fence but only if an auxiliary facing, like the one sketched in **Figure 4-13**, is provided. Rabbets on narrow stock are formed by feeding the work with a miter gauge. Use a hold-down, if one is available, to keep the work snugly in place throughout the pass (**Fig. 4-14**). Rabbets that are wider than the maximum setting of the cutting tool are accomplished by making repeat passes.

A rabbet being done an a radial arm saw is shown in **Figure 4-15**.

**4-12 Rabbeting goes quickly when the saw is equipped with a dadoing tool.**

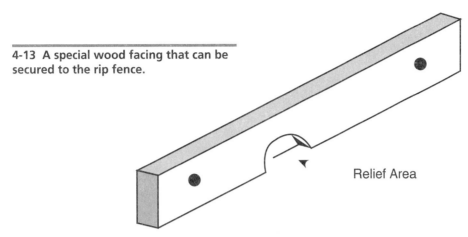

4-13 A special wood facing that can be secured to the rip fence.

Relief Area

4-14 Using a dadoing tool to form a rabbet on narrow stock. A hold-down ensures that the work will stay put while being cut.

4-15 Rabbeting on a radial arm saw. The elevation of the cutter above the table determines the depth of the cut.

**4-16 Forming a rabbet on a jointer. The homemade pusher hold-down is used to ensure accuracy, and for safety.**

On long cuts, the machine is set up as it would be for ripping operations. That is, the dadoing tool is set parallel to the fence and the work is moved *against* the direction of rotation of the cutter.

Another way to produce clean, accurate rabbets is to work on a *jointer* as shown in **Figure 4-16**. Most jointers are equipped with a *rabbeting ledge* that makes the application possible. Set the machine's fence to gauge the width of the cut; lower the infeed table for the cut depth you want. Be aware that on rabbeting operations the machine's guard can't be used. This calls for extra careful work. A combination pusher hold-down or a clamped-on hold-down like the one in **Figure 4-17** are requisites.

**Figure 4-18** shows a rabbet being formed with a portable router. Since the bit being used is a straight shank type, the router is guided by a straightedge. Special rabbeting bits for routers are available (**Fig. 4-19**). These have *pilots* that ride against the edge of the work and so control the width of the cut. Some pilots are integral; others are ball bearings. The latter type turns independently of the cutter's shank and so eliminates the burning that can occur when a solid pilot is riding against the edge of the stock.

**4-17 A clamped block of wood that will keep the work snugly down on the table is another way to work.**

4-18  A portable router is a good tool to use for rabbeting. Here, the router is guided by a straightedge.

4-19  A router bit that is designed specifically for forming rabbets.  The ball-bearing pilot, which is free to turn on its own, eliminates the burning that can occur when a bit has an integral pilot.

4-20  The arrow points to the area that is preformed with a chisel when a hand plane is used to form a stopped rabbet.

## STOPPED RABBETS

The procedure for stopped rabbets formed with a hand plane follows closely the one described for stopped dadoes. The end of the cut, where the rabbet stops, is formed with a chisel. The balance of the job is done with the plane (**Fig. 4-20**). For this work, the blade of the plane is set in the forward or "bullnose" position. Actually, once the starting cavity is made, the remaining waste can be removed with cuts made with a backsaw or dovetail saw.

Short stopped rabbets, often referred to as *notches*, can be used in the type of joint shown in **Figure 4-21**. The shapes can be produced by using a handsaw and chisels or with a router or a power tool that is equipped with a dadoing tool. The router or the power saw is used to remove the bulk of the waste; chisel work completes the job.

Stopped rabbets can be faked by making the cut full length and then blocking one end with a filler strip (**Fig. 4-22**). This makes the job easier to do, but it introduces an additional joint line. The filler strip should be cut to match the grain pattern and direction of the parent stock.

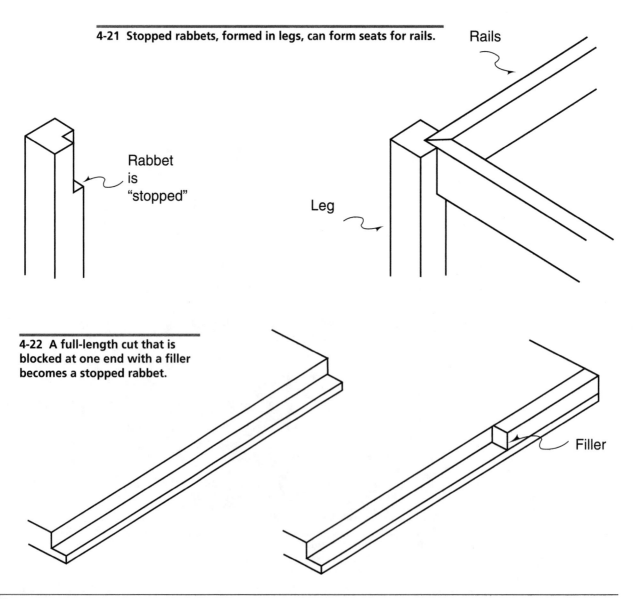

**4-21 Stopped rabbets, formed in legs, can form seats for rails.**

Rails

Rabbet is "stopped"

Leg

**4-22 A full-length cut that is blocked at one end with a filler becomes a stopped rabbet.**

Filler

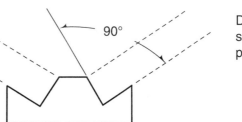

**4-23 Components with angled rabbets can be used to join parts that do not turn 90 degrees.**

90°

Dotted lines show insert pieces

## ANGLED RABBETS

Angled rabbets, like the examples in **Figure 4-23**, are needed when adjacent pieces do not make a 90-degree turn. Notice that the shoulders of the rabbet still form a 90 degree angle even though the form itself is not square to adjacent areas.

A typical application is shown in **Figure 4-24** where rabbeted connectors are used as joint components in a segmented project. Many woodworkers find this technique easier to do than simple or splined miters, but a major incentive is that the rabbeted posts provide a design element. Like rabbeted corner covers, parts like this can be embellished with chamfers, flutes or reeds and other details.

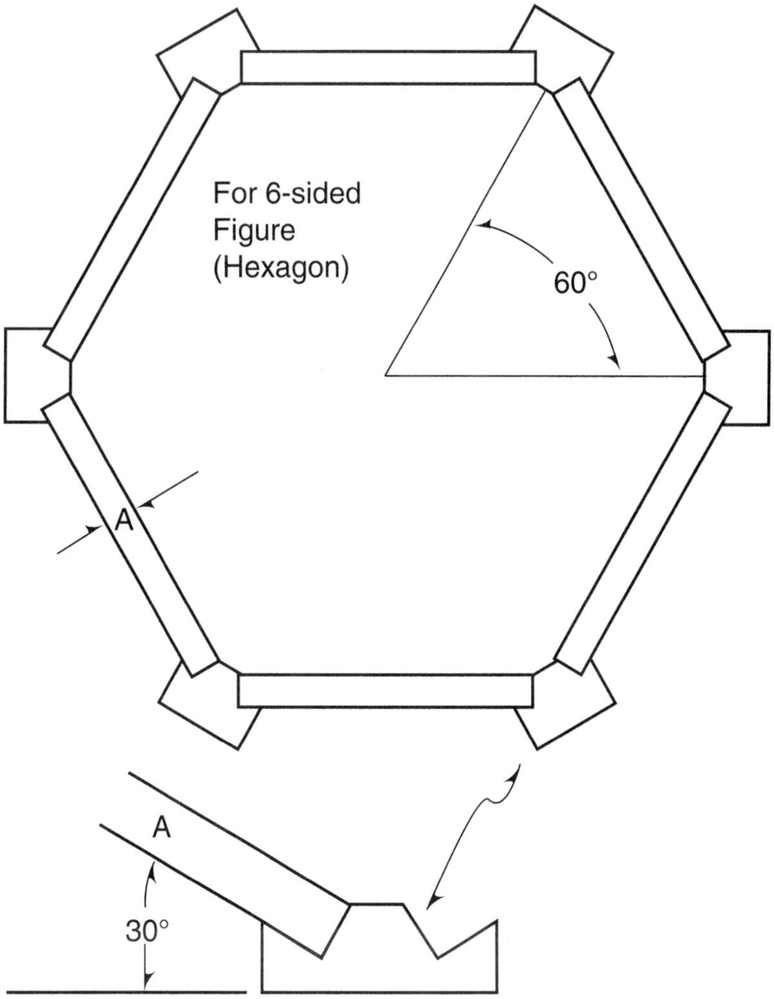

**4-24 Components with angled rabbets may be used to join the parts of a segmented assembly.**

For 6-sided Figure (Hexagon)

60°

A

A

30°

4-25 How a radial arm saw is organized to cut angled rabbets. Be sure to note the use of a guard.

One way to form angles rabbets is demonstrated in **Figure 4-25** where the cutting is being done on a radial arm saw that is equipped with a dadoing tool. Once the setup is established, any number of pieces can be passed through. All cuts will be duplicates.

**Figure 4-26** suggests a way to work when many duplicate parts are needed. Form the rabbets on a long piece and then separate it into the number of pieces that are needed. Always work with the guard and use push sticks when the workpiece is narrow. Push sticks are easy to make and replace. Your fingers are not.

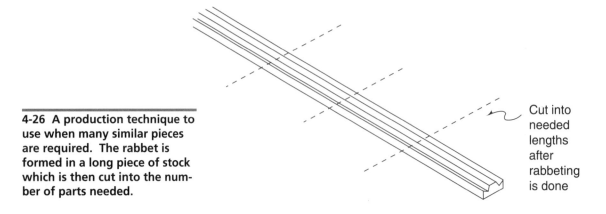

4-26 A production technique to use when many similar pieces are required. The rabbet is formed in a long piece of stock which is then cut into the number of parts needed.

Cut into needed lengths after rabbeting is done

# 5

# MITER JOINTS

Accuracy Is Critical • The Miter Box • Table Saw Work • Radial Arm Saw Cuts • Reinforcements *(Splines, Feathers, Dowels)* • Compound Miter Joints *(With Hand Tools, With Power Tools, With Splines, On a Radial Arm Saw)* • Special Miter Joints *(Tongue-and-Groove Miter, Housed Rabbet-Miter, True Rabbet-Miters, Locked Rabbet-Miter)*

well-executed miter joint is pleasing to the eye because it leaves a virtually unbroken grain pattern at the corner and shows minimum joint line (**Fig. 5-1**). Another advantage of the design is demonstrated in **Figure 5-2**, where it is compared with a butt joint to show how it conceals end-grain. This is accomplished even when the parts have different widths by cutting miter angles (**Fig. 5-3**) that complement each other.

The layout method to use when the components have different widths is shown in **Figure 5-4**. Place one part over the other as shown in detail (**A**) and make a mark to indicate the width of the overlay. The cut-line (**B**) is drawn from the mark to the corner. After the first piece is cut, used it as a pattern to mark the cut-line on the mating part.

The simple miter, however, is not a very strong connection. For one thing, the mating

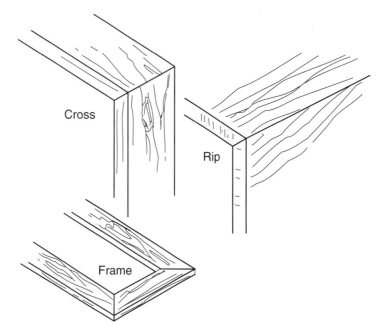

**5-1 The grain pattern on parts joined with a miter can be closely matched by careful planning.**

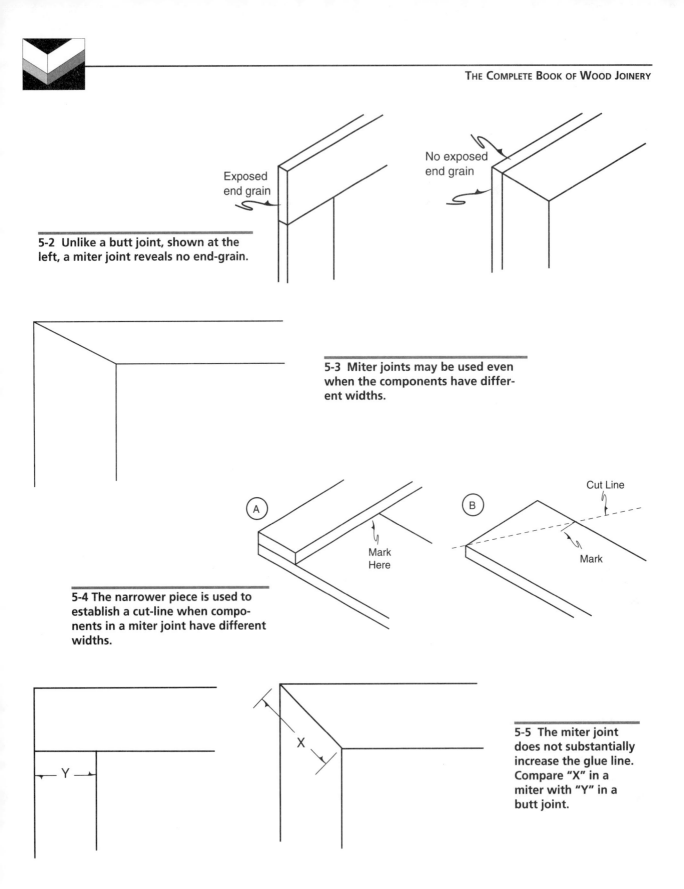

**5-2 Unlike a butt joint, shown at the left, a miter joint reveals no end-grain.**

Exposed end grain

No exposed end grain

**5-3 Miter joints may be used even when the components have different widths.**

A

B

Mark Here

Cut Line

Mark

**5-4 The narrower piece is used to establish a cut-line when components in a miter joint have different widths.**

X

Y

**5-5 The miter joint does not substantially increase the glue line. Compare "X" in a miter with "Y" in a butt joint.**

surfaces of frame and cross miters are virtually end grain, which doesn't contribute much strength to a glue bond. A second point is that the increase in contact surface, which is a variable that depends on the width and the thickness of the stock, is not impressive. A comparison with a butt joint supports the observation; "X" in **Figure 5-5** is not much

**5-6 Miters must be accurate and the best way to begin is with good layout procedures.**

longer than "Y." By actual measurement on a board that is 10 inches wide, the increase in a 45 degree miter is about 4 inches. On narrow pieces, which is usually the case with frame miters, the increase is much less.

Miter joints on projects like lightweight picture frames are usually assembled with glue and finishing nails. Heavier constructions, assemblies where durability is part of the intent, call for reinforcement procedures. These often involve dowels or splines. Sometimes, as will be shown later in this chapter, the joint is modified to include an interlock or simply to increase glue area.

## ACCURACY IS CRITICAL

If the miter joint is to form a 90 degree corner, each of the cuts must be 45 degrees. Careless cutting can result in small mistakes that add up to an enormous error when the four components of a frame, case, or cabinet are assembled. It will be very difficult to keep the project square and even if it is managed, there will be obvious gaps in the joint lines. The truth is, it's as feasible to work accurately as it is to be too casual. Careful layout and accurate sawing are not difficult techniques. Don't assume, for example, that the settings made on a power tool are precise. Make a test cut on scrap stock and check it carefully before sawing the project material.

Mark the guide lines for a miter cut by using an adjustable square (**Fig. 5-6**). When the length of the blade isn't long enough to span the width of the stock, remember that the diagonal of a square layout forms a 45 degree angle. By way of example, let's assume a 45 degree cut is required at the end of a piece of plywood that is 20 inches wide. Mark a line parallel to the end of the stock and 20 inches away. A 45 degree guide line appears when opposite corners are connected.

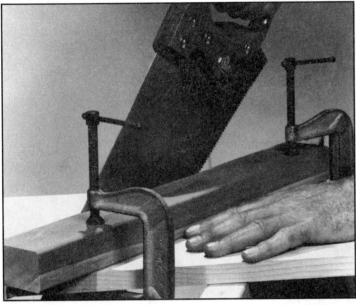

A guide line offers something to follow when sawing by hand or with power and it is an on-going check of accuracy. Any discrepancy will be immediately obvious. It's better to make adjustments when cutting than to realize the error at assembly time.

Whenever possible, especially when sawing by hand, establish a guide that will minimize the possibility of human error. The guide doesn't have to be complicated. Just a straight strip of wood clamped to the work, as shown in **Figure 5-7**, will do. The guide will keep the saw on the cut-line and will also help to produce an edge that is square to adjacent surfaces.

**5-7** Always use a clamped guide block when cutting with a handsaw.

**5-8** Nomenclature of a miter box. Such a box can be purchased or custom made.

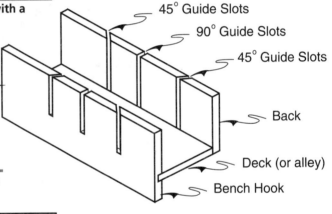

**5-9** A well-made miter box, used carefully, will ensure accurate cuts.

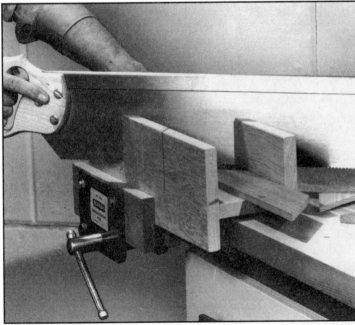

## THE MITER BOX

The common *miter box* is a wooden, U-shaped, holding device that has paired guide slots for a saw so left- or right-hand miters can be cut more accurately than is possible when sawing freehand. Most units include a set of guide slots for 90 degree cuts (**Fig. 5-8**). Some commercial units do not have the extra wide front that provides the *bench hook*. This is unfortunate since the hook helps to keep the accessory secure either by holding or clamping it against the edge of a workbench or by gripping it in a vise (**Fig. 5-9**).

Top View Showing
Guide Slot
Arrangement

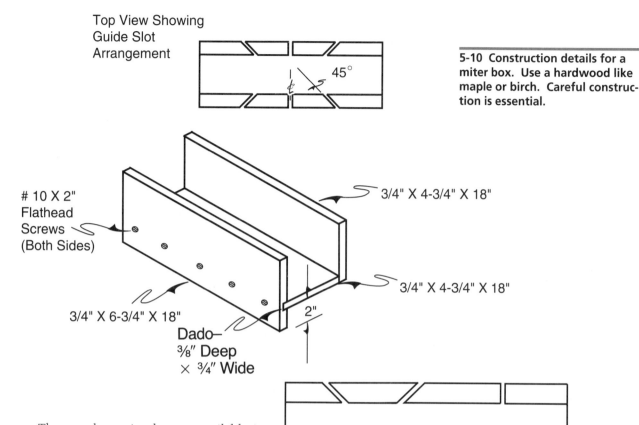

45°

**5-10 Construction details for a
miter box. Use a hardwood like
maple or birch. Careful construction is essential.**

3/4" X 4-3/4" X 18"

# 10 X 2"
Flathead
Screws
(Both Sides)

3/4" X 4-3/4" X 18"

3/4" X 6-3/4" X 18"

Dado—
3/8" Deep
× 3/4" Wide

2"

**5-11 Another way to arrange the guide slots
in a miter box.**

The wooden units that are available in stores, especially those found on bargain counters, leave something to be desired in terms of accuracy and construction. That's why most careful woodworkers will make their own, designing them along the lines of the project detailed in **Figure 5-10**. One dimension to check before making one is the height of the front and back when measured from the surface of the deck. This should be a bit less than the width of the backsaw measured from the bottom edge of the spine to the tips of the teeth, that will be used. This is necessary so the saw will be able to cut completely through the workpiece.

Cutting the guide slots accurately is the most critical factor. If they are not correct, the accessory won't be of much help. Mark the cut-lines carefully across the top edges and down the sides of the front and back parts. Form the slots with the saw that will be used with the box. Use a clamped-on guide to ensure that the slots will be perpendicular. The slots can be formed by clamping front

and back pieces together before assembly. If so, be sure alignment is precise before attaching parts permanently.

**Figure 5-11** suggests an alternate method of arranging the guide slots. An advantage of this design is that the uprights will be stronger because of the greater space between guide slots. A disadvantage is that the work, on some cuts, will not have as much support as it gets when slots are centered. Of course, to compensate, the length of the project can be increased.

The miter box is most useful for cutting frame miters, cross miters on narrow stock, and miter cuts on molding. In all cases, the normal procedure is to hold or clamp the work tightly so it is down on the deck and

**5-12** A high quality unit like this, also called a miter box, has many built-in features that make it easy to do many sawing jobs accurately.

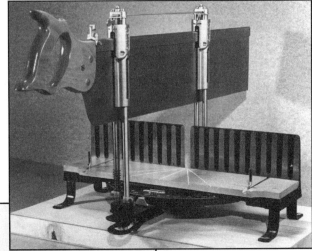

**5-13** Other examples of miter boxes that are available commercially. They vary in price, features, and rigidity.

snug against the back and to keep it so until the cut is complete. The teeth on backsaws are not designed for the fastest type of sawing, so rushing and forcing will accomplish nothing but inaccuracies and rough cuts.

The tools shown in **Figures 5-12** and **5-13** are also miter boxes, but they are commercial units with built-in features that make sawing easier and more accurate. Index plates, on some, have positive locks that automatically position the saw for miter cuts other than the common 45 degrees. The saw guides are adjustable to accommodate different blade gauges, and stops are provided to limit cut-depth when necessary. This is helpful, for example, when the tool is used to make the shoulder cuts for a dado.

**5-14** A relative newcomer for miter cutting, in the home workshop area anyway, works with a power driven circular saw blade. Features include indexing plates and adjustable hold-downs.

An example of a relative newcomer in the field of miter cutting, shown in **Figure 5-14**, is called a power miter box. It has an attached, pivoting motor that drives a circular saw blade. The advantages in minimizing physical effort are obvious, and since the machine has built-in stops that automatically set the angularity of the blade, there are gains in accuracy also. Some machines allow the blade to be tilted; this permits cutting compound miters as well as simple ones.

## TABLE SAW WORK

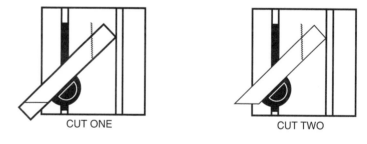

5-15 Cutting a frame miter on a table saw. A miter gauge hold-down will keep the work in place throughout the pass.

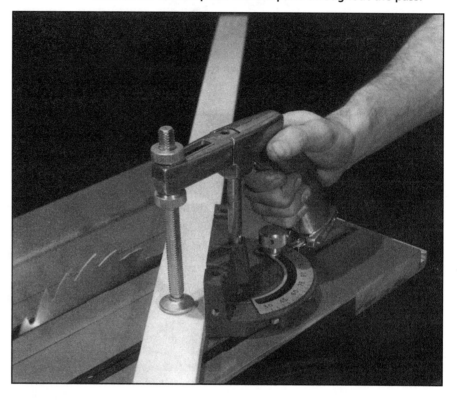

Frame miters are cut on a table saw by setting the miter gauge to the necessary angle and making the pass, preferably with a hold-down as shown in **Figure 5-15**. The operation is being done with the gauge in a closed position, but an open position — when the miter gauge is at the opposite 45 degree stop — can also be used. The latter position is preferred by some workers since it helps to keep hands farther away from the blade. It is critical to keep the work firmly in place throughout the pass to guard against the tendency of the blade to pivot the work about the front edge of the miter gauge. When the stock is flat, there is no need to reset the gauge for the second cut. The work is flipped end-for-end for the second pass as shown in **Figure 5-16**. The material is face up for the first cut, face down for the second one.

In any situation where the stock must remain face up, as is the case with moldings, the second cut must be made after resetting the miter gauge to the opposite 45 degree stop and using the miter gauge on the other side of the saw blade (**Fig. 5-17**). Having to reset the miter gauge offers another opportunity to make a mistake so cutting good stock should follow tests made on scrap material.

The direction of the pass, which is against the blade's rotation, creates a force that tends to pivot the work or move it along the gauge. The technical term for this negative action is *creep*. Holding the work firmly as the cut is made or using a hold-down are essential procedures. Adding an extension, which can be purchased or made, to the miter gauge is a wise move. The extension provides good

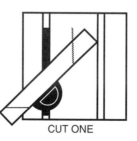

CUT ONE

CUT TWO

5-16 Frame miters on flat stock can be sawed without changing the miter gauge setting.

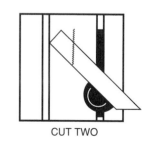

CUT ONE

CUT TWO

5-17 Extra care is required when mitering shaped pieces like moldings since the position and the setting of the miter gauge must be changed. Some workers keep an extra miter gauge on hand for work like this.

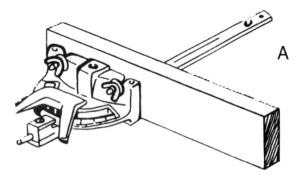

5-18 A miter gauge extension, faced with fine sandpaper, helps to keep work in place during miter sawing. Actually, using an extension is good practice on most any sawing operation.

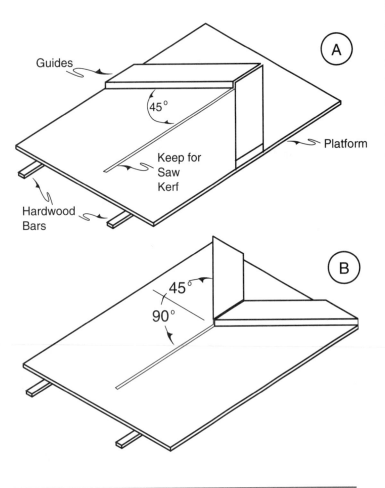

5-19 Well-made sliding tables can be used indefinitely for accurate miter sawing. The possibility of creep is eliminated since jig and work move together.

support and when faced with fine sandpaper, as shown in **Figure 5-18**, will help guard against creep.

Units known as *sliding tables* are easy to construct and will produce accurate cuts indefinitely if they are made carefully. The advantage of the jigs is that they eliminate the possibility of human error. Two examples of sliding tables that can be dimensioned to suit the saw being used are shown in **Figure 5-19**. The procedure for making either is the same.

Use 3/8-inch or 1/2-inch plywood for the platform, hardwood for the bars that will ride in the table slots. Size the bars for a good slip-fit and place them in the slots. Place the platform so its long centerline will be over the blade and parallel to the cut-path of the blade and tack-nail it to the bars. Next, clamp the platform in place and raise the blade so it cuts a slot through the platform. Then, remove the clamps and elongate the slot. Turn the project over and attach the bars permanently with glue and short flathead screws.

The guides must be positioned accurately in relation to the slot. Make a layout with a large square and then add the guides temporarily by tack-nailing. Make some test cuts and adjust the guides if necessary before attaching them permanently.

The sliding table in use in **Figures 5-20** and **5-21** is a more sophisticated model, having individual, removable guides and a single platform, but the two depicted in **Figure 5-19** work the same way. In one case,

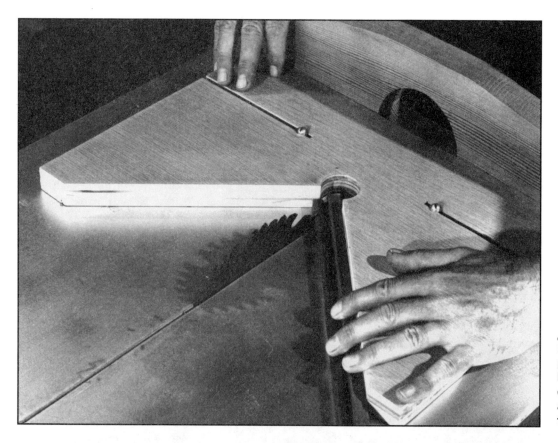

**5-20** Frame pieces that have been pre-cut to length are mitered this way.

**5-21** Cutting consecutively from a single piece is accomplished in this manner. The sliding table used in this and the previous illustration is equipped with removable mitering guides.

the frame pieces are precut to length; in the other, parts are cut consecutively from a single length of material. In both cases, since miter cuts at each end of a part point in opposite directions, both bearing edges of the guides come into play.

Since the purpose of sliding tables is to produce smooth, accurate cuts, it's wise to use them with a quality planer-type saw blade.

*Cross miters* are cut as shown in **Figure 5-22**. The setup is the same as that used for cross-cutting except that the blade is tilted. Good work security is essential so using a hold-down is wise. Make the pass more slowly than you would normally and place the work so its good side is up.

Sawing a *rip miter,* which is essentially a bevel, follows the same procedure used for simple ripping. (**Fig. 5-23**). Be sure the edge of the stock that rides the rip fence is smooth and straight and that the alignment of the fence to the saw blade is correct.

**5-22 Cross miters are done on a table saw by tilting the blade to the necessary angle. The pass is made with the miter gauge and, preferably, with a hold-down.**

**5-23 Rip miters are cut by using the fence as it would be for a rip cut. A combination pusher hold-down is an asset on operations like this.**

## RADIAL ARM SAW CUTS

Frame miters are cut on the radial arm saw by swinging the arm of the machine to the angle needed and then pulling the blade through as you would for a crosscut (**Fig. 5-24**). An advantage of the radial arm saw is that the work stays put; the rotation of the blade tends to keep the work back against the fence, and since the work is stationary, there is no danger of creep. Once test cuts are made to check out the setting, a stop block can be secured to the fence so that any number of duplicate pieces can be sawed (**Fig. 5-25**). This will work whether pieces are precut to length or cut consecutively from a single piece. When cutting consecutively, the stock is flipped over for each cut.

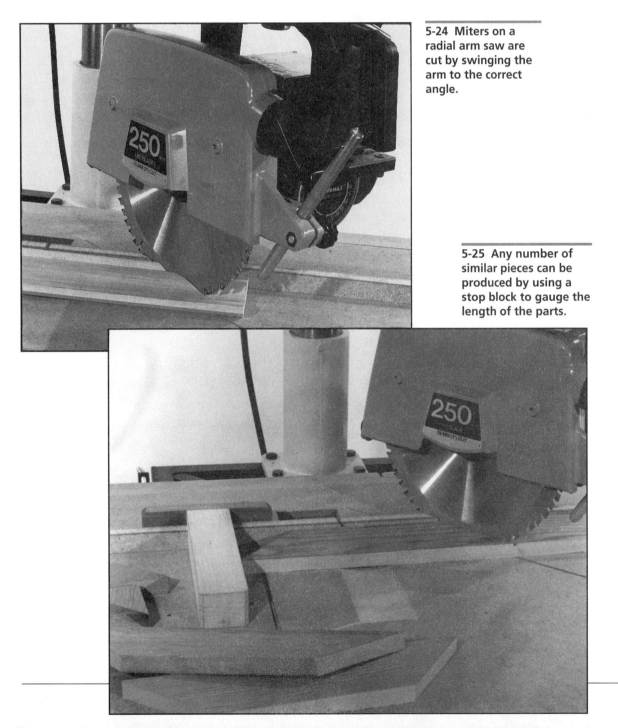

5-24 Miters on a radial arm saw are cut by swinging the arm to the correct angle.

5-25 Any number of similar pieces can be produced by using a stop block to gauge the length of the parts.

5-26 The radial arm saw stays in crosscut mode when a mitering jig is used. Left and right guides must be 45 degrees to the cut-line.

Working with a jig that is tack-nailed or clamped to the table is a preferred method of working (**Fig. 5-26**). With this arrangement, the arm is used in normal crosscut fashion. The guides on the auxiliary table provide for accuracy. The jig may be used for flat pieces or molding, but in each case the parts must first be cut to length.

The only difference between straight cross-cutting and ripping and cross and rip miters is that for the miters, cuts are made with the blade set at an angle. Work is held against the fence and the blade is pulled through for a cross miter; for a rip miter, the blade is set parallel to the fence and the work is moved against the blade's direction of rotation.

## REINFORCEMENTS

*Corrugated nails* and "Skotch" fasteners are often used to reinforce miter joints (**Fig. 5-27**). They are not very attractive items but adequate for utility projects and for joints that will be concealed.

A more sophisticated fastener, shown in **Figure 5-28**, is a *clamp nail*. Its special configuration pulls parts together tightly. Its design, however, calls for a narrow groove which, in commercial practice, is usually formed with a special 22-gauge saw blade. An alternate method, when the size of the stock permits, is to cut the grooves on a band saw since its blade cuts a much finer kerf than, say, a con-

5-27 Corrugated nails and "Skotch" fasteners are often used to reinforce miter joints.

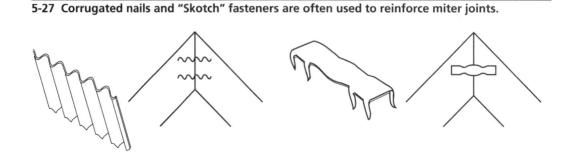

ventional circular saw blade. Another suggestion is to cut the grooves with a backsaw or dovetail saw. A simple test on scrap stock will tell whether the kerfs are suitable. The average clamp nail is 9/16-inch wide, so kerfs about 5/16-inch deep will accommodate them while providing some clearance.

Clamp nails can be driven into both ends of the joint if the stock is wide and, like finishing nails, they can be set below the surface of the wood and concealed with wood dough.

Clamp Nail

5-28 Clamp nails are more sophisticated devices for strengthening miter joints.

## Splines

Splines (**Fig. 5-29**) have many advantages. They supply considerable strength, help to keep parts united during assembly, are not objectionable when left exposed, especially if they are made of a contrasting material, and they can be used for any type of miter joint.

As shown in **Figure 5-30**, the splines fit into matched grooves that are cut in the mating pieces. It's always best to work with splines that are longer than necessary, so they can be trimmed and sanded flush after the glue dries.

Splines used in cross and rip miters usually work well if their width is equal to the thickness of the stock. It's good practice to install

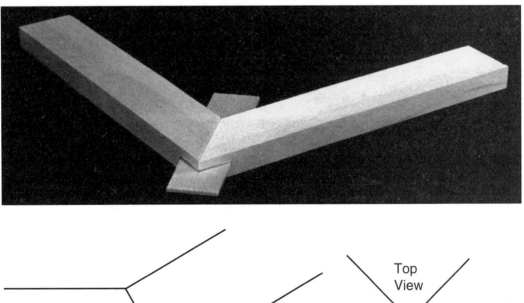

5-29 Splines, that can be solid wood, plywood or hardboard, strengthen miter joints and also make it easier to assemble parts.

Top View

Spline

Spline

5-30 How splines are used in a frame miter. The excess is trimmed and sanded flush after the glue dries. When wood is used as spline material, the grain should run across the width of the spline.

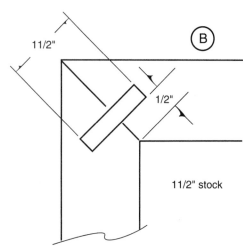

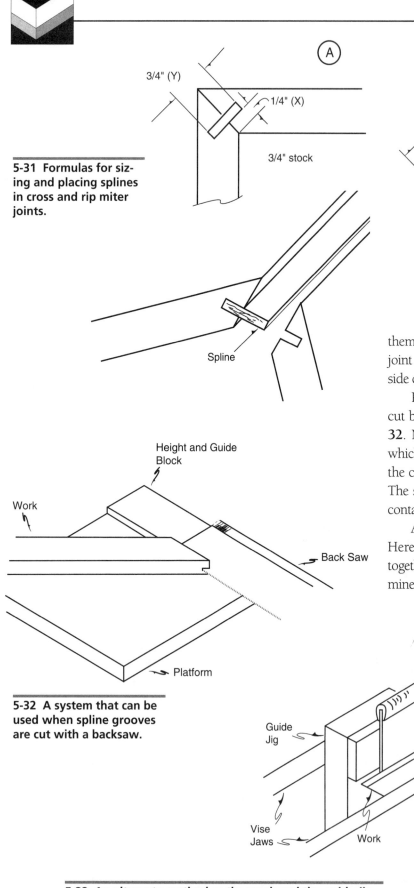

**5-31 Formulas for sizing and placing splines in cross and rip miter joints.**

**5-32 A system that can be used when spline grooves are cut with a backsaw.**

them so that they favor the inside corner of the joint (**Fig. 5-31**). Placing them close to the outside corner will result in some weak areas.

Kerfs for splines in frame miters can be cut by using a setup like the one in **Figure 5-32**. Note that the thickness of the block on which the saw rests will control the location of the cuts, while its width will gauge cut-depth. The saw will stop penetrating when its spline contacts the edge of the guide block.

Another system is shown in **Figure 5-33**. Here, the guide and the work are clamped together in a vise. Again, the guide block determines the location and the depth of the cuts.

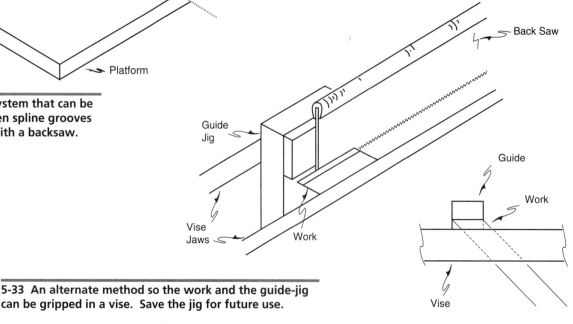

**5-33 An alternate method so the work and the guide-jig can be gripped in a vise. Save the jig for future use.**

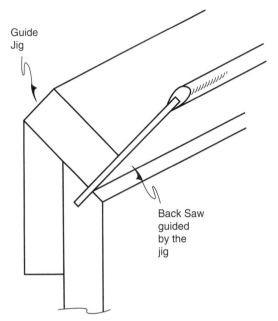

Guide
Jig

Back Saw
guided
by the
jig

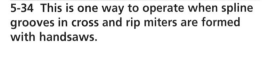

**5-34** This is one way to operate when spline grooves in cross and rip miters are formed with handsaws.

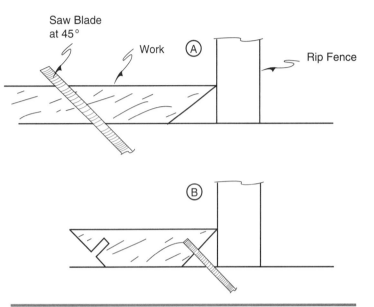

Saw Blade
at 45°

Work (A)

Rip Fence

(B)

**5-35** Sawing spline grooves with a table saw. The angle of the blade is the same for the miter cut and the spline groove.

**Figure 5-34** suggests one way to organize when spline grooves are needed in cross and rip miters. The important consideration is that the grooves must be perpendicular to the miter-cut. The depth of the groove is controlled with a stop block clamped to the saw. Grooves cut with a backsaw or coping saw are pretty narrow, but they can be widened by resawing with a crosscut or even a rip saw.

**Figure 5-35** demonstrates how spline grooves are cut on a table saw. Detail (**A**) shows the setup for the miter cuts. For the grooves (**B**), keep the blade at the same angle but adjust its projection for the depth of the groove.

If the grooves are required for a frame miter, sawing is done as shown in **Figure 5-36**. The first pass (**A**) is made with the work forming a closed angle with the table at the front edge of the blade. The second pass (**B**), at the opposite end of the stock, is made with the same side of the work against the fence but with the angle open. Even though the depth of the cuts is usually shallow, this kind of freehand sawing must be done very carefully for the sake of accuracy and safety. Making the passes with the same side of the work against the fence will ensure that the grooves will match, even though they may not be exactly centered.

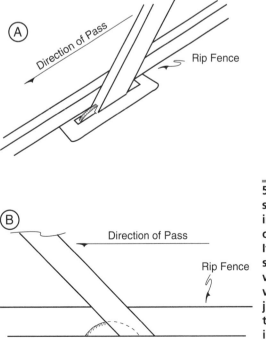

(A)

Direction of Pass

Rip Fence

(B)

Direction of Pass

Rip Fence

**5-36** Cutting spline grooves in frame miters on a table saw. It's better and safer to do work like this with a special jig, like the one that is detailed in Figure 5-39.

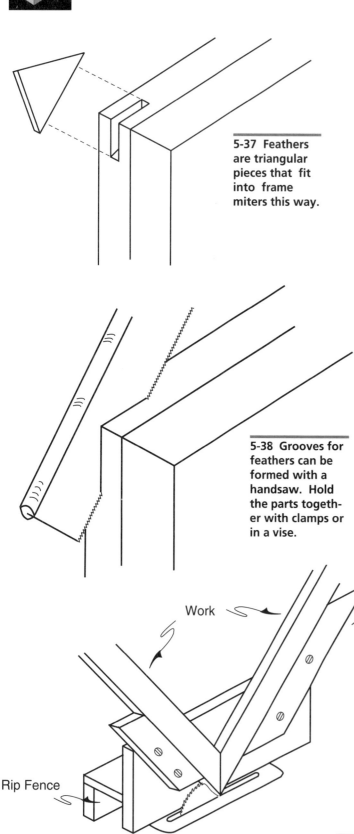

**5-37 Feathers are triangular pieces that fit into frame miters this way.**

**5-38 Grooves for feathers can be formed with a handsaw. Hold the parts together with clamps or in a vise.**

## Feathers

*Feathers,* which are, in a sense, partial splines, are often used to reinforce frame miters (**Fig. 5-37**). Feathers, in final form, are triangular, but it's better to cut them as rectangles so they can be trimmed and sanded flush after they have been installed.

Whenever possible, hold the joint parts together with clamps or in a vise, so the groove for the feather can be cut in both parts at the same time (**Fig. 5-38**). The depth of the groove, while it should not be excessive, is not critical since the feathers can be sized to suit.

**Figure 5-39** shows how grooves for feathers can be cut simultaneously in mating parts accurately and safely. The jig is made so it will slide smoothly, but without wobble, on the rip fence. The work, positioned by the guides that are installed at the angles shown in the drawing, is clamped to the jig. The jig with only one of the guides, can also be used to form spline grooves in frame miters.

Grooves for feathers or splines can be cut on a radial arm saw if the work is elevated on a platform and the saw blade set parallel to

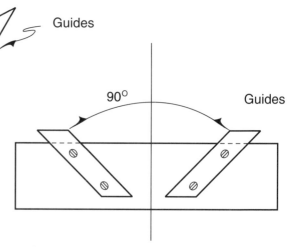

**5-39 A jig to make for forming feather-grooves on a table saw. The jig should also be used for cutting spline grooves in frame miters.**

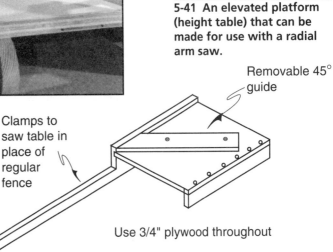

**5-40 A special, elevated platform is used for cutting feather or spline grooves with a radial arm saw.**

**5-41 An elevated platform (height table) that can be made for use with a radial arm saw.**

Removable 45° guide

Clamps to saw table in place of regular fence

Use 3/4" plywood throughout

the machine's table (**Fig. 5-40**). The jig can be made by adopting the design offered in **Figure 5-41**. If the guide is installed with screws, so it is removable, the jig can be used for cutting grooves across the end of square stock and for other chores like making cheeks cuts for tenons and rabbets.

## Dowels

Holes for dowel reinforcements in frame miters must be perpendicular to the cut. The holes can be bored freehand, but it's always better to provide a guidance system. A doweling jig like the one that was described in Chapter 1 can be used when the drilling tool is a hand brace; custom-designed guide blocks can be used with portable electric drills. A good setup for doing the work on a drill press is shown in **Figure 5-42**. Tilting the table to 45 degrees will position the work so

**5-42 Using the drill press for dowel holes in a miter. The small, clamped strip positions the pieces so holes in all components will have the same location.**

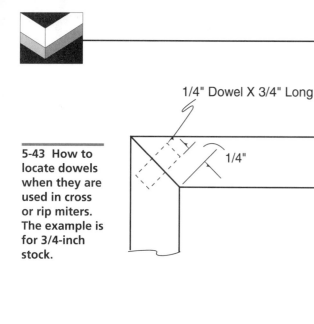

1/4" Dowel X 3/4" Long

1/4"

**5-43 How to locate dowels when they are used in cross or rip miters. The example is for 3/4-inch stock.**

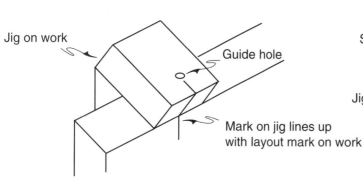

Jig on work

Guide hole

Mark on jig lines up with layout mark on work

**5-44 A jig made this way can be used for drilling holes with a brace or electric drill.**

the drill bit will enter perpendicular to the mitered edge. A straight strip that is clamped to the table, positioned so drilling will occur on the work's centerline, serves as a fence.

Dowels, used on cross and rip miters, should be installed as shown in **Figure 5-43**. Like splines, they should be positioned to favor the inside corner of the joint. The jig that is shown in **Figure 5-44** can be used with a hand brace or electric drill. In either case, a stop on the bit is used to control the depth of the hole.

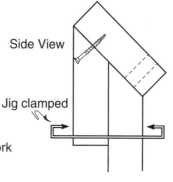

Side View

Jig clamped

A quick and practical way to use conventional dowels as frame-miter reinforcements is to hold the parts together and drill through both of them. Use a dowel that is longer than necessary so it can be trimmed and sanded flush after the glue dries (**Fig. 5-45**)

*Right angle dowels,* or *miter dowels* as they are often called, shown in **Figure 5-46A**, are relatively new items that facilitate the installation of dowel reinforcement in all miter joints. Since the special dowels are bent at 90 degrees, holes can be formed before sawing the miter. This allows working as shown in **Figure 5-46B**, an easier system than drilling into a mitered edge. The same thought applies when right angle dowels are used in a frame miter (**Fig. 5-47**). Miter dowels are made of plastic so they resist bending. Common sizes are 1/4-inch and 3/8-inch in diameter.

**5-45 Reinforcement dowels can be installed while the parts are held together.**

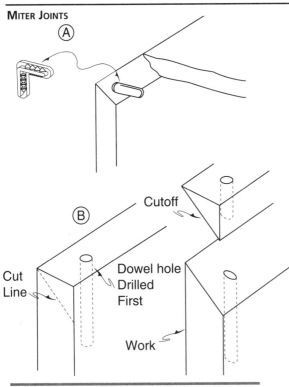

**5-46 The procedure to follow when miter dowels are used.**

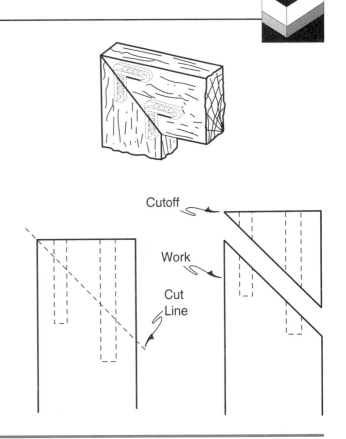

**5-47 The same procedure works when miter dowels are used in a frame miter.**

## COMPOUND MITER JOINTS

Compound miter joints are required whenever a project has sloping sides (**Fig. 5-48**). A four-sided peaked roof for a bird house, rails for a table with splayed legs, and a simple box with sloping sides are typical examples of projects requiring compound angle cuts. Actually, the joint is more difficult to visualize than it is to execute.

The box with straight sides shown in **Figure 5-49** doesn't require more than simple miters. But if the box is made with sloping sides, a cut that combines a miter and a bevel is needed. **Figure 5-50** demonstrates how the two cuts combine to form a compound miter. The cuts are not done separately, except in one particular technique that can be employed with hand tools.

Note that the top and bottom edges of the sloping sides will not be horizontal unless they are pre-beveled (**Fig. 5-51**). This is not critical on some projects, but if it is, the beveling can be done before cutting the compound miters and assembly work.

**5-48 Compound miter joints are required whenever a project has sloping sides.**

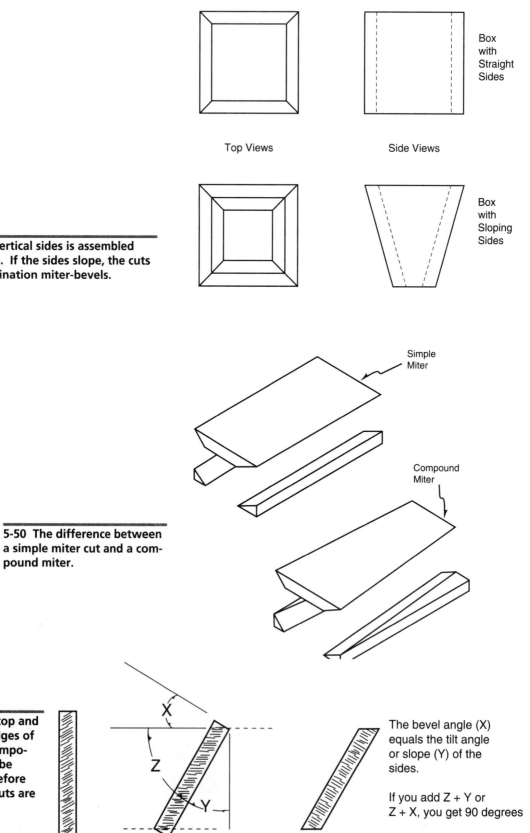

Box with Straight Sides

Top Views

Side Views

Box with Sloping Sides

**5-49** A box with vertical sides is assembled with simple miters. If the sides slope, the cuts required are combination miter-bevels.

Simple Miter

Compound Miter

**5-50** The difference between a simple miter cut and a compound miter.

**5-51** The top and bottom edges of sloping components can be beveled before the joint cuts are made.

The bevel angle (X) equals the tilt angle or slope (Y) of the sides.

If you add Z + Y or Z + X, you get 90 degrees

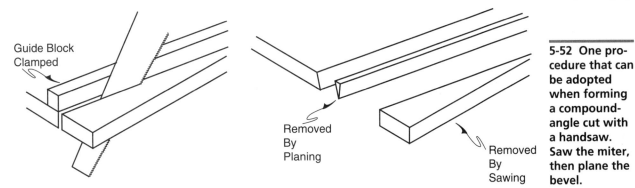

Guide Block Clamped

Removed By Planing

Removed By Sawing

**5-52 One procedure that can be adopted when forming a compound-angle cut with a handsaw. Saw the miter, then plane the bevel.**

## With Hand Tools

A two-step procedure when using hand tools is shown in **Figure 5-52**. The first cut, the miter, is a straightforward sawing job; the second step, done with a plane, produces the bevel. It's obvious that some very careful work is required. A better way to work is with a pre-beveled guide block that is clamped to the work at the correct miter angle (**Fig. 5-53**). Careful sawing will result in a compound angle cut in a single operation.

The angle of the miter and the bevel can't be arbitrary if the slope angle must be exact, but there are times — a shadow box picture frame is a case in point — when the slope angle is not critical so long as it is visually acceptable. When the work is held at a particular angle while a simple miter cut is made, the result will be a compound angle. **Figure**

5-54 shows how this is done with a miter box. A strip of wood, clamped to the bed of the tool, serves to brace the work at a slope angle that seems appropriate. The cut is made with the saw set at 45 degrees just as it would be for a simple miter.

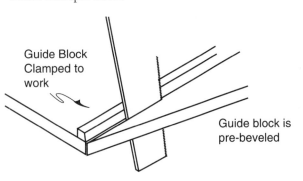

Guide Block Clamped to work

Guide block is pre-beveled

**5-53 A faster, easier way to make a compound cut with a handsaw is to work with a pre-beveled guide. Miter and bevel are made in one operation.**

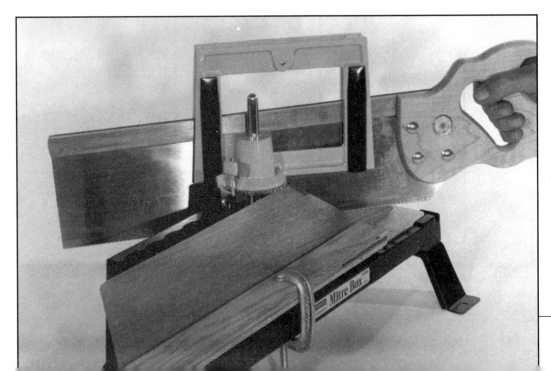

**5-54 When the work is braced at a slope angle and a 45 degree miter cut is made, a compound angle results.**

## With Power Tools

Compound cuts on a table saw are done by establishing both a miter gauge setting and a blade tilt (**Fig. 5-55**). Being accurate with both settings is critical. A slight error will be repeated many times, even if the project has only four sides.

The chart in **Figure 5-56** tells what the blade tilt and miter gauge settings must be for most commonly used slope angles. Note that some are to a fraction of a degree, a precision that isn't easy to achieve by relying entirely on the machine's stamped marking. Test cuts are in order before sawing good stock.

When the work is too wide for easy and safe handling with a miter gauge, the cuts should be made using a *taper jig* (**Fig. 5-57**). This type of accessory is available commercially, but one can be homemade by using the plan shown in **Figure 5-58**. The mark that is

**5-55** A compound angle cut on a table saw calls for a miter gauge setting and a blade tilt.

**5-56** Blade and miter gauge settings to use when cutting compound angles on a table saw.

| Work Slope Angle | 4-Sided Figure | | 6-Sided Figure | | 8-Sided Figure | |
|---|---|---|---|---|---|---|
| | Blade | Miter Gauge | Blade | Miter Gauge | Blade | Miter Gauge |
| 10 deg. | 44 1/4 | 80 1/4 | 29 1/2 | 84 1/4 | 22 | 86 |
| 20 deg. | 41 3/4 | 71 1/4 | 28 1/4 | 79 | 21 | 82 |
| 30 deg. | 37 3/4 | 63 1/2 | 26 | 74 | 19 1/2 | 78 1/4 |
| 40 deg. | 32 1/2 | 57 1/4 | 22 3/4 | 69 3/4 | 17 | 75 |
| 50 deg. | 27 | 52 1/2 | 19 | 66 1/4 | 14 1/4 | 72 1/2 |
| 60 deg. | 21 | 49 | 14 1/2 | 63 1/2 | 11 | 70 1/4 |

NOTES:  • Blade and arm settings are in degrees
• Settings are called out to the closest 1/4 degree.

5-57 Use a taper jig when the work is too large for safe handling with a miter gauge.

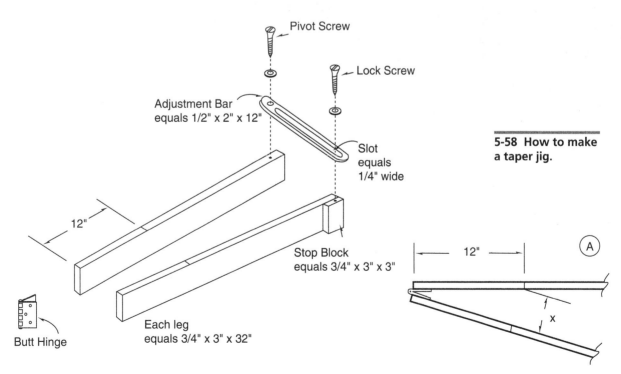

Pivot Screw

Lock Screw

Adjustment Bar
equals 1/2" x 2" x 12"

Slot
equals
1/4" wide

5-58 How to make a taper jig.

12"

Stop Block
equals 3/4" x 3" x 3"

Butt Hinge

Each leg
equals 3/4" x 3" x 32"

12"

x

(A)

made 12 inches from the hinged end of the project is used to set the tool for the amount of taper per foot. If the legs are locked — so there is 1 inch between the marks — the taper will be 1 inch per foot.

A convenient way to make compound cuts when the slope angle can be arbitrary is shown in **Figure 5-59**. The system calls for a jig that is secured to the miter gauge and that braces the work at a particular slope angle. The miter gauge is set at 45 degrees and advanced, as it would be for a simple miter. The jig is made and positioned on the miter gauge as shown in **Figure 5-60**. The stop does not have a fixed position, but is tack-nailed where needed to gauge the slope of the work. Attach the jig by driving screws through the holes or the slots that are in the miter gauge.

**5-59 An easy way to cut compound angles on a table saw when the slope of the work is not critical.**

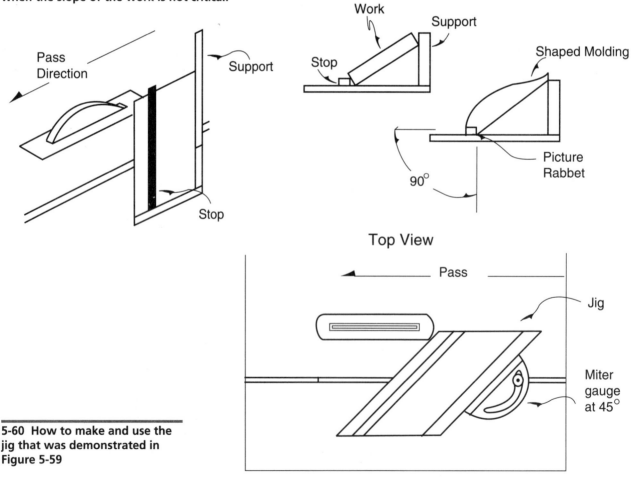

**5-60 How to make and use the jig that was demonstrated in Figure 5-59**

## With Splines

Splines add strength to compound angle joints and make it easier to assemble the segments (**Fig. 5-61**). The grooves for the splines are cut in the manner shown in **Figure 5-62**. The guide is a length of thick material that is beveled at the same angle used for the segments. Notches are cut at both ends of the guide so it can be clamped to the rip fence.

The guide provides good support and keeps the work at the correct angle. Be sure the stock is thick enough to span the slot in the table insert so it will have adequate support during the cut. If necessary, make a special insert of plywood or hardboard with a slot that is just wide enough for the blade to poke through. Keep the work snugly in the pocket between guide and table throughout the pass.

**5-61** Splines add strength to compound angle joints, and they help make assembly work easier.

**5-62** Forming spline grooves in a compound angle cut. Make a special insert, if necessary, to provide ample bearing surface for the work.

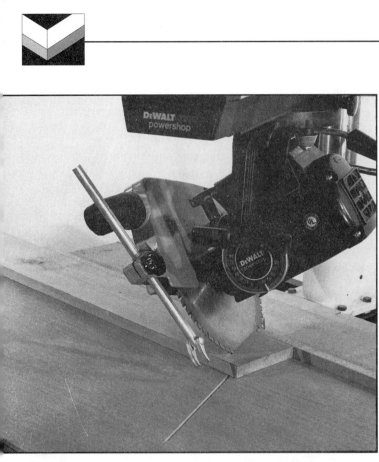

**5-63 Compound cuts on a radial arm saw are done by swinging the arm for the miter and tilting the blade for the bevel.**

## On a Radial Arm Saw

Compound cuts on a radial arm saw require swinging the arm for the miter setting and tilting the blade for the bevel (**Fig. 5-63**). Correct settings for most commonly used slope angles are listed in **Figure 5-64**.

One way to work more easily is to cut segments consecutively from one board. Make an end cut first and then flip the stock for following cuts. A stop block on the fence can be used to control the length of the segments (**Fig. 5-65**).

The following methods can be used when the slope angle of the work is not critical. Use the jig that was described for simple miter sawing but add a stop block that will brace the work at the slope angle (**Fig. 5-66**). The saw blade is set and pulled through as it would be for a crosscut.

**5-64 The arm and blade settings to use for compound angle cuts on a radial arm saw.**

| COMPOUND ANGLE SETTINGS TO USE ON A RADIAL ARM SAW | | | | | | |
|---|---|---|---|---|---|---|
| Work Slope Angle | 4-Sided Figure | | 6-Sided Figure | | 8-Sided Figure | |
| | Blade | Arm | Blade | Arm | Blade | Arm |
| 10 deg. | 44 $\frac{1}{4}$ | 9 $\frac{1}{4}$ | 29 $\frac{1}{2}$ | 5 $\frac{1}{2}$ | 22 | 4 |
| 20 deg. | 41 $\frac{3}{4}$ | 18 $\frac{1}{4}$ | 28 $\frac{1}{4}$ | 11 | 21 | 8 |
| 30 deg. | 37 $\frac{3}{4}$ | 26 $\frac{1}{2}$ | 26 | 16 | 19 $\frac{1}{2}$ | 11 $\frac{3}{4}$ |
| 40 deg. | 32 $\frac{1}{2}$ | 32 $\frac{1}{4}$ | 22 $\frac{3}{4}$ | 20 $\frac{1}{4}$ | 17 | 15 |
| 50 deg. | 27 | 37 $\frac{1}{2}$ | 19 | 23 $\frac{3}{4}$ | 14 $\frac{1}{4}$ | 17 $\frac{1}{2}$ |
| 60 deg. | 21 | 41 | 14 $\frac{1}{2}$ | 26 $\frac{1}{2}$ | 11 | 19 $\frac{3}{4}$ |

NOTES:   • Blade and arm settings are in degrees
          • Settings are called out to the closest $\frac{1}{4}$ degree.

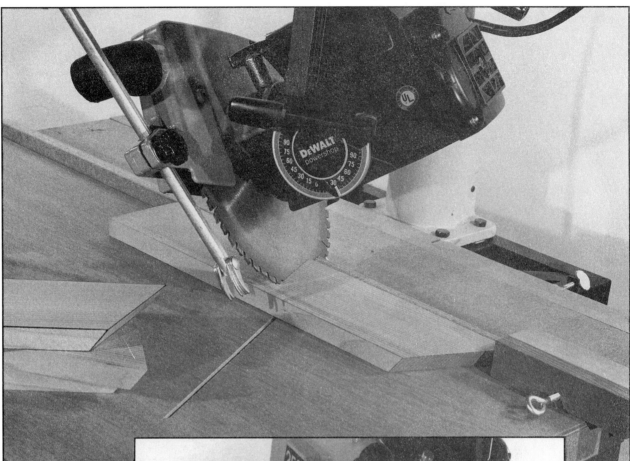

5-65 Compound angles can be cut consecutively from one board. A stop block, clamped to the fence, can be used to control the length of the segments.

5-66 The jig that was made for frame miters can also be used for compound cuts. A tack-nailed stop block holds the work at a selected slope angle.

**5-67** A U-shaped jig, secured at 45 degrees to the normal crosscut path of the blade, positions stock for a compound angle cut.

**5-68** The position of the height block determines the slope angle of the work.

A U-shaped jig, clamped to the table so it is 45 degrees to the line of a crosscut, can be used to hold the work in a tilted position (**Fig. 5-67**). The distance between the vertical members of the jig is suited to the angle at which the part should be held. Here too, the machine is used as it would be for a crosscut.

A quick method calls for clamping or tack-nailing a height block to the table so the work can be braced between the block and the fence (**Fig. 5-68**). In this case, the machine is set for a 45 degree cut. The cut-angles in the examples we've described indicate that the project will have four sides. The cut-angle changes as the number of segments in the project changes.

## SPECIAL MITER JOINTS

The designs that follow are for joints that can be used anywhere, but because they require extra time and more care than basic designs, they are usually limited to choice pieces of cabinetwork and to high quality furniture.

## Tongue-and-Groove Miter

A tongue-and-groove element in the joint adds glue area and provides an interlock. The joint is illustrated in **Figure 5-69**. The series of steps to follow after the mating parts have been mitered are listed in **Figure 5-70**.

**Step 1** — Set a dadoing tool to cut the width of the groove that is needed.Tilt the dado to 45 degrees and form the groove in part one. The projection of the dado determines the depth of the groove.

**Step 2** — With the dado at the same angle but with its projection adjusted as shown, make two cuts in part two. This is the beginning of the tongue.

**Steps 3 and 4** — Remove the remainder of the waste with the dado or by switching to a saw blade.

The settings must be made very carefully and similar cuts should be made in all components before changing settings for following cuts. It's wise to have test pieces on hand so cuts can be checked before working on good stock.

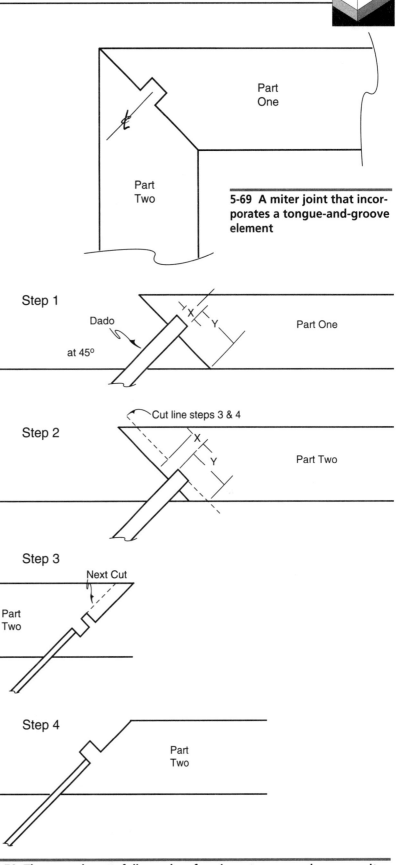

**5-69 A miter joint that incorporates a tongue-and-groove element**

**5-70 The procedure to follow when forming a tongue-and-groove miter joint. As always, accurate settings are critical.**

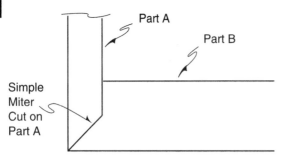

Part A

Part B

Simple
Miter
Cut on
Part A

5-71 The housed rabbet miter is a good connection to use when components differ in thickness.

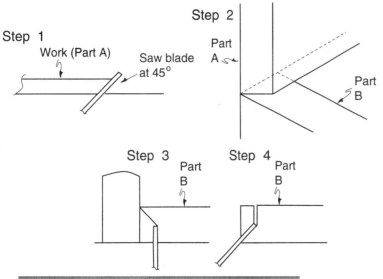

Step 1
Work (Part A)
Saw blade at 45°

Step 2
Part A
Part B

Step 3
Part B

Step 4
Part B

5-72 How the housed rabbet-miter joint is formed.

5-73 An example of a true rabbet-miter joint.

## Housed Rabbet-Miter

A housed rabbet-miter is a good joint to use when joining parts that are not equal in thickness and where the good appearance of a miter plus the additional glue area afforded by a rabbet are assets (**Fig. 5-71**). The sequence of steps to follow are listed in **Figure 5-72**.

**Step 1** — Saw a simple cross miter on the thinner component — part A.

**Step-2** — Use part A as a pattern to mark the outline of the cut that is needed in part B.

**Step 3** — Set the rip fence so the distance from it to the *outside* of the saw blade equals the thickness of part A. Set the projection of the saw blade so it will just meet the intersection of the lines that were marked in step 2, and make the cut as shown.

**Step 4** — The miter cut on B starts exactly at the corner of the stock and just touches the bottom inside corner of the cut that was made in step 3. Be very careful with blade projection so cuts will meet nicely to leave clean lines.

## True Rabbet-Miter

There are two types of true rabbet-miters. The simple design is shown in **Figure 5-73**; the more complicated locked design that incorporates a tongue-and-groove interlock is shown in **Figure 5-74**.

5-74 The locked rabbet-miter joint includes a tongue-and-groove interlock.

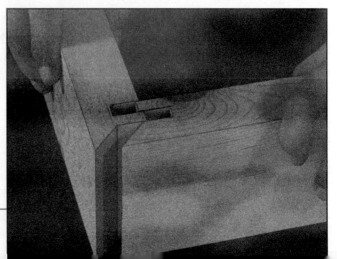

The best way to form the shapes that are required for the mating parts is to follow the formula suggested in **Figure 5-75**, which will apply regardless of the thickness of the stock. You can't go wrong working this way, but on the other hand, there's no reason why you can't deviate from the formula to suit a particular situation. For example, changes might be made for deeper rabbet cuts or shorter tongue-and-groove patterns.

The program in **Figure 5-76** details the formation of the simple rabbet-miter.

**Step 1** — Adjust the projection of the saw blade so it equals one-half the the thickness of the stock. Set the rip fence so the distance from it to the *outside* of the blade equals the thickness of the stock.

**Step 2** — Make the first cut in part one with the stock butting against the rip fence. Be sure that narrow stock is advanced with the miter gauge.

**Step 3** — Make a similar cut on the same piece but with the stock pulled away from the fence so the cut will be more than halfway to the end of the work. The second cut must be made to the left of the centerline, between the fence end of the work and the cut that was made in step 2. Make repeat passes with the saw blade to remove the stock that remains between the two cuts.

**Step 4** — Use the same saw-blade projection but reset the rip fence so the distance from it to the *outside* of the blade equals one-half the thickness of the stock.

**Step 5** — Butt the end of the mating piece against the fence and make the cut that is shown. Use the miter gauge when advancing stock that is too narrow for adequate bearing surface against the fence.

**Step 6** — Tilt the saw blade to 45 degrees and make a miter cut on the part that was kerfed in step 5. Set the blade projection carefully since the miter cut must just meet the inside corner of the kerf.

**Step 7** — Make the same miter cut on the mating piece. The projection of the blade is not critical in this step but the cut must start at the corner of the work.

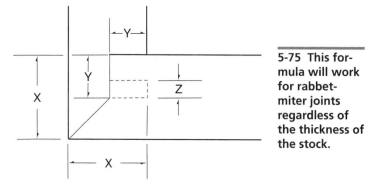

**5-75** This formula will work for rabbet-miter joints regardless of the thickness of the stock.

### The Basics of Rabbet-Miter Joints

- All cuts fall within a square whose sides are equal to the thickness of the stock
- $X$ equals the thickness of the stock
- $Y$ equals $1/2$ ($X$)
- $Z$ equals $1/2$ ($Y$)
- The diagonal line equals $1/2$ the full diagonal of the square
- When the lock tenon is included (dotted lines), its length equals $Y$ and its width ($Z$) equals $1/2$ ($Y$)

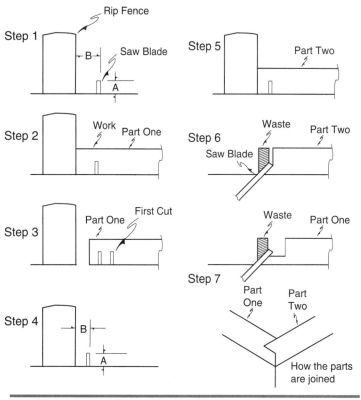

**5-76** The steps to follow when forming the true rabbet-miter joint.

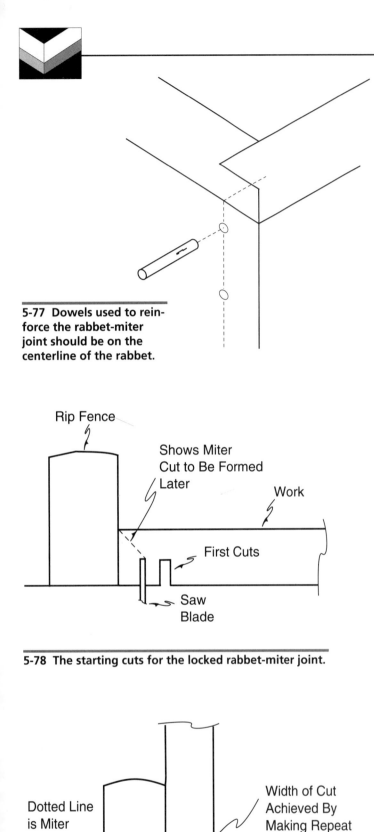

**5-77 Dowels used to reinforce the rabbet-miter joint should be on the centerline of the rabbet.**

Rip Fence

Shows Miter Cut to Be Formed Later

Work

First Cuts

Saw Blade

**5-78 The starting cuts for the locked rabbet-miter joint.**

Dotted Line is Miter Cut to Be Formed Later

Width of Cut Achieved By Making Repeat Passes

Saw Blade

The rabbet-miter joint can be reinforced with dowels as shown in **Figure 5-77**. Drill the dowel holes so they are on the centerline of the rabbet.

## Locked Rabbet-Miter

The locked rabbet-miter joint incorporates a tongue-and-groove element so the cutting procedure differs from that already described, even though the shapes are formed within a square whose sides equal the thickness of the stock.

The first steps, on one part, are shown in **Figure 5-78**. There is no cleaning out operation here. Instead, the distance from the rip fence to the blade is adjusted for cuts that will leave a tongue on the work. The projection of the saw blade is still one-half the thickness of the stock. In the cut shown in the illustration, the distance from the rip fence to the outside surface of the blade is also one-half the stock thickness.

The groove in the mating piece is formed with the stock on edge as shown in **Figure 5-79**. The distance from the fence to the *inside* face of the blade equals one-half the stock thickness. The projection of the blade *equals* the stock thickness. Form the groove by making repeat, overlapping passes. Be sure the width of the groove equals the thickness of the tongue formed on the first piece.

Making cuts with the stock on edge is acceptable *only* if the work is large enough to provide good bearing surface on the table. When there is the least doubt, or to be sure in any event, make the cuts with a tenoning jig. The jig provides a good safety factor and helps do the work accurately.

**5-79 The mating part of the locked rabbet-miter joint is formed this way.**

# 6

# LAP JOINTS

he term *lap joints* is used to describe a category of woodworking joints that are similar visually, but differ radically in relation to strength and construction methods. Literally, a lap joint is made by lapping one component over another and fastening them together in the area of contact. Technically, such a connection is a *surface lap*. The strength of the joint when done only with glue depends entirely on the amount of contact area (**Fig. 6-1**). Without reinforcement, the joint will not resist lateral or twisting stresses for too long. The design may be adequate for crates and rough carpentry where, often, reinforcement is just heavy nails, but it won't be found too often in cabinet work and furniture.

The lap joints that have more visual appeal and more strength are the *half-lap* and the *full-lap*. An example of a half-lap joint is

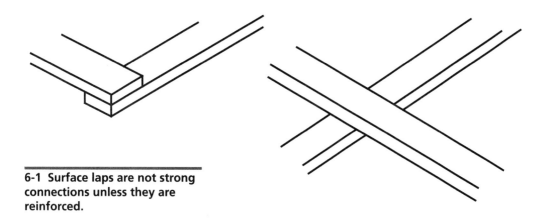

**6-1 Surface laps are not strong connections unless they are reinforced.**

**6-2** Half-laps form an interlock that resists stresses. Reinforcements can be added—in this case, screws that were concealed with buttons.

shown in **Figure 6-2**. In a common half-lap joint, the thickness of each piece is reduced by one-half in the contact area so that when the parts are assembled, surfaces will be flush and the joint forms an interlock. In the example, the connection joins a one-piece back-and-leg part to a one-piece seat-and-leg component of a lounge chair. Since the joint will be severely tested, it is reinforced with screws that are hidden with buttons.

Full-laps are often used when the parts differ in thickness. The seat cut, which is essentially a wide dado or rabbet, is formed in the thicker member to suit the width and the thickness of the mating piece.

## FRAME HALF-LAPS

Frame half-laps are often called *end-laps* since they appear at the corners of frame projects (**Fig. 6-3**). The cuts required in both pieces are rabbets that are sized according to the formula in the illustration. The joint shown in (**A**) is a full-lap. In this case, the rabbet cut is made only in the thicker part and is dimensioned to suit the thickness and width of the insert.

**Figure 6-4** shows how the cuts can be made with a backsaw. First mark the work

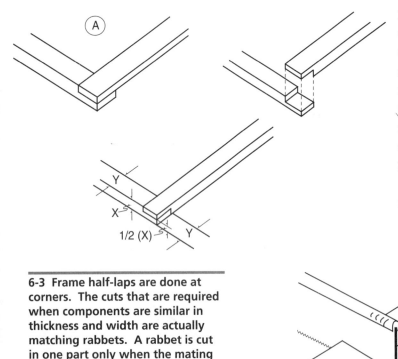

**6-3** Frame half-laps are done at corners. The cuts that are required when components are similar in thickness and width are actually matching rabbets. A rabbet is cut in one part only when the mating piece is thinner, as in the full-lap shown in A.

**6-4** How to use a backsaw to form the rabbet cuts for a frame half-lap.

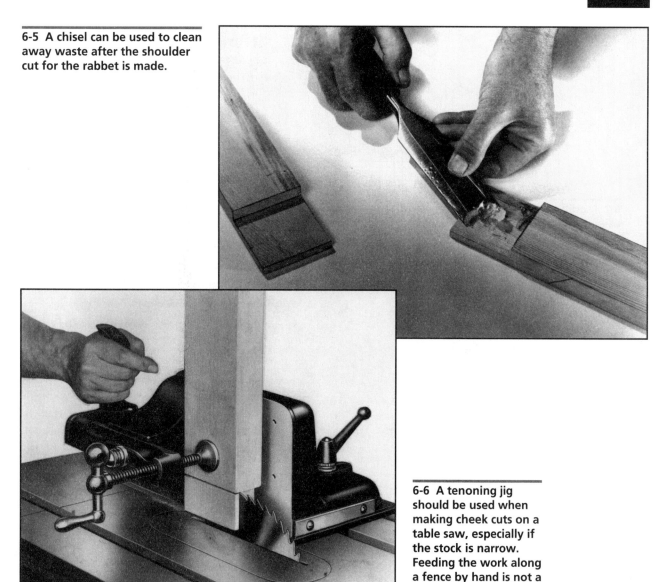

**6-5** A chisel can be used to clean away waste after the shoulder cut for the rabbet is made.

**6-6** A tenoning jig should be used when making cheek cuts on a table saw, especially if the stock is narrow. Feeding the work along a fence by hand is not a safe procedure.

carefully with a square and then make the shoulder cuts, using a block of wood clamped to the saw as a depth gauge. The second, or *cheek,* cut is done with the stock held vertically in a vise. A good procedure is to clamp the mating pieces edge-to-edge so the saw cuts can be made in both pieces in one operation. Many woodworkers skip the saw cuts for the cheeks, doing only shoulder cuts, and removing the waste with a chisel (**Fig. 6-5**).

There are several ways to do the job on a table saw. Use a dadoing tool with its projection set to one-half the thickness of the stock. Make one pass to produce the shoulder area

and then make additional cuts to clear away the waste. If you hold or clamp the parts together edge-to-edge, you can cut both pieces at the same time.

A regular saw blade can be used. Make the shoulder cut first with the stock flat on the table and then the cheek cut with the stock held on edge. The latter cut should not be made freehand, especially if the material is narrow. Using a homemade or commercial tenoning jig allows the work to be done safely and accurately (**Fig. 6-6**). When using a tenoning jig, a starting shoulder cut can be eliminated if the shape is produced by mak-

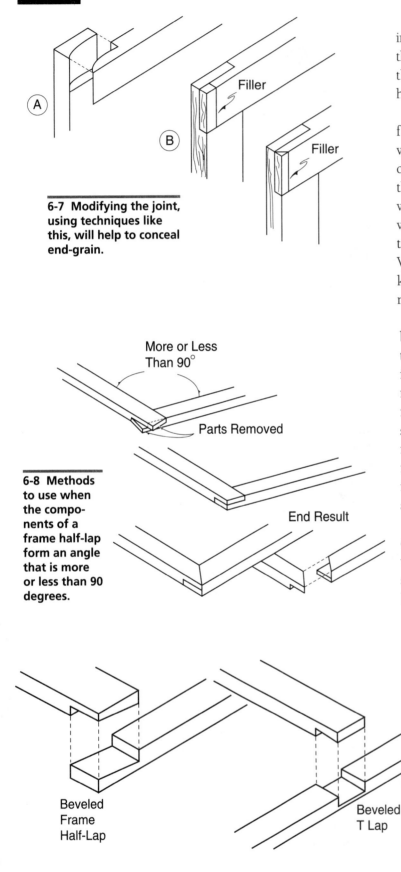

**6-7 Modifying the joint, using techniques like this, will help to conceal end-grain.**

**6-8 Methods to use when the components of a frame half-lap form an angle that is more or less than 90 degrees.**

Beveled Frame Half-Lap

Beveled T Lap

ing repeat passes. If you use a dadoing tool, the cut can be done in a single pass, assuming that the projection of the cutter can be set high enough for the cut.

Essentially, the same procedures can be followed on a radial arm saw. The work/machine relationship changes because of the characteristics of the tool. When using the two-pass method, make the shoulder cut with the stock flat on the table, the cheek cut with the saw blade situated parallel to the table and the work secured on a height table. When a dadoing tool is used, the work is kept flat on the table and the cut is cleared by making repeat passes.

The techniques shown in **Figure 6-7** can be adopted to hide end-grain. In detail (**A**), the cut in one part, done with a dadoing tool, is stopped just at the edge of the work. The mating piece has a full cut, but the end is rounded off so the parts will mesh. Detail (**B**) shows how one part can be cut short or end-mitered to accommodate a filler block. The result is effective only if the filler is made and installed very carefully. Match grain patterns as closely as possible.

Frame half-laps that form a closed or open angle can be produced as shown in **Figure 6-8**. Make the shoulder cut at the necessary angle but locate it so the cheek will be longer than necessary. Excess material is trimmed and sanded flush after assembly.

Often, cheek cuts are sloped as shown in **Figure 6-9**. The mating bevels add a degree of interlock that strengthens the joint. The same illustration shows how the idea applies to a T half-lap.

**6-9 Incorporating a bevel provides a degree of interlock for added strength.**

## END-TO-END HALF-LAPS

End-to-end half-laps aren't common on cabinets and furniture but the technique is handy for joining pieces of wood that might otherwise be discarded to make a longer usable board. The cuts are the same as those required for frame half-laps (**Fig. 6-10**). The longer the joint line, the stronger the union will be.

A similar procedure can be used when a circular component that can't be cut from a single board is needed (**Fig. 6-11**). Straight segments are joined with end half-laps that are cut at the correct angle in relation to the number of pieces in the project. The illustration shows six segments, so the joint angle is 30 degrees. If fasteners are used, be sure to locate them so they won't interfere with final sawing. The circular cutting can be done on a scroll saw or band saw.

## MIDDLE, OR T, HALF-LAPS

Middle, or T, half-laps are used when one end of a component must join another part at some point (**Fig. 6-12**). One part requires a dado whose depth equals one-half the thickness of the stock. The second piece, when the parts are equal in thickness, is rabbeted to fit snugly in the dado. If the insert piece is thinner, it simply sits in a dado that is sized to suit it.

Angled lap joints are used when the insert is not perpendicular. The major factor, of course, is that the dado and the shoulder of the rabbet must be cut at the correct angle. **Figure 6-13** shows a basic angled lap joint and a modified version that adds strength to the connection. In both cases, it's good procedure to cut the rabbet in the insert longer than necessary so it can be trimmed and sanded flush after assembly.

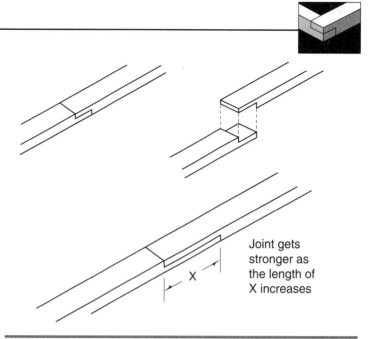

Joint gets stronger as the length of X increases

**6-10 Half-laps can be used to join parts end-to-end. The longer the lap, the stronger the connection.**

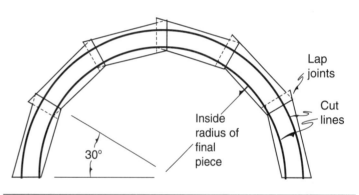

Lap joints

Cut lines

Inside radius of final piece

30°

**6-11 End-laps can be used to join segments to prepare stock for circular forms.**

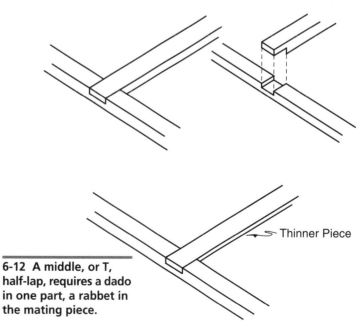

Thinner Piece

**6-12 A middle, or T, half-lap, requires a dado in one part, a rabbet in the mating piece.**

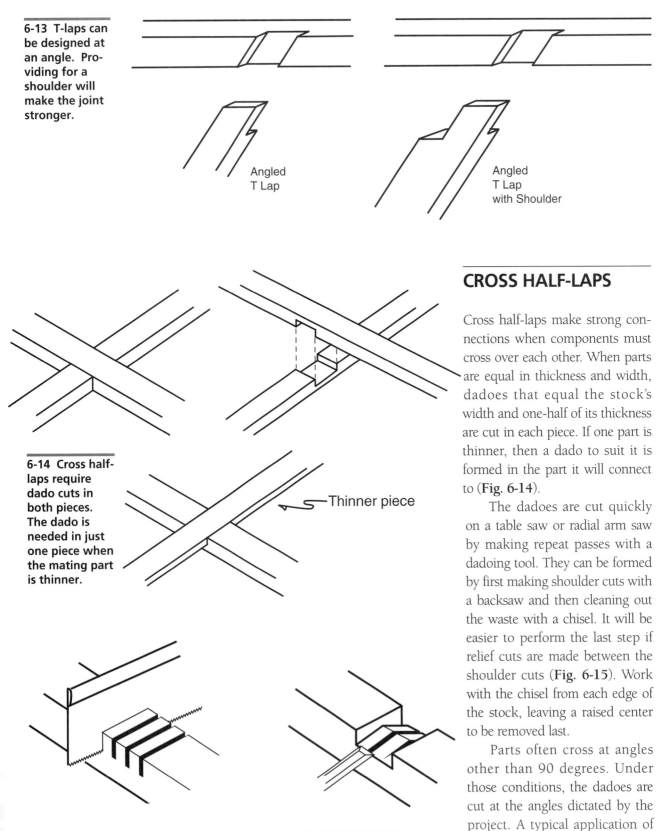

**6-13 T-laps can be designed at an angle. Providing for a shoulder will make the joint stronger.**

Angled
T Lap

Angled
T Lap
with Shoulder

**6-14 Cross half-laps require dado cuts in both pieces. The dado is needed in just one piece when the mating part is thinner.**

Thinner piece

**6-15 Dadoes for a cross half-lap can be formed by making shoulder cuts with a backsaw and then clearing the waste with a chisel.**

## CROSS HALF-LAPS

Cross half-laps make strong connections when components must cross over each other. When parts are equal in thickness and width, dadoes that equal the stock's width and one-half of its thickness are cut in each piece. If one part is thinner, then a dado to suit it is formed in the part it will connect to (**Fig. 6-14**).

The dadoes are cut quickly on a table saw or radial arm saw by making repeat passes with a dadoing tool. They can be formed by first making shoulder cuts with a backsaw and then cleaning out the waste with a chisel. It will be easier to perform the last step if relief cuts are made between the shoulder cuts (**Fig. 6-15**). Work with the chisel from each edge of the stock, leaving a raised center to be removed last.

Parts often cross at angles other than 90 degrees. Under those conditions, the dadoes are cut at the angles dictated by the project. A typical application of

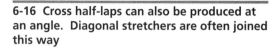

**6-16 Cross half-laps can also be produced at an angle. Diagonal stretchers are often joined this way**

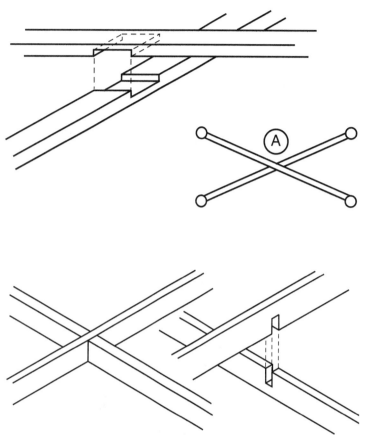

the cross half-lap is shown in **Figure 6-16**. Detail (**A**) is a top view of diagonal stretchers that add rigidity to the legs of a table project.

## EDGE HALF-LAPS

Edge half-laps differ from cross half-laps in that the dadoes are cut into the edge of the stock, instead of its surfaces (**Fig. 6-17**). Because the dadoes are usually narrow and deep, they are often referred to as *notches*. The formula for sizing the cuts departs from what has been shown so far. Here, the width of the dado equals the thickness of the stock and the depth of the dado equals one-half the width.

A miter box is a good tool to use when hand-sawing the shoulder cuts (**Fig. 6-18**). To control the depth of the cuts, clamp a strip of wood to the saw. Be sure the stop block will span across the sides of the miter box. The illustration shows one part being cut, but it's feasible to gang pieces so sawing can be done on several at the same time. Remove the waste in sections with a chisel (**Fig. 6-19**), taking shallower bites as you get closer to the bottom of the notch.

**6-17 The cuts required for edge half-laps are often called notches since they are usually narrow and deep.**

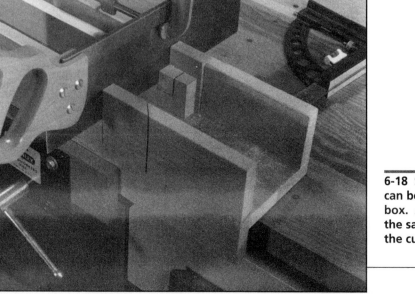

**6-18 Shoulder cuts for notches can be formed by using a miter box. A guide strip, clamped to the saw, will control the depth of the cuts.**

**6-19 Use a chisel to remove the waste between the shoulder cuts.**

Notches can be cut easily and quickly on a power tool by working with a dadoing tool. The width of the dado is set to match the thickness of the stock, its cut-depth to one-half the stock's width. When just a few pieces are needed, it's feasible to do the notching by making repeat passes with a saw blade as is being done with a radial arm saw in **Figure 6-20**. Note that parts are clamped together for simultaneous cutting.

Gang-cutting is the way to go when edge half-laps are needed for egg crate or grid patterns (**Fig. 6-21**). The formula given in the illustration applies regardless of the width and thickness of the stock. The sawing can be done freehand, guided by a careful layout of the notches on the front piece of the stack, but a method that provides a mechanical means of achieving accuracy is to work with a jig that is secured to the table saw miter gauge (**Fig. 6-22**). Make the first cut by butting the stock against the guide block. Make other cuts by placing the last notch that was cut *over* the guide block. This system ensures that spacing between all notches will be the same; no layout is necessary.

Edge half-laps are often used as the connection between sides of a project (**Fig. 6-23**). The joint provides a good interlock for a permanent assembly, but it's also a way to provide for projects that can be disassembled.

**6-20 Mating pieces can be clamped together for simultaneous sawing. Here, the notch is being formed by making repeat passes with a saw blade.**

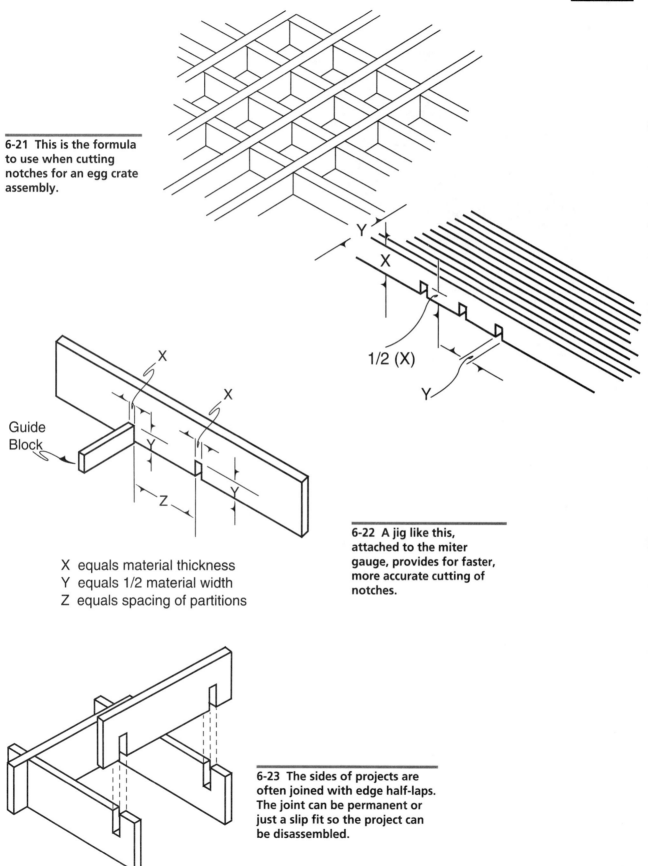

**6-21** This is the formula to use when cutting notches for an egg crate assembly.

Y

X

1/2 (X)

Y

Guide
Block

X

X

Y

Z

Y

X  equals material thickness
Y  equals 1/2 material width
Z  equals spacing of partitions

**6-22** A jig like this, attached to the miter gauge, provides for faster, more accurate cutting of notches.

**6-23** The sides of projects are often joined with edge half-laps. The joint can be permanent or just a slip fit so the project can be disassembled.

**6-24 The fingerlap joint is attractive and very strong because of the substantial glue area.**

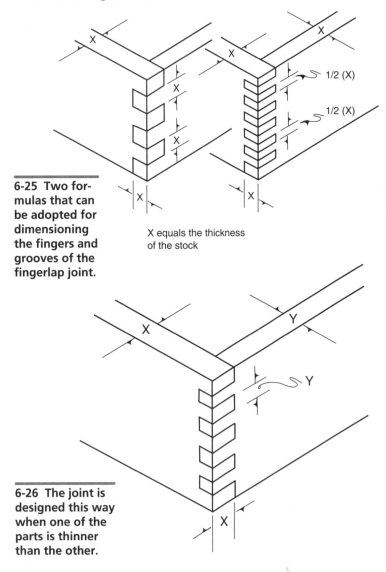

**6-25 Two formulas that can be adopted for dimensioning the fingers and grooves of the fingerlap joint.**

X equals the thickness of the stock

**6-26 The joint is designed this way when one of the parts is thinner than the other.**

## THE FINGERLAP JOINT

The fingerlap joint (**Fig. 6-24**) is often called a *box joint*. It is found on many classic pieces, sometimes exposed as an indication of craftsmanship, other times used in hidden areas simply because it has much strength. It does not have the interlock feature of a dovetail joint, but it does have structural appeal because of the unusual amount of glue area. It also has visual appeal because of the way the fingers mesh.

A common recommendation for the design of the joint is that the width of the fingers and the notches should equal the thickness of the stock. The formula works okay, but it doesn't always result in the most attractive joint. Reducing the width of the fingers and notches to one-half the stock's thickness or even less often contributes to a better looking project (**Fig. 6-25**). On shallow projects — small boxes and drawers and the like, narrow fingers are more appropriate visually and stronger structurally.

The fingerlap joint may also be used to join components that differ in thickness (**Fig. 6-26**). The result will be more appealing if the width of the fingers equals the thickness of the thinner part.

## Cutting by Hand

To cut by hand requires time and care, but the joint should not be ignored just because hand tools are used. A recommended procedure is given in the series of steps in **Figure 6-27**.

**Step 1** — Clamp the parts together in a vise so they are offset by the width of one finger. Make a layout to indicate the width and depth of the cuts.

**Step 2** — Bore holes where indicated through both pieces. Use a bit that matches or is a little smaller than the width of the notches.

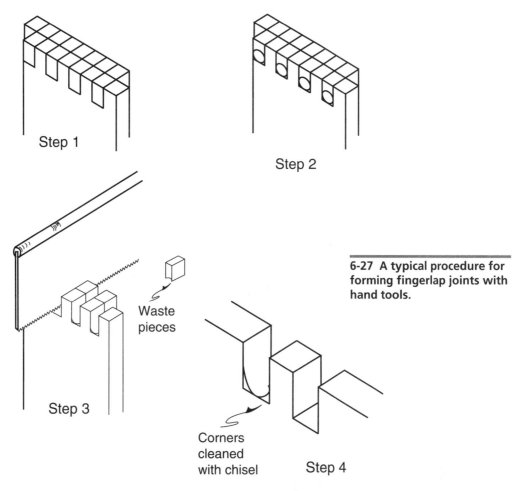

Step 1

Step 2

Step 3

Waste
pieces

**6-27  A typical procedure for forming fingerlap joints with hand tools.**

Corners
cleaned
with chisel

Step 4

Clamp a scrap block to the back of the assembly to guard against splintering when the bit breaks through. Drill slowly and be sure the bit is perpendicular to the surface of the work.

**Step 3** — Use a backsaw or dovetail saw to make the shoulder cuts. Stay a fraction away from the line so that sandpaper, wrapped around a small block of wood, can be used later to smooth the cuts.

**Step 4** — Use a chisel or a square file to clean out the corners.

## Cutting With Power Tools

The fingerlap joint is formed on a radial arm saw by using an auxiliary height table as shown in **Figure 6-28**. The mating pieces are

**6-28  Forming the fingerlap on a radial arm saw.  Here, the width of the grooves is just the kerf-width of the blade.  The design provides a delicate appearance that is ideal for small projects.**

held together and clamped to a fence that is part of the table. The cuts shown in the illustration are no wider than the kerf of the saw blade. This means that for each cut, the blade is raised a distance that is equal to twice the width of the kerf. Careful adjustment of the

**6-29** This jig is used on a table saw for faster, more accurate cutting of fingerlap joints.

3/4" x 3 1/2" x 4

1 1/2"

Guide Block

3/4" x 4" x 16

Hardwood bars sized and spaced to fit miter gauge grooves

tool for each of the cuts is critical. Wider cuts are made by substituting a dadoing tool for the saw blade. Adjust the guard so it will be as close to the cutting area as possible. Do not make height adjustments while the saw is running.

Cutting on a table saw can be guided by a layout on the work, but the system leaves a lot of room for human error. A much better way is to make the special jig shown in **Figure 6-29**. This machine has twin bars to ride in the table slots so it is used independently of the miter gauge as shown in **Figure 6-30**. The distance from the side of the guide block and the adjacent side of the blade equals the width of the fingers. The height of the guide block equals the depth of the cuts. The length of the guide block is not critical, but it should not be less than twice the thickness of the stock. The series of steps that are detailed in **Figure 6-31** tell how to use the jig.

**6-30** The jig, having its own bars to ride in the table slots, works independently of the miter gauge. The angle between the jig's fence and the cutting tool must be 90 degrees.

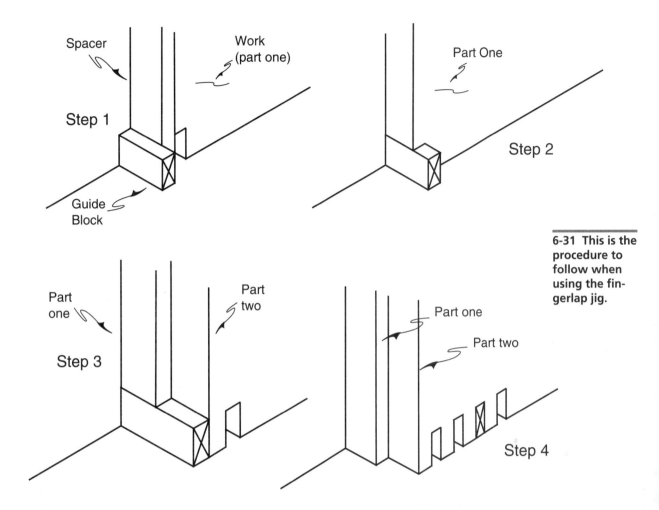

Step 1 — Spacer, Work (part one), Guide Block

Step 2 — Part One

Step 3 — Part one, Part two

Step 4 — Part one, Part two

Step 1 — Make a spacer that is as thick as the width of the grooves and place it between the guide block and the edge of one of the parts. Hold the spacer and the work firmly in place and advance the jig to make the first cut.

Step 2 — Remove the spacer and move the work so the first cut sits firmly against the guide block.

Step 3 — Add the mating piece by butting it against the guide block and make a second pass that will form the groove in both pieces.

Step 4 — Continue to make cuts by placing the last groove that was formed over the guide block.

Figure 6-32 shows the same type of jig but made so it can be attached to the miter

6-32 This version of the fingerlap jig is secured to the miter gauge.

**6-33** This fingerlap jig also attaches to the miter gauge, but it is adjustable to suit various cut-widths.

**6-34** A good procedure is to form grooves deep enough so the fingers will project a bit. Then they are sanded flush after assembly.

gauge. **Figure 6-33** shows a version of the jig that can be adjusted for various groove-widths. It is also attached to the miter gauge, but with screws that pass through a slot that permits lateral adjustments. Notice that the guide is a thin piece of hardboard instead of a full size block. This is necessary in order for the jig to handle various groove-widths. In practice, the cuts, viewed from the operator's side, should show the *left* side of the notch already formed, placed against the *left* side of the guide, which positions the work for the next cut. This is so for each cut.

## Finishing the Joint

The fingerlap joint does show some end-grain. In order to minimize its impact, cut the notches a bit deeper than necessary so the fingers will project a bit (**Fig. 6-34**) and can be sanded flush after assembly.

The joint will have an unique appearance if notches are cut deep and the fingers are allowed to project prominently (**Fig. 6-35**). Chamfering the edges of the fingers as shown

**6-35** Allowing the fingers to project prominently provides an extra design element.  Chamfering the ends of the fingers is an extra touch.

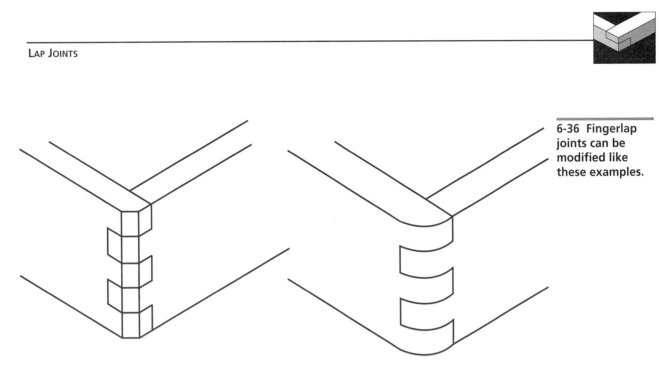

6-36 Fingerlap joints can be modified like these examples.

in (**A**) of the same illustration can add another design element.

**Figure 6-36** suggests two ways the fingerlap joint can be treated after assembly. On large projects, the work can be done with portable sanders. If the project is small enough, the modifications can be accomplished more easily on a stationary belt or disc sander.

## Locking the Joint

**Figure 6-37** shows how a dowel can be used to secure a fingerlap joint so it will never come apart.

**6-37 Incorporating a dowel provides an extra strength factor.**

## MAKING A SWIVEL JOINT

The swivel joint uses a dowel as a pivot (**Fig. 6-38**). Drill the hole for the dowel while the parts are held together. Then, separate the parts and shorten the fingers a bit by sanding them. The last step is to round off or chamfer the corners of the fingers so the parts can turn freely.

## MAKING GRILLS OR GRIDS

The fingerlap jig can be used to form the notches that are required for the type of assembly shown in **Figure 6-39**. Opposite frame pieces are held together so cuts can be made in both simultaneously. This ensures accuracy not only in the size of the notches but also in their alignment.

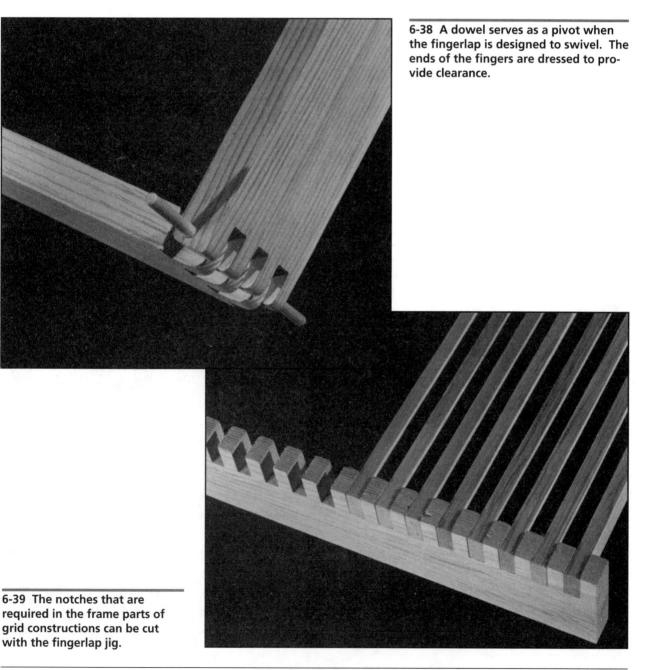

**6-38** A dowel serves as a pivot when the fingerlap is designed to swivel. The ends of the fingers are dressed to provide clearance.

**6-39** The notches that are required in the frame parts of grid constructions can be cut with the fingerlap jig.

# 7

# MORTISE-TENON JOINTS

The Basic Mortise-Tenon • Forming a Hinge Mortise • Forming a True Mortise With Hand Tools • Mortising on a Drill Press • Mortising Round Stock • Other Mortising Methods • Open Mortise • Cutting Tenons *(Cutting By Hand, Power Tool Work)* • Integral Round Tenons • How to Lock a Tenon • Tusks • Angled Joints • Mitered Tenons • Other Mortise-Tenon Designs

The mortise-tenon joint ranks with the dovetail in terms of high quality construction. It's a craftsman's connection that can be used for doors, leg-stretcher or leg-rail assemblies for tables, cabinets, and a host of other projects. It's a joint that is appreciated because of its resistance to racking or twisting forces from any direction. In addition to the interlocking feature provided by the tenon, the design provides for a substantial amount of gluing area.

There are many variations of the mortise-tenon joint, some of which are shown in **Figure 7-1**, but

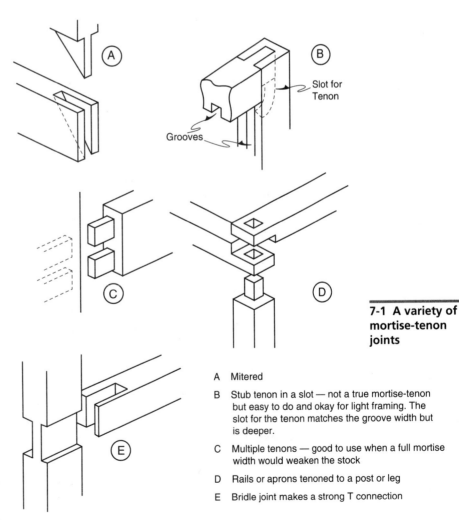

**7-1 A variety of mortise-tenon joints**

A  Mitered

B  Stub tenon in a slot — not a true mortise-tenon but easy to do and okay for light framing. The slot for the tenon matches the groove width but is deeper.

C  Multiple tenons — good to use when a full mortise width would weaken the stock

D  Rails or aprons tenoned to a post or leg

E  Bridle joint makes a strong T connection

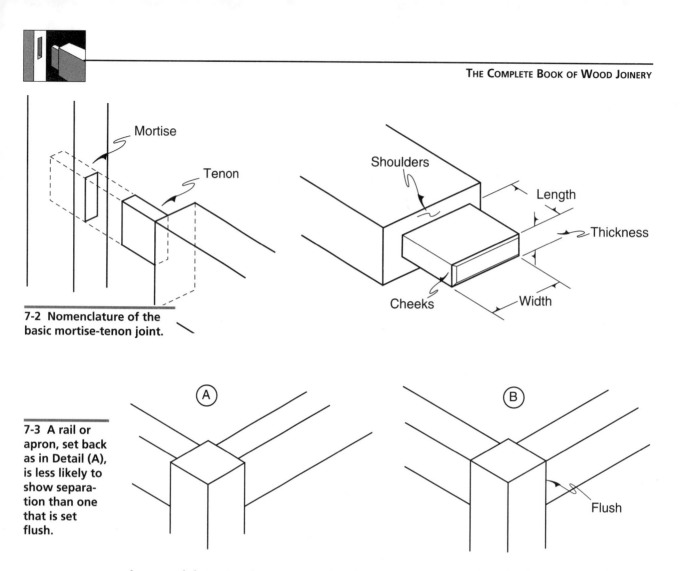

**7-2 Nomenclature of the basic mortise-tenon joint.**

**7-3 A rail or apron, set back as in Detail (A), is less likely to show separation than one that is set flush.**

the general design involves an integral projection on one part that suits, usually, a square or rectangular cavity formed in the mating piece. The cavity is the *mortise*, the projection is the *tenon*. Knowledge of how to form the two components is necessary for the construction of any type of mortise-tenon joint.

In some instances, only a mortise is needed. An example is the seat that is required for the leaf of a butt hinge. While this is not a wood-to-wood joint, the cutting procedure will be shown since the operation is an important one for any project that has swinging doors.

## THE BASIC MORTISE-TENON

The parts of the joint are detailed in **Figure 7-2**. The mortise may be *blind* or *through* and this determines the length of the tenon. When the

tenon passes through the part with the mortise, it should be cut a bit longer than necessary and sanded flush after assembly.

When the parts are joined, the visible joint line is not more than if the parts were simply butted together. The surfaces of the components will be flush when the pieces are of equal thickness. When this is not so — a typical example being the connection between legs and rails (or aprons) — the rails should be installed to leave a small shoulder where the parts meet (**Fig. 7-3**). This is advisable so that a hairline crack that might eventually appear will not be obvious.

A basic rule says that the thickness of the tenon should not be more than one-third to one-half the thickness of the part it enters. There can be variation in the tenon's length and width. Its length depends on the width of the mating piece and whether the mortise is through or blind.

Usually, the maximum width of a tenon should not exceed about 5 inches. The limit is established because an oversize mortise can weaken the part it is cut in. A standard method of working when a situation calls for a very wide tenon is to form two or more tenons with ample space between them as shown in **Figure 7-1C**.

The length of a tenon should be 1/32-inch or so shorter than the depth of a blind mortise and its edges should be rounded a bit or chamfered to provide space for excess glue. A tenon must not fit loosely, nor should excessive force be required to seat it. A slip fit, one that can be accomplished with only hand pressure, is best. It will provide adequate contact and will not introduce additional stresses in the area.

The mortise is formed first so the tenon can be sized to fit. This makes sense, especially when the cavities are formed with mortising bits and chisels on a drill press. The mortising cutters are not adjustable, but tenons can always be custom-cut to suit the situation.

**7-4 Start a mortise for a hinge by using the unit as a template.**

**7-5 Score the marked lines with a knife deeply enough to sever surface fibers.**

## FORMING A HINGE MORTISE

This seemingly prosaic operation requires as much care as any joint if doors are to fit nicely and function smoothly. Start by using the hinge itself as a template to mark the outline for the mortise (**Fig. 7-4**). Use a hard, sharp pencil and be sure the hinge is positioned parallel to the work. Incise the lines with a knife, using a square as a guide and favoring the hinge side of the pencil mark (**Fig. 7-5**). Score several times so surface fibers will be severed. If the mortise must be quite shallow, scoring can be done to the full depth of the cut. If not, or if the wood is very dense, deepen the scored lines with a chisel.

Work with a chisel and mallet to make cuts across the mortise as shown in **Figure 7-6**, so waste removal will be easier to do. The extra chisel cuts can be considered optional since it's feasible to use the chisel immediately after the scoring (**Fig. 7-7**). Remove the bulk of the waste by holding the chisel with its bevel edge down. Finish with just hand pressure, taking light, shaving cuts with the chisel's bevel up.

**7-6 Incising cross-lines with a chisel will make it easier to remove waste.**

**7-7 It's also feasible to remove the waste simply by shaving it away.**

# FORMING A TRUE MORTISE WITH HAND TOOLS

The procedure to follow with hand tools is shown in **Figure 7-8**. Lay out the shape of the mortise by using a marking gauge for the lines that are parallel to edges and a square to mark end points. Use a knife to score the lines deeply enough to sever surface fibers and then use a brace and bit to bore overlapping holes that will remove the bulk of the waste. Use a stop on the bit if the mortise is blind. If the cut is through, place a scrap piece under the work to guard against the splintering and feathering that can occur when the bit breaks out.

Remove the remaining waste with a chisel as shown in **Figure 7-9**. It isn't necessary to square the ends of the mortise since the tenon can be rounded off to conform.

When drilling a mortise, plan its width so the waste holes can be formed with a standard-size bit. This does not impose limitations since bit sizes change by sixteenths of an inch.

If the mortise will be formed by working solely with chisels, it is started as shown in **Figure 7-10**. Remove the surface waste after the marked lines have been deeply scored. The intent is to make the entrance as clean as possible. Complete the job by following the steps shown in **Figure 7-11**. Make the angle cuts in series, applying pressure on the chisel toward the center of the cavity. Do the final cleaning of the sides by using the chisel vertically.

Jobs like this are easier to do when an assortment of chisels is available so that one of suitable width can be selected for the cutting. Removing a little material at a time is better than chewing out big chunks. *Sharp* chisels are a must.

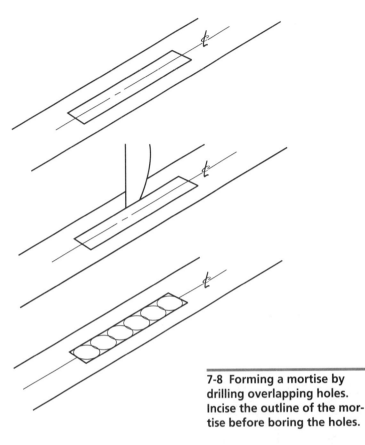

**7-8 Forming a mortise by drilling overlapping holes. Incise the outline of the mortise before boring the holes.**

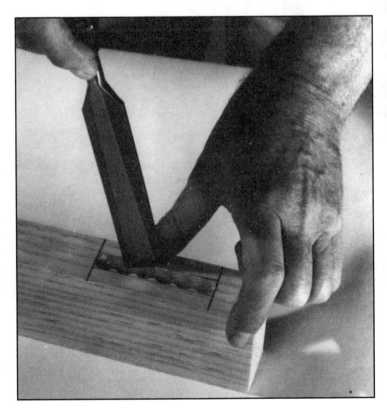

**7-9 Use a chisel to remove the remaining waste.**

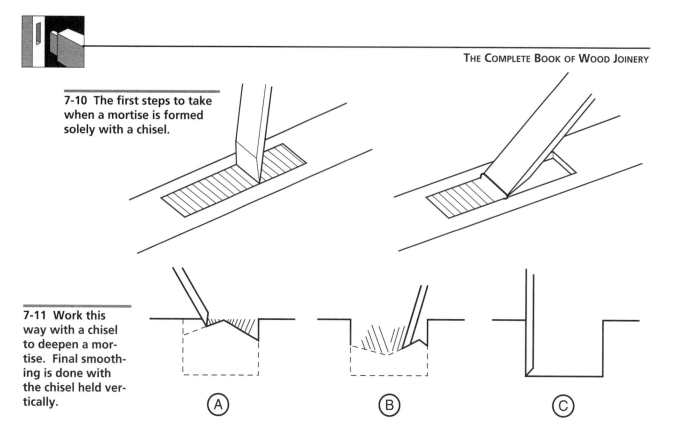

**7-10** The first steps to take when a mortise is formed solely with a chisel.

**7-11** Work this way with a chisel to deepen a mortise. Final smoothing is done with the chisel held vertically.

Ⓐ    Ⓑ    Ⓒ

## MORTISING ON A DRILL PRESS

The drill press must be equipped with a special mortising accessory that provides a fence and hold-down and a device that mounts on the spindle to hold the mortising chisels and bits (**Fig. 7-12**). The bit, which is encased in the chisel, works much like a regular drill bit to remove stock, but the chisel moves with it to

**7-12** Always make the end cuts first when mortising on a drill press.

**7-13** Finish the job by making a series of overlapping cuts.

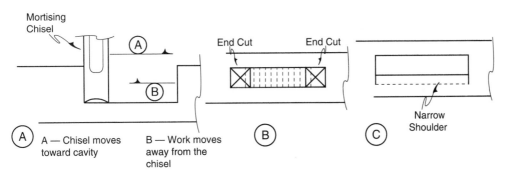

**7-14 Part of the job when doing drill press mortising is keeping the cutting tools from moving out of position.**

clean out the corners that remain. By working together, the units produce a square hole.

Standard chisel sizes include 1/4-inch, 5/16-inch, 3/8-inch, and 1/2-inch, so it's a good idea to size the width of mortises accordingly. The length of the mortise is variable. The speed of the drill press is adjusted in relation to the size of the chisel and the density of the wood. A general rule for chisels up to 1/2-inch is to use a speed range of 1800 to 2800 rpm for softwood and 800 to 1500 rpm for hardwood. The *best* speed is determined by the operator and based on how well the cutting tools are functioning.

Excessive *feed pressure,* the force needed for the cutting tools to enter the wood, should not be necessary, but since the chisel cuts with only feed pressure, a timid touch won't do either. A critical factor when setting up is to be sure the side of the chisel is square to the fence. Also, to avoid excessive friction, there must be a gap of about 1/32-inch between the end of the bit and chisel. Information of this nature is supplied with the accessory.

Start the operation by marking lines on the work to indicate where the mortise will start and end. The edge distance of the mortise is determined by the position of the fence. Make the end cuts first, as shown in **Figure 7-12**, and then remove the waste between them by making a series of overlapping cuts (**Fig. 7-13**). The procedure fights the tendency of the cutting tools and the work to move (**Fig. 7-14**).

Ideally, the cuts should overlap about

three-quarters of the chisels width. This isn't always feasible but stay as close to it as possible. Don't leave narrow shoulders if the mortise that is needed is wider than the largest chisel available.

Making narrow cuts can cause the chisel to slant toward the open area. It's better to use a smaller chisel so overlapping cuts can be made across as well as along the length of the mortise.

Mortising is not limited to straight pieces of stock. Shaped components and even assemblies can be mortised so long as they can be positioned correctly and held securely (**Fig. 7-15**).

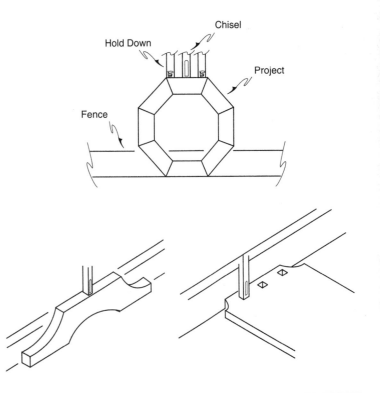

**7-15 Any shaped part or assembly can be mortised if it can be positioned correctly.**

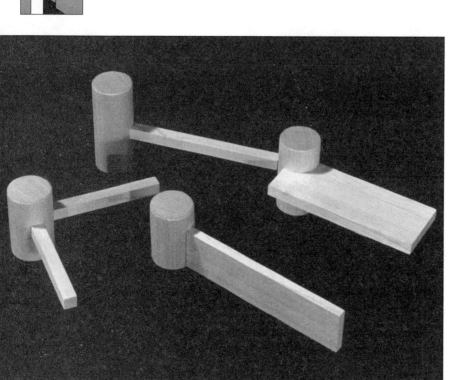

**7-16 A special jig that is custom-made is used to do mortising in round stock.**

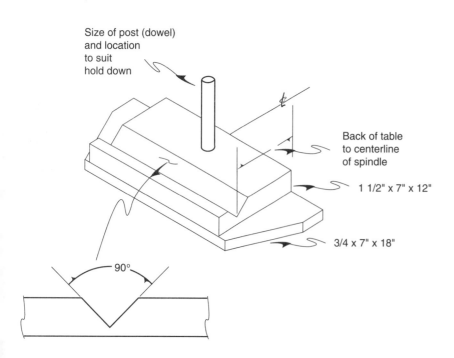

Size of post (dowel) and location to suit hold down

Back of table to centerline of spindle

1 1/2" x 7" x 12"

3/4 x 7" x 18"

90°

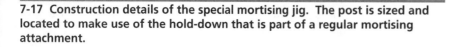

**7-17 Construction details of the special mortising jig. The post is sized and located to make use of the hold-down that is part of a regular mortising attachment.**

## MORTISING ROUND STOCK

A special jig that must be custom made is used to produce mortise-tenon joints like the examples in **Figure 7-16**. Mortising can be done to attach rails and stretchers to round legs; even radial mortises are possible so corners of shelves can be inserted in round posts. A plan for the jig is offered in **Figure 7-17**.

While the jig is used in place of the commercial mortising accessory, it does not call for any change in speed or feed pressure that is normally required. The purpose of the jig, essentially, is to provide a holding device so cylinders can be held securely and positioned accurately (**Fig. 7-18**). Be sure, when clamping the jig, that the spindle and the "V" in the jig have a common center-line and that the side of the chisel is square to the long line of the "V". Start by making one end-cut and then, using the cut as a guide, draw a longitudinal line that the chisel can follow for ensuing cuts.

**Figure 7-19** demonstrates how radial mortises are formed. Make end-cuts first and then clean out the stock between them with overlapping cuts as you rotate the stock. The strip of wood, tack-nailed across the "V" in the jig, ensures correct edge-distance for the mortise.

**Figure 7-20** suggests another use for the jig — forming mortises in a corner of square components.

**7-18** The work nestles in the V-block. Provide a guide line for the chisel to follow.

**7-19** Radial mortises are formed by rotating the stock for overlapping cuts. The strip of wood is a stop that controls edge distance. Make end-cuts first.

**7-20** The same jig can be used for forming mortises into the corners of square stock.

**7-21 This special joint is made by forming square holes with a mortising bit and chisel.**

Being creative can lead to many unusual but practical additional uses for mortising bits and chisels. For example, consider the multi-tenon joint shown in **Figure 7-21**. It makes a strong connection and introduces extra design elements when the tenons are allowed to project.

## OTHER MORTISING METHODS

A portable router will cut clean, smooth mortises, but the operation must be organized so the tool will have adequate bearing surface on the work. One method is to broaden the work edge by clamping it between blocks and using an edge-gauge to guide the tool. Another technique is to attach a custom-made, L-shaped guide to the base of the router for extra support and for gauging edge-distance (**Fig. 7-22**). When a conventional router is used, the tool is held at an angle and then swung down for cutting. If slots are cut in the guide for the attachment screws, it will be adjustable for various edge-distances. The advent of *plunge routers* makes this kind of work much easier to do since the tool can be positioned on the stock before the bit is made to enter.

Don't attempt deep mortises in a single pass. It's always better to make repeat passes, adjusting for a deeper bite after each one. Mortises formed with router bits will have round ends so the tenon must be shaped to match.

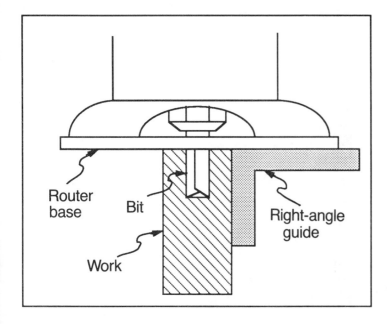

Router base · Bit · Work · Right-angle guide

**7-22 Forming a mortise with a portable router that is equipped with a homemade guide. Work of this nature can be done more easily with a plunge router.**

## OPEN MORTISE

An open mortise calls for a slot in one component to receive the tenon on the mating piece (**Fig. 7-23**). This concept is easier to form than other designs but accuracy requirements are just as critical. With hand tools, use a backsaw to form the shoulders and then remove the waste with a chisel, or first remove the bulk of the waste with a coping saw and then finish with a chisel.

Use a custom-made or commercial tenoning jig if cutting is done on a table saw (**Fig. 7-24**). Usually, the slot is centered. To do it accurately, make one shoulder cut and then reverse the stock's position so its opposite face is against the jig. Clean out remaining material by making additional passes.

The job is done on a radial arm saw by using a height table to position the stock (**Fig. 7-25**). Here too, make outline cuts first, flipping the stock for the second cut and then clearing the waste with other passes.

A dadoing tool can be used on either machine if sufficient projection for the cut-depth required is available. Remember that dadoing removes a lot of material, so passes must be made more slowly than usual and, if necessary, by making more than one pass to achieve full cut-depth.

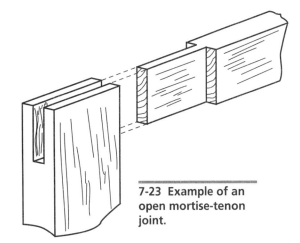

**7-23 Example of an open mortise-tenon joint.**

**7-24 Using a custom-made tenoning jig to form the slot for an open mortise.**

**7-25 A height table is used to position the work when a slot for an open mortise is formed on a radial arm saw.**

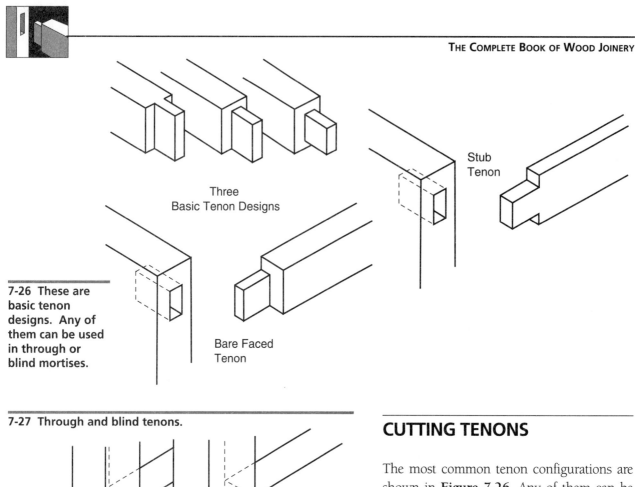

Stub Tenon

Three Basic Tenon Designs

**7-26** These are basic tenon designs. Any of them can be used in through or blind mortises.

Bare Faced Tenon

**7-27 Through and blind tenons.**

Through

Blind

## CUTTING TENONS

The most common tenon configurations are shown in **Figure 7-26**. Any of them can be either *blind* or *through* (Fig, **7-27**). Start by using a marking gauge to draw the lines for the cheek cuts (**Fig. 7-28**) and then switch to a square to draw shoulder locations.

## Cutting by Hand

First use a backsaw to form the shoulders. If the stock is narrow enough, several pieces can be held edge-to-edge for simultaneous sawing. Clamp a stop block to the saw to control the depth of the cut, or clamp a block of suitable thickness to the work. Either idea will control cut-depth and will help to keep the saw perpendicular. Twin cheek cuts finish the job (**Fig. 7-29**).

If the tenon requires four shoulders, then shoulder and cheek cuts are necessary on the edges of the stock as well as its surfaces.

**7-28 Use a marking gauge to draw the cheek lines for a tenon. Use a square to mark lines for the shoulder cuts.**

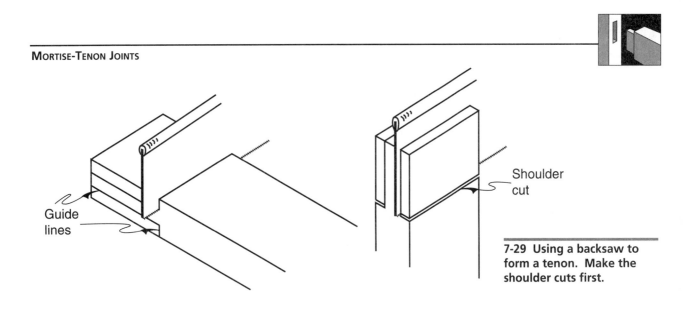

7-29 Using a backsaw to form a tenon. Make the shoulder cuts first.

## Power Tool Work

On a table saw, make the shoulder cuts first, using the setup shown in **Figure 7-30A**. The distance from the fence to the *outside* of the blade equals the length of the tenon; the projection of the blade will determines the tenon's thickness. Work like this must always be done with a miter gauge unless the stock is wide enough to provide sufficient bearing surface against the fence.

If the tenon must have four shoulders, adjust the projection of the saw blade if necessary, and then repeat the operation but with the stock on edge. *Always* use the miter gauge when stock is held on edge.

The cheek cuts are made with the stock

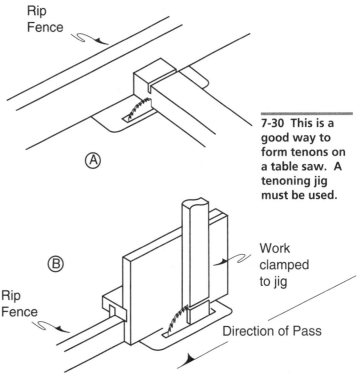

7-30 This is a good way to form tenons on a table saw. A tenoning jig must be used.

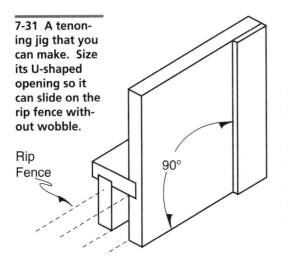

7-31 A tenoning jig that you can make. Size its U-shaped opening so it can slide on the rip fence without wobble.

on edge, *always* with a tenoning jig used for safety and accuracy (**Fig. 7-30B**). Commercial units for this type of work are available, or you can custom make a basic one by adopting the design shown in **Figure 7-31**. The jig must fit precisely over the rip fence but not so tight that moving it is a problem. It's a good idea to polish the fence and the contact surfaces of the jig with hard, paste wax to provide for

**7-32** Using a dado assembly on a table saw to form a square tenon on square stock. The projection of the cutting tool remains the same for all four cuts. A change would be required for two opposing cuts if a rectangular tenon was the intent.

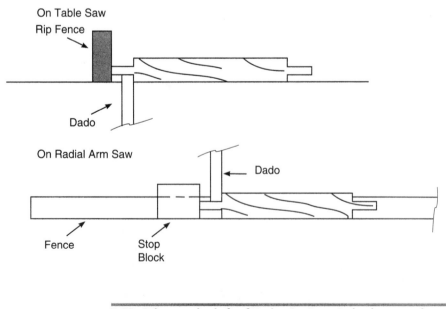

**7-33** Other methods for forming tenons. In both cases, the stock is flipped for opposing cuts.

On Table Saw
Rip Fence
Dado

On Radial Arm Saw
Dado
Fence
Stop Block

smooth action. Establish the position of the 90 degree guide with a square while the jig is in place on the fence.

Tenons can also be formed with a dadoing tool. In fact, it's the way to go when forming square tenons on square stock (**Fig. 7-32**). The tenon is formed with four passes, each pass after the stock has be turned to an adjacent surface. Use stop rods to keep the work in correct position.

**Figure 7-33** suggests how a dadoing tool can be

used to form tenons on a table saw or radial arm saw. The distance from the rip fence, or stop block in the case of the radial arm saw, to the *outside* of the cutter equals the length of the tenon. Make shoulder cuts first; clean out waste with additional passes after moving the stock away from the rip fence or the stop block.

Tenons that must fit round-end mortises are dressed like the example in **Figure 7-34**. Round off the corners by first using a file and then sandpaper.

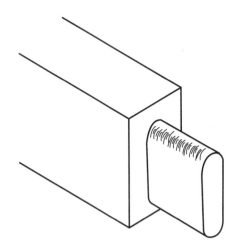

**7-34 Tenons for round-end mortises are shaped to suit the cavity.**

## INTEGRAL ROUND TENONS

Integral round tenons can be formed on cylinders or square stock with hand tools by following the procedure shown in **Figure 7-35**.

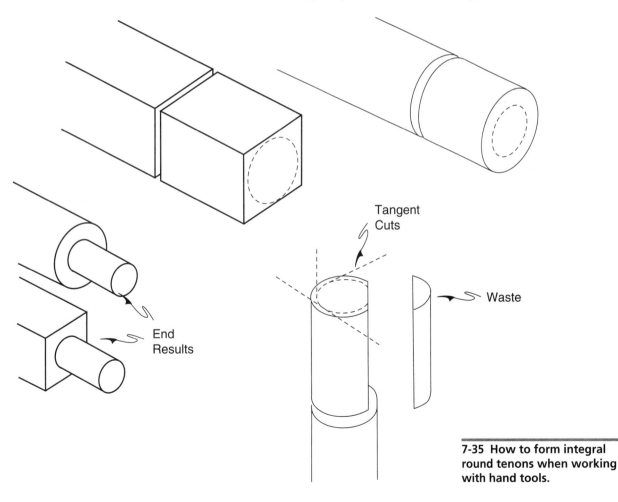

Tangent Cuts

Waste

End Results

**7-35 How to form integral round tenons when working with hand tools.**

**7-36 Shoulder cuts are made first when an integral round tenon will be formed with a plug cutter.**

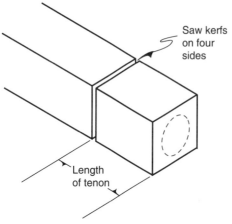

Shoulder cuts to determine the length of the tenon are cut first with a backsaw. Control the depth of the cut with a strip of wood clamped to the saw regardless of whether the work is

round or square. The second step is to make a series of tangent cuts to remove the bulk of the waste. Finish the job by working with a file and then sandpaper. The greater the number of tangent cuts, the less the waste material that remains. Final smoothing is done with a narrow strip of sandpaper, buffing as you would a shoe with a polishing cloth.

Integral round tenons are easier to form if you use a plug cutter in a drill press. The first step is to cut kerfs that form the shoulders of the tenon and that determine its length (**Fig. 7-36**). The depth of the kerfs determine the diameter of the tenon. The next step is to organize the power tool so a plug cutter can be used to form the cylinder (**Fig. 7-37**). Be sure to organize the setup so the plug cutter and

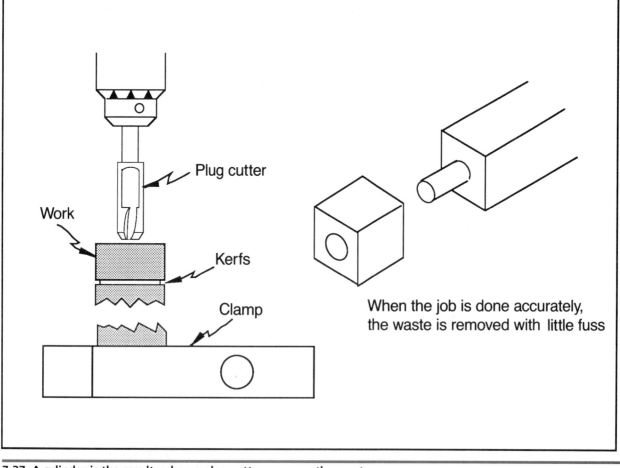

**7-37 A cylinder is the result when a plug cutter removes the waste.**

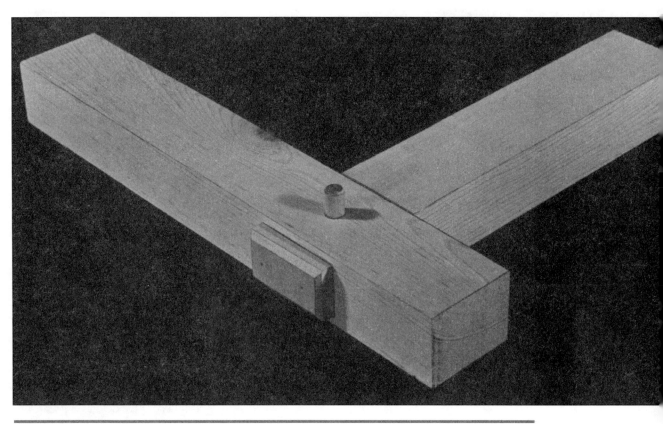

**7-38 A mortise-tenon joint locked with a through dowel.**

the workpiece have a common, vertical centerline. The average speed for using the plug cutters is between 1,500 and 2,000 rpm.

When the work's length allows, it can sit vertically on the table under the spindle, held securely with, say, a handscrew clamp that is, in turn, clamped to the table. When this isn't feasible, tilt the table 90 degrees so the work can be clamped vertically.

The sizes of integral tenons that can be formed with plug cutters that are generally available will range from ¼ inch to ½ inch in diameter and up to 2 inches in length.

## HOW TO LOCK A TENON

The easiest way to provide extra security for a mortise-tenon joint is to drill through it for a dowel while the parts are held together (**Fig.**

7-38). A better technique, one that will pull the parts together tightly, is shown in **Figure 7-39**. The holes for the dowel are drilled in each part before assembly with one of the holes offset about 1/32-inch. When the dowel

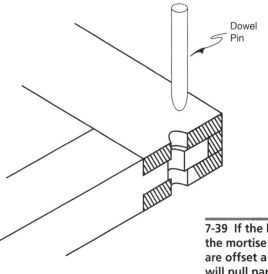

Dowel Pin

**7-39 If the holes through the mortise and the tenon are offset a bit, the dowel will pull parts tightly together.**

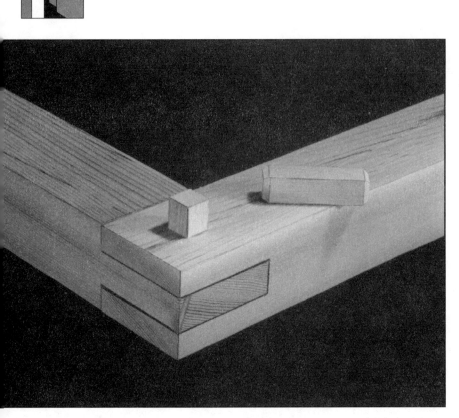

is tapped into place it will pull one part tightly against the other. Round off one end of the dowel so it will be easier to drive through the misaligned holes. Be sure that the length of the tenon is a bit less than the depth of the mortise.

**Figure 7-40** shows how a square peg can be used the same way. The square hole is formed with a mortising bit and chisel. The peg can be sanded flush or it can be precut to exact length with chamfered ends so it can project as a decorative detail.

Tenons can be locked with wedges if they are slotted as shown in **Figure 7-41**. The best procedure is to hold the parts together with clamps as the wedges are driven. The wedges must not be too large. Their purpose is to expand the tenon to fit the mortise tightly, but not to introduce a negative stress. The length of the wedges must be controlled when they are used in a blind connection.

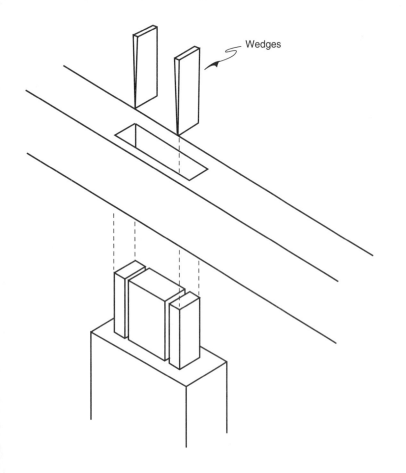

Wedges

**7-41** A wedged mortise-tenon joint. Wedges are also feasible for blind mortises. Just cut the wedges a bit shorter than the depth of the mortise.

Tusked
Tenon

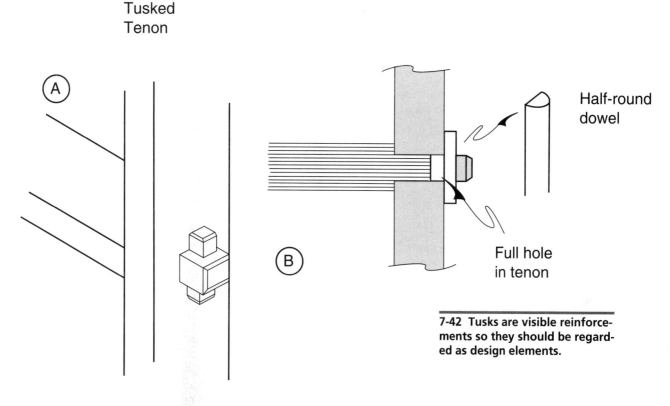

Half-round
dowel

Full hole
in tenon

7-42 Tusks are visible reinforcements so they should be regarded as design elements.

## TUSKS

Examples of tusked tenons are shown in **Figure 7-42**. In both cases, the cavity through the tenon is located so that driving the tusk or the half-dowel will pull the parts of the joint tightly together. A square or rectangular tusk should have a slight taper so it can be installed more easily. Notice that the hole in the assembly in **Fig. 7-42B** can match the diameter of the lock dowel. Its location in the tenon must be precise, but it's possible to rectify errors by shaping the lock dowel to fit.

## ANGLED JOINTS

The connection between stretchers or rails and slanted legs can be designed along the line shown in **Figure 7-43**. The mortise is square to the contact surface; the tenon and its shoulders are cut to conform.

Another technique for angled joints is to form the mortise so its sides are on a horizontal plane. This can be done on a drill press if a height block is used under the work (**Fig. 7-44**). The thickness of the height block establishes the slant angle, but the block must be

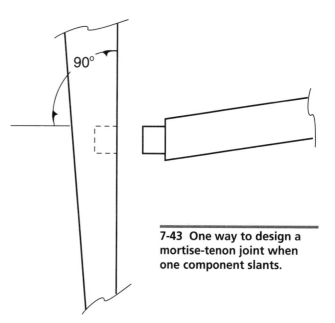

7-43 One way to design a mortise-tenon joint when one component slants.

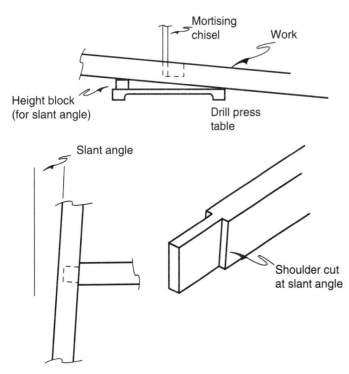

**7-44** When the mortise is formed this way, the connection will be normal except for the slanted shoulders on the tenon.

attached to the work, *not* the table, in order for the mortise to have a flat bottom. In this case, the end of the tenon can be square; only the shoulders are cut at an angle to suit the slant on the mating piece.

## MITERED TENONS

Mortise-tenon joints are frequently used to connect aprons or rails to legs. In some situations, especially when the rail or apron is flush with the leg, a standard tenon may not be as long and, therefore, not as strong as one that is mitered to fit as shown in **Figure 7-45**. The cutting procedures do not change. The only modification is the miter cut on the end of the tenon.

It's not important whether the joint shown in **Figure 7-46** is called a mitered mortise-tenon or simply described as a miter joint reinforced with a tenon. What is important is that the connection combines good strength with good appearance when used on frame constructions. Cutting the tenon is a matter of making angled shoulder cuts first and then cheek cuts that remove triangular-shaped waste pieces. Shorten the tenon by making saw cuts down through its edge and then finishing with a chisel. **Figure 7-46B** shows the procedure to use for the mortise. Form a regular blind mortise and then make a miter cut to finish the job.

The joint shown in **Figure 7-47** is something like a lap miter that incorporates a tenon. The design provides a considerable amount of glue area. One side has the appearance of a frame half-lap; the other, more attractive side, appears as a miter.

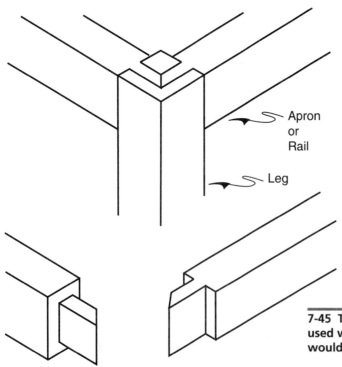

**7-45** Tenons with mitered ends are often used when a regular tenon, being shorter, would not supply enough strength.

## OTHER MORTISE-TENON DESIGNS

*Haunched tenons* are often used in the corner of frame constructions that are grooved to receive a panel (**Fig. 7-48**). The principal purpose of the haunch is to fill the gap that is visible because of the full length grooves in the frame members. Note that the width of the mortise and the frame grooves and the thickness of the tenon are similar. This makes for easier construction procedures.

**7-46  A mitered mortise-tenon combines strength with good appearance.**

Cut Line

Mortise

Ⓐ

Ⓑ

**7-47  This joint design provides a lot of glue area.  It looks like a half-lap on one side, a miter on the other.**

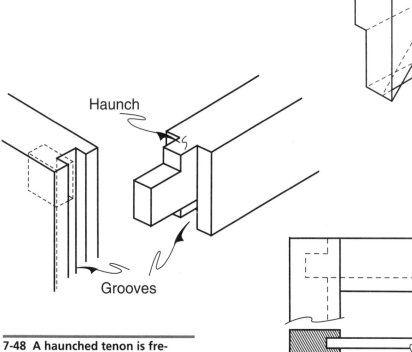

Haunch

Grooves

**7-48  A haunched tenon is frequently used to hide the gap caused by a groove that is the full length of frame components.**

Panel

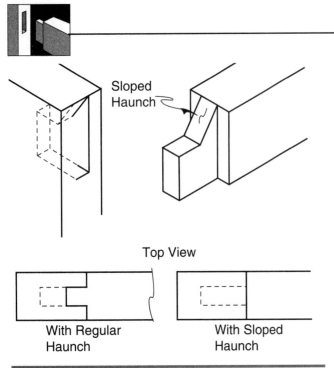

Top View

With Regular Haunch

With Sloped Haunch

Sloped Haunch

**7-49** A haunch provides some extra strength, and if it is sloped, it will not contribute to visible joint lines.

Haunched tenons are frequently used on basic frame assemblies because of the strength they contribute. Many times the haunch is sloped, as shown in **Figure 7-49**, to avoid adding visible joint lines.

Tenons with unequal shoulders are used with a mortise in framework or sash assemblies where a rabbet is required (**Fig. 7-50**). Detail (**B**) in the same illustration is the cross-section of a frame member that illustrates how the rabbet serves as a seat for a glass or wood panel insert.

**Figure 7-51** shows the shapes that are formed on the mating components.

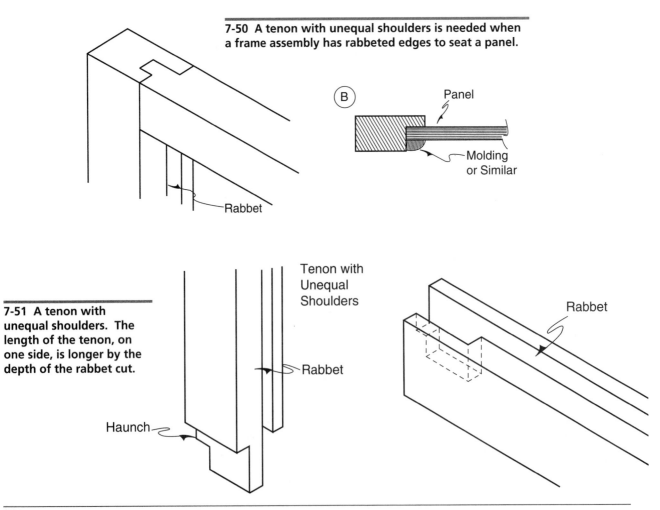

**7-50** A tenon with unequal shoulders is needed when a frame assembly has rabbeted edges to seat a panel.

B

Panel

Molding or Similar

Rabbet

**7-51** A tenon with unequal shoulders. The length of the tenon, on one side, is longer by the depth of the rabbet cut.

Tenon with Unequal Shoulders

Rabbet

Haunch

Rabbet

# 8

# EDGE-TO-EDGE JOINTS

Making the Joint • Reinforcements *(Dowels, Splines)* • Tongue-and-Groove Joint • Rabbet Joint • The Glue Joint • Decorative Joints • End Boards

**T**he edge-to-edge joint is commonly used to assemble individual pieces of lumber as solid slabs for table and desk tops, chair and bench seats, sides of case goods, and so on. Boards that are more than 12 inches wide are difficult to find, and even when they are available, it isn't too wise to use them as is. Unless plywood or some other man-made panel material is used, wide slabs are produced by joining relatively narrow boards edge-to-edge.

Since wide boards can warp, it's fairly standard practice among woodworkers to rip them into, say, three pieces, and then reassemble them after inverting the center section. Alternating the direction of the annual rings causes opposing stresses that, in theory, will prevent a cumulative warp (**Fig. 8-1**).

A reason given for *not* inverting alternate pieces is that distortion in each one might result in a rippled or washboard surface that would be difficult to hold down without a lot

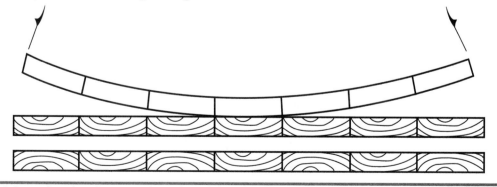

**8-1 Inverting the alternate pieces in a slab assembly is one method used to avoid cumulative warp.**

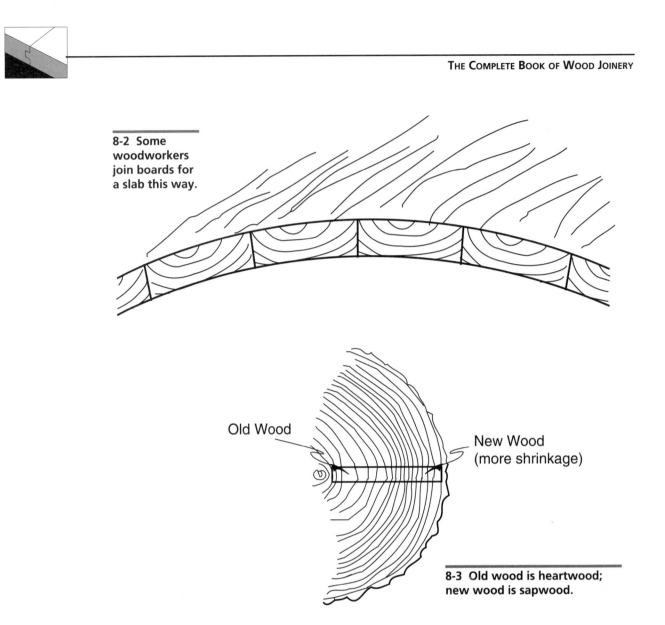

**8-2 Some woodworkers join boards for a slab this way.**

Old Wood

New Wood (more shrinkage)

**8-3 Old wood is heartwood; new wood is sapwood.**

of screws. It seems an extreme point since any waves that might occur can be eliminated with a plane or belt sander. If the parts are joined as shown in **Figure 8-2**, a prominent arch might result and this certainly would call for mechanical fasteners to achieve levelness — and the fasteners would not eliminate the existing stresses.

An important factor to consider is how the characteristics of a tree affect the boards that are cut from it. A tree grows by adding cells at its circumference. The old wood (*heartwood*) is at the core of the tree. The new wood (*sapwood*) is at outer areas (**Fig. 8-3**). Sapwood, being more porous than heartwood, is more affected by changes in humidity.

The different degrees of expansion and contraction should be considered when joining boards. A basic approach is to assemble so that old wood is against old wood and new wood abuts new wood (**Fig. 8-4**). This procedure will do much to minimize, if not eliminate, the effects of natural distortions.

Pay attention to grain patterns that will result after parts are joined. Set them together loosely so you can study the effects. Change their positions; move them longitudinally to achieve most attractive results. Mark across them lightly with a pencil and number them so that after cutting procedures they can be returned to the positions you have selected.

**8-4 Assembling a slab with parts joined this way will do much to minimize distortions.**

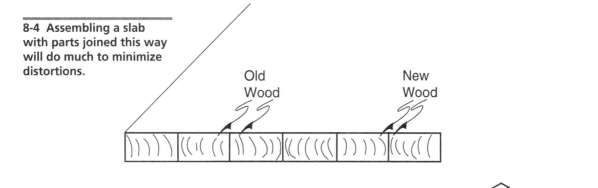

Old Wood    New Wood

## MAKING THE JOINT

Boards have a tendency to shrink more at ends where more open pores exist than at mid-points. One way to counteract the shrinkage or splitting is to use a *spring type* joint like the example in **Figure 8-5**. This puts the ends of the board under compression to guard against distortion that can occur in those areas. The shaving that is removed must be very fine. The chore can be accomplished efficiently with a hand plane that is set to remove a translucent shaving (**Fig. 8-6**) or on a jointer, if one is available.

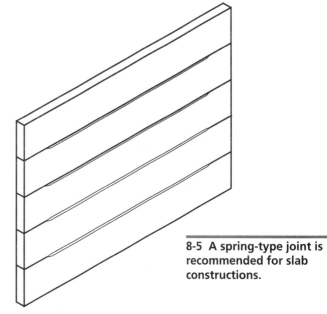

**8-5 A spring-type joint is recommended for slab constructions.**

**8-6 Using a hand plane to remove a see-through shaving. The job can also be done on a jointer.**

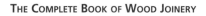

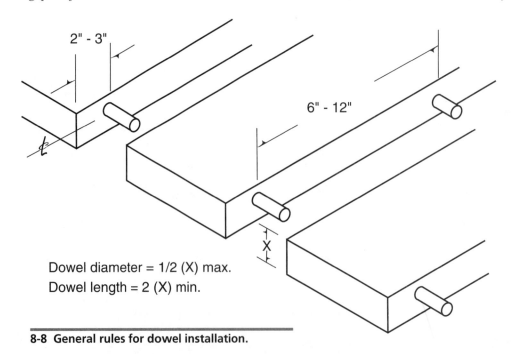

**8-7 Mating edge of components in a slab must be square in order for the project to have an even surface.**

Boards for slabs should be tested for fit and alignment before any further work is done or before glue is applied (**Fig. 8-7**). Don't depend on clamp pressure to compensate for poor cutting since it will only result in additional stresses that contribute to failure or gaps in joint lines.

## REINFORCEMENTS

A good, spring-type, edge-to-edge joint will make a bond as strong as the wood itself. Destruction tests show that adjacent areas may fail before the joint does. So why reinforce it? For one thing, reinforcement adds a safety factor that helps combat stresses caused by use. Another reason is that most reinforcement procedures provide a type of interlock that helps keep parts in alignment while they are being clamped. Anyone who has assembled a considerable number of pieces using only butt joints will appreciate how helpful an interlock can be.

## Dowels

The number of dowels used in a joint is not as critical as the care that should be used to locate them. If dowel holes are not aligned precisely, they will do more harm than good.

Some general rules for locating dowels are shown in **Figure 8-8**. They should not, however, be viewed as bible. Many wood-

2" - 3"

6" - 12"

Dowel diameter = 1/2 (X) max.
Dowel length = 2 (X) min.

**8-8 General rules for dowel installation.**

workers will avoid using dowels at the end of parts and will increase spacing to as much as 18 or 20 inches. This approach utilizes the dowels more for alignment than for reinforcement. Conversely, some workers go to the opposite extreme, broadcasting dowels over the entire assembly in staggered fashion as shown in **Figure 8-9**. There may be some justification for this approach on heavy-duty projects subjected to considerable abuse, but it would be a bit much for components like desk and table tops.

Hole centerlines should be established by gauging edge distance from the similar surface of each piece. Even if the holes are not centered exactly, they will have the same edge distance and will align correctly.

Mark the hole spacing on one component with dividers or a compass (**Fig. 8-10**). Here too, a slight error will not be significant so long as the first piece is used as a gauge for its mates. Hold the parts firmly together, with clamps if necessary, and then use a square to carry the line across all edges (**Fig. 8-11**). Centerlines are not required if the holes will be bored on a drill press. The location of a fence, clamped to the drill press table, will establish edge distance correctly on all pieces

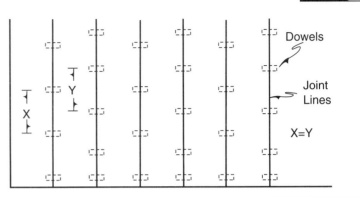

**8-9 Dowels are often broadcast and staggered when the slab is for heavy-duty use.**

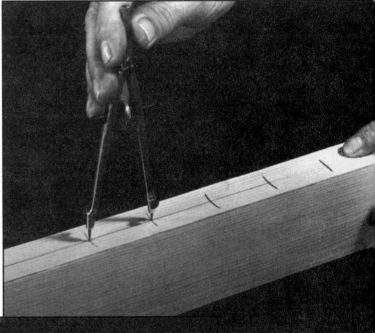

**8-10 Use a compass or dividers to mark the spacing between holes.**

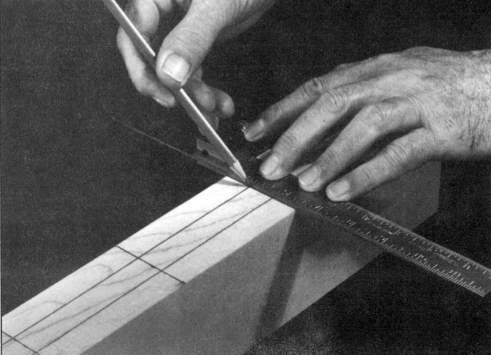

**8-11 Use a square to mark hole locations across all edges.**

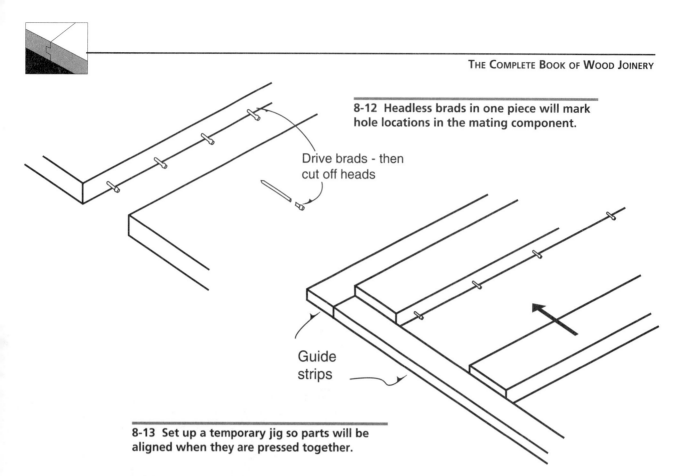

**8-12 Headless brads in one piece will mark hole locations in the mating component.**

Drive brads - then
cut off heads

Guide
strips

**8-13 Set up a temporary jig so parts will be aligned when they are pressed together.**

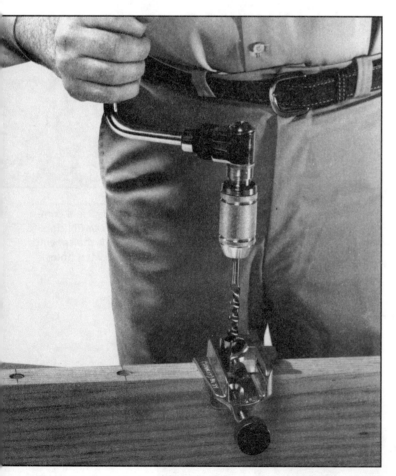

so long as the similar surface of each one is against the fence when drilling.

A good way to establish hole alignment when drilling with a hand tool is shown in **Figure 8-12**. Spot the holes in one piece and then tap in short brads. Snip the heads off the brads and then press the part and its mate together, thus leaving marks on the mate piece for the holes. Alignment of the parts will be assured by improvising a jig like the one suggested in **Figure 8-13**. Tack-nail guide strips to form a 90 degree angle. Place the guide piece in the corner of the jig and then press the mating part against it.

A similar way to work is to locate and bore the holes in the pattern piece with a brace and doweling jig (**Fig. 8-14**). Be sure the same side of the jig is against the face side of the stock for each hole. Dowel centers can then be used to mark hole locations on the mating piece (**Fig. 8-15**).

**8-14 Boring dowel holes by working with a doweling jig. Be consistent when placing the jig for each hole.**

The jig that is detailed in **Figure 8-16** is handy since it will automatically locate holes in the center of edges regardless of the stock's thickness. Drill 1/16-inch pilot holes when using the jig and drill as deep as the dowel must penetrate. The pilot hole is then enlarged to suit the dowel. **Figure 8-17** shows a more sophisticated version of the centering jig. Here, a steel bushing is used for the pilot hole so that it can't be enlarged by

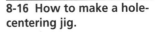

**8-15 One part with dowel centers placed in drilled holes can be used as a pattern to mark other pieces.**

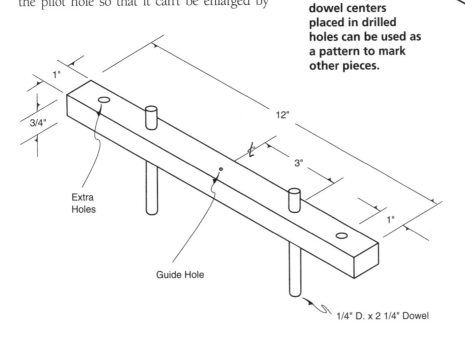

1"
3/4"
12"
3"
1"
Extra Holes
Guide Hole
1/4" D. x 2 1/4" Dowel

**8-16 How to make a hole-centering jig.**

**8-17 A more sophisticated hole-centering jig. The steel bushing provides consistent accuracy — more so than just a hole through wood**

**8-18 Drilling dowel holes on a drill press. A clamped fence positions the work for correct edge distance. Hole spacing is controlled by aligning lines on the work with the line on the clamped guide block.**

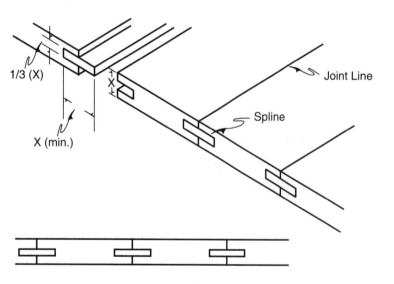

**8-19 General rules for spline installations.**

repetitive use. A centering jig can be used, of course, regardless of the tool used to do the final drilling.

Accuracy is easier to achieve and holes can be formed with less fuss by working on a drill press (**Fig. 8-18**). Clamp a fence to the table to control edge distance and to help keep the part vertical. A second block, clamped to the table, is marked so the work can be moved the correct spacing for each hole. Be sure that a similar surface of each piece is placed against the fence.

## Splines

Edge-to-edge joints often incorporate splines (**Fig. 8-19**). Splines may be cut from lumber or they can be plywood or hardboard of suitable thickness.

The width of the spline can be a bit less than the combined depth of the grooves, but

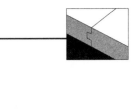

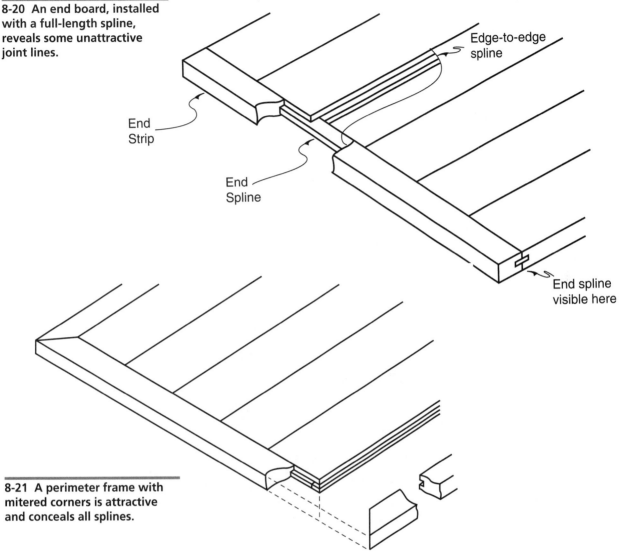

**8-20** An end board, installed with a full-length spline, reveals some unattractive joint lines.

End Strip

End Spline

Edge-to-edge spline

End spline visible here

**8-21** A perimeter frame with mitered corners is attractive and conceals all splines.

it must never be more. Obviously, a spline that is too wide will not allow the parts to butt together.

*End strips,* used on splined slabs, serve a double purpose. They conceal the splines and they cover the end-grain of the components. Form the end pieces as if they will be part of a spring-type joint. Many workers use glue only at the center area of end pieces regardless of how the joint is designed. The logic is that the length of the end boards will be stable while the width of the slab parts might change because of humidity variations. If

parts can move a bit, they won't split. If this plan is followed, it's recommended that a dowel be used in the center area.

End boards that are attached with splines, or with a tongue-and-groove arrangement, will still reveal some objectionable joint lines as indicated in **Figure 8-20**. Using a blind spline to attach the end boards, or designing the slab for a perimeter frame as shown in **Figure 8-21**, will eliminate the objection.

Grooves for splines, or for tongue-and-groove joints, can be formed on a table saw

**8-22 Forming grooves for splines by making repeat passes with a saw blade. Make initial cuts on all parts before changing the fence position for other cuts that may be needed to clear away waste.**

by making repeat passes with a saw blade (**Fig. 8-22**). To be sure the groove will be centered, establish edge distance by measuring from the fence to the facing side of the blade. Then make two passes, each with an opposite surface of the stock against the fence. If stock remains between the two cuts, it can be removed by making additional passes after the fence position is adjusted.

The groove can be formed in a single pass by working with a dadoing tool. In this case, make all cuts so the same surface of each piece will be against the fence.

Splines in edge-to-edge joints can be hidden if the grooves for them are stopped. The radius that is at the ends of the stopped groove poses no problem since the splines are easily shaped to fit (**Fig. 8-23**).

## TONGUE-AND-GROOVE JOINT

The tongue-and-groove connection is much like a splined joint (**Fig. 8-24**), except that the tongue is an integral part of one component. General dimensioning rules are offered in **Figure 8-25**. Both the tongue and the groove can be formed in conventional fashion

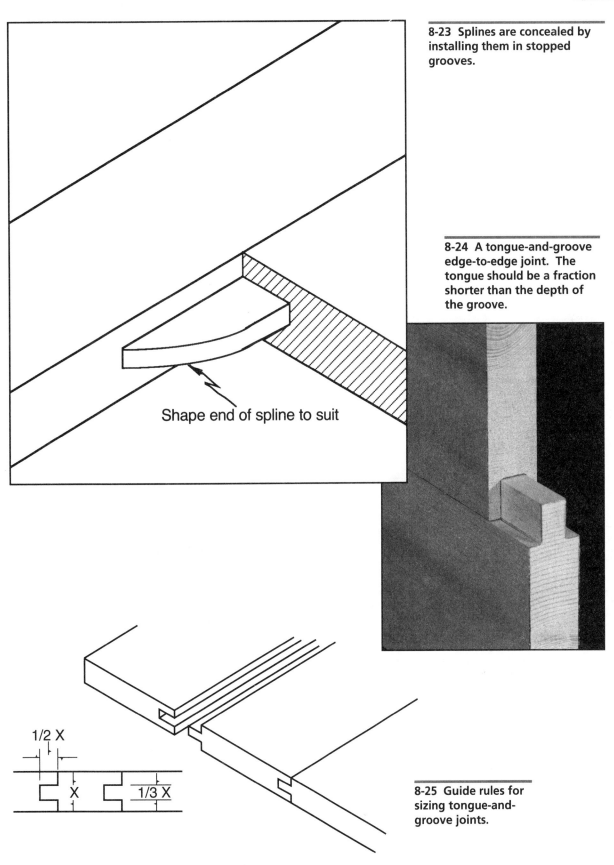

**8-23** Splines are concealed by installing them in stopped grooves.

Shape end of spline to suit

**8-24** A tongue-and-groove edge-to-edge joint. The tongue should be a fraction shorter than the depth of the groove.

1/2 X

X     1/3 X

**8-25** Guide rules for sizing tongue-and-groove joints.

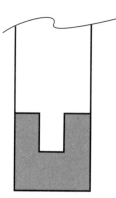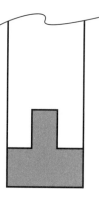

Tongue Cutter          Groove Cutter

**8-26 A matched set of cutters can be used to form the tongue-and-groove joint. They are available as 3-lip shaper cutters for use with a shaping machine or as knives that can be used in a molding head.**

Matched Set

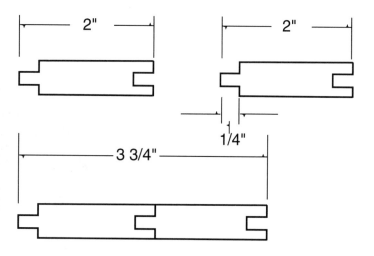

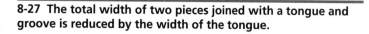

**8-27 The total width of two pieces joined with a tongue and groove is reduced by the width of the tongue.**

by working with a regular saw blade on a table saw. The tongue is formed by doing a two pass rabbeting operation on opposite edges of the stock, the groove by making repeat passes. Faster production is possible by working with a dadoing tool or, if a molding head is available, by using a matched set of cutters designed for the purpose (**Fig.8-26**). Cutters of this nature are also available for use on a shaping machine.

An important consideration when making tongue-and-groove joints is that the width

of the tongue must be considered when determining the width of the assembly. Note in the example in **Figure 8-27**, that though the parts are 2 inches wide, their total width when assembled is reduced by 1/4-inch.

## RABBET JOINT

Rabbet joints (**Fig. 8-28**) can be formed in any one of numerous ways. Use a two pass technique on a table saw or work with a dadoing tool, or do the job on a jointer. There are also cutters available for doing rabbeting on a shaping machine or with a portable router, and when working by hand, there is the rabbet plane. The width considerations that affect the tongue-and-groove joint also apply to rabbet joints (**Fig. 8-29**).

## THE GLUE JOINT

The *glue joint* is the popular name for a milled joint that is accomplished with a molding head on a table saw or, as shown in **Figure 8-30**, with a 3-lip cutter on a shaper. The cutter is designed so the shaped edges will fit per-

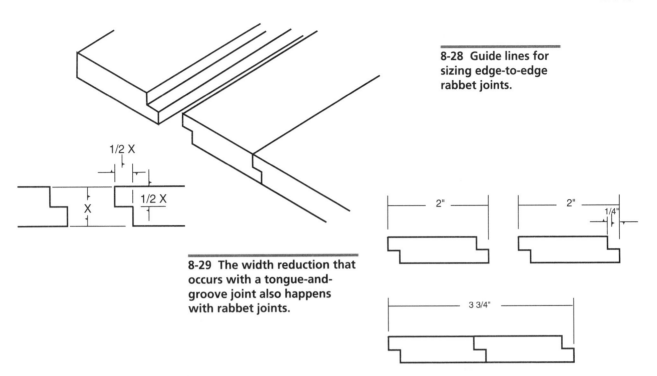

**8-28 Guide lines for sizing edge-to-edge rabbet joints.**

**8-29 The width reduction that occurs with a tongue-and-groove joint also happens with rabbet joints.**

**8-30 Using a glue joint 3-lip cutter on a shaper.**

fectly if the second piece is flipped for the mating cut.

The joint provides quite a bit of glue area and a degree of interlock. The joint is neat and not too objectionable if ends are left exposed. The mating edges of the stock must be prepared for a tight fit before they are shaped. Irregularities will be followed by the cutter. Shaper fences are organized so they will be in line with the smallest diameter of the cutter. Make a test cut so the depth of the cut and the height of the spindle can be adjusted correctly. You will know that adjustment is needed if test cuts do not go together with flush surfaces. Once the setup is correct, cutting proceeds as shown in **Figure 8-31**.

## DECORATIVE JOINTS

Cross-shaped splines can be used, as shown in **Figure 8-32**, to serve as parts of the joint and to provide an attractive inlay effect.

Results are more interesting when the splines are made of a contrasting wood. The grooves in the slab components are cut in routine fashion, but the best way to form the splines is to first shape a board as shown in **Figure 8-33**. Careful layout and a precise machine setup are necessary. Cutting is being done with blank knives in a molding head, but a dadoing tool can be used as well. Be certain that the thickness of the web in the cross-pieces is substantial. The best way to separate the splines is to cut them apart with a hand-saw or on a scroll saw or band saw.

A V-joint is another way to add a decorative touch to slabs (**Fig. 8-34**). The "V" can be formed with a saw blade, but it will be easier to form with greater accuracy if it is milled with a shaper cutter or even V-knives mounted in a molding head. Form the insert piece as a square. Trim and sand it flush after assembly. The result will be accent strips on the surfaces of the slab and diamond shapes at the ends.

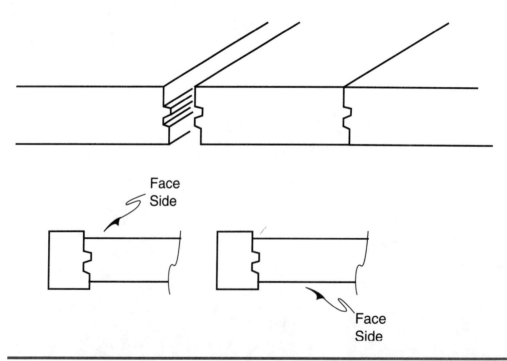

**8-31** The single 3-lip cutter is used to do the forming on mating edges. Make test cuts before working on project material.

8-32 Cross-shaped splines add an inlay effect to slabs. They are more effective when made of a contrasting material.

8-33 The cross-splines can be formed with blank knives in a molding head. Separate the splines with a hand saw or on a scroll saw or band saw.

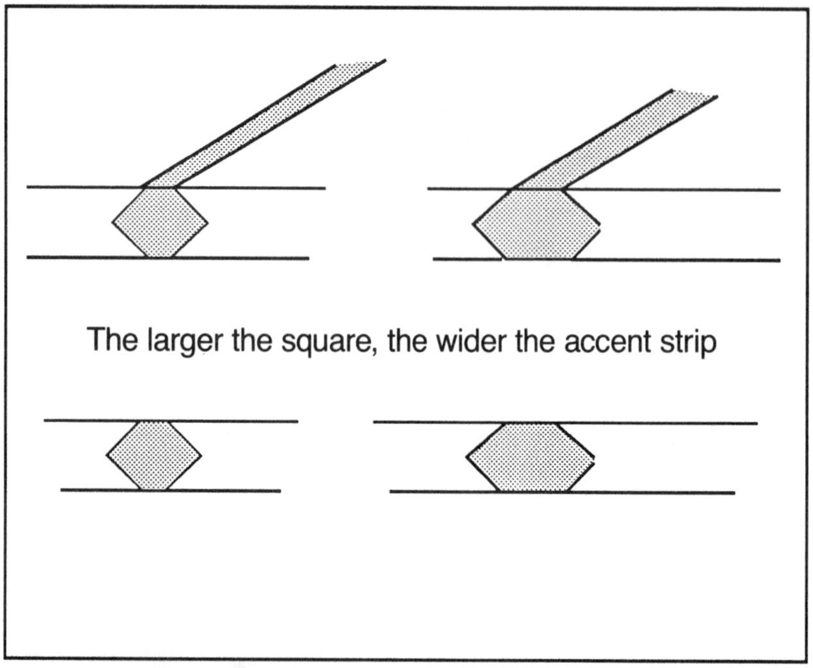

The larger the square, the wider the accent strip

**8-34 Inserts in V-cuts can be square and then trimmed and sanded flush, or they can be shaped beforehand.**

## END BOARDS

End boards are usually used to conceal end-grain but, as shown in **Figure 8-35**, they can be shaped to provide lips or to make the slab look heavier. One of the sketches suggests how a slab can be made more attractive without an end board. A sharp bevel, which can be formed by planing or sawing after assembly, puts the bulk of the joint lines below the line of sight.

Narrow strip glued in place

Molding or a specially shaped strip provides a lip

A sharp bevel puts the joint lines below the line of sight

Rabbeted frame pieces hide the joint lines and also make the slab look thicker

A strip of contrasting wood, inset in a rabbet cut, serves as a decorative detail while concealing the joint lines

Rabbet Cut

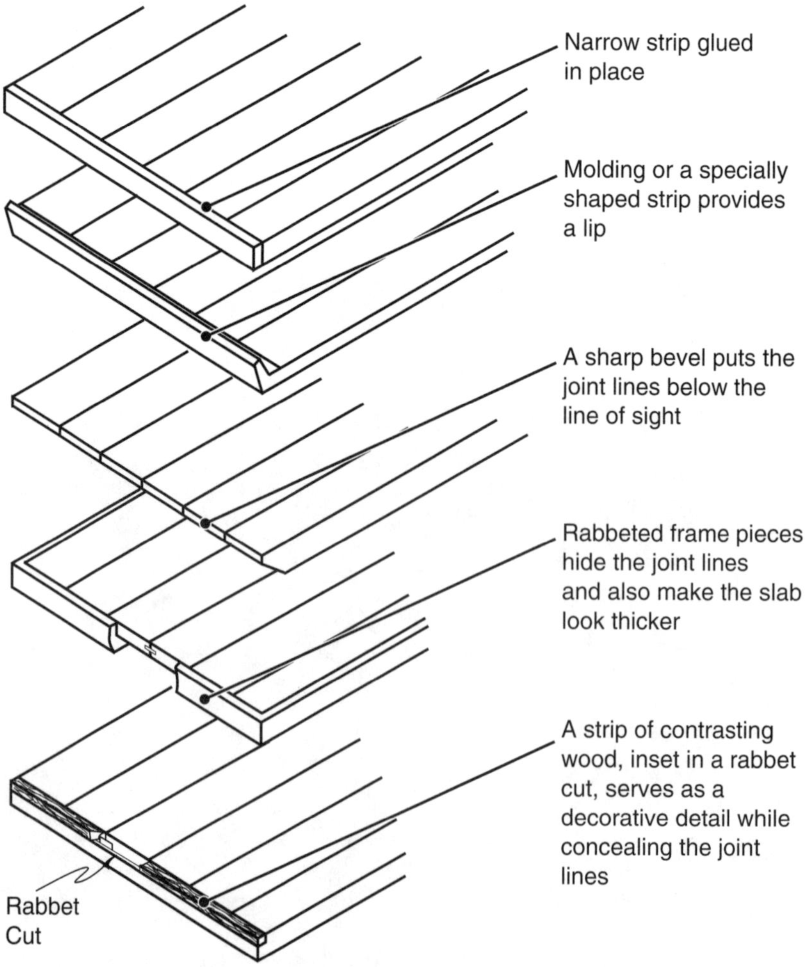

**8-35 Various ways to finish the ends of slabs.**

# 9

# DOVETAIL JOINTS

Multiple Dovetails • Design and Layout • Half-Blind Dovetails • Dovetailed T-Joints • Dovetail Slots • Pocket Dovetails • Dovetail Splices • Dovetail Keys and Splines

**D**ovetail joints are classic wood connections because they are attractive, reliable, and have an interlock so parts can stay together even if the glue fails. When woodworking machines were scarce, or yet to appear, dovetails were formed painstakingly, and lovingly, by hand. Many individual woodworkers still function so today by choice, not need, since the joint can be produced on stationary and portable power tools faster and with less fuss than hand-tooling requires. This brings up a debatable point. Are handmade dovetails better than those produced by machine? The dovetail design exists regardless of how they are made. A plus for hand-tooling is that it allows exclusive treatment in areas such as size and spacing. Dovetail joints produced by machine, like those in **Figure 9-1** that were formed with a jig and portable router, are, usually, uniform in size and spacing.

**9-1 Multiple half-blind dovetails can be produced quickly and with minimum fuss by working with a portable router and a dovetail jig.**

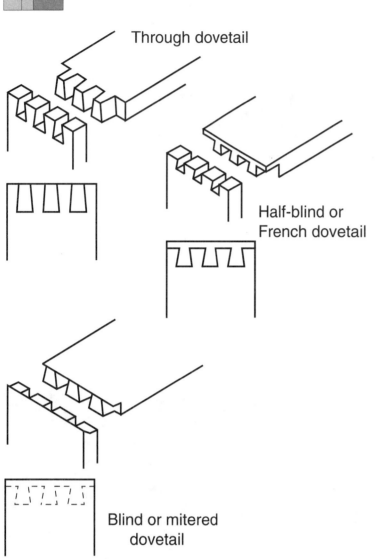

Through dovetail

Half-blind or
French dovetail

Blind or mitered
dovetail

**9-2 Type of dovetail joints. Through and half-blind are the designs that are used most often.**

Although design originality is certainly an asset, construction quality is paramount, as it is in all phases of joinery. An attractive result doesn't compensate for careless work regardless of the method adopted.

## MULTIPLE DOVETAILS

The basic designs of multiple dovetails are shown in **Figure 9-2**. Those that are used most often are the *through dovetail* and the *half-blind dovetail*. Another type, the *blind dovetail,* looks like a simple miter joint when assembled. The blind dovetail calls for an exceptional amount of work and attention, so it is usually found on very special projects, done by very persnickety craftsmen.

The nomenclature of the dovetail joint can be confusing unless you study the shapes of the interlocking parts. In construction procedures, components are referred to as *pins* and *sockets* (**Fig. 9-3**). Often, the solid piece between the sockets is called a *tail*.

The *half-pins* are named so because they slope only on one side. It's not mandatory that they be half the size of the whole pins. This is important when the joint is designed with very narrow pins since a half-pin, literally, would be very weak and could easily be chipped off. However, all dovetail joints should start and end with half-pins as opposed to half-tails. Tails get their strength by glue contact with pins. They don't gain much if they connect to end-grain.

## DESIGN AND LAYOUT

The slope of the dovetail can have a ratio that ranges from one-to-five to one-to-eight. Greater angles are needed more on soft wood than on hardwood, but many woodworkers adopt the one-to-eight layout generally, because they feel it has more visual appeal.

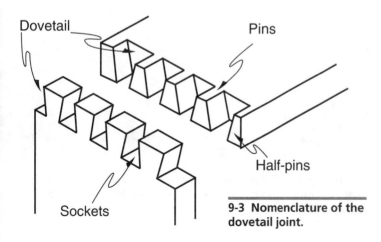

Dovetail

Pins

Half-pins

Sockets

**9-3 Nomenclature of the dovetail joint.**

**9-4 How to make a layout that determines the slope angle for a dovetail. The procedure is explained in the text.**

**Figure 9-4** shows a layout method that can be used to determine the slope angle. Assuming a one-to-eight proportion, draw a parallel line 8 inches away from the edge of a board and then use a square to establish a perpendicular line. Mark 1 inch away from the intersection of the two lines and then draw the diagonal. A T-bevel, set to conform with the diagonal line, can be used to mark the work. A technique that will be revealed later will show how to make and use a template for faster layout and with less chance of human error.

There can be a lot of variation in the size and spacing of dovetails, especially when they are formed with hand tools. Some workers prefer a uniformity that is achieved by following the formula shown in **Figure 9-5**. The thickness of the stock determines the depth of the sockets. Uniformity in size and spacing is also the rule when dovetails are formed by using a conventional dovetail jig.

Many workers prefer to depart from uniformity. There are many examples of non-conforming dovetails found in older pieces of furniture and it's not unusual to find modern woodworkers that work in similar fashion, using, for example, just a few dovetails even on wide connections (**Fig. 9-6**). In a sense, this is a way of interpreting the concept of the joint and applying individual preferences and sense of style to the project.

There is an on-going debate about what to make first — the pins or the tails. Either way, the first piece that is formed serves as a pattern

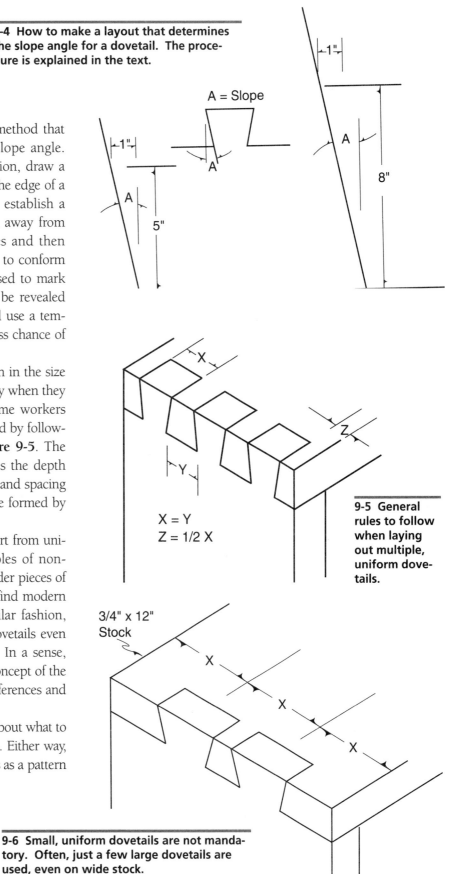

**9-5 General rules to follow when laying out multiple, uniform dovetails.**

$$X = Y$$
$$Z = 1/2 \ X$$

3/4" x 12" Stock

**9-6 Small, uniform dovetails are not mandatory. Often, just a few large dovetails are used, even on wide stock.**

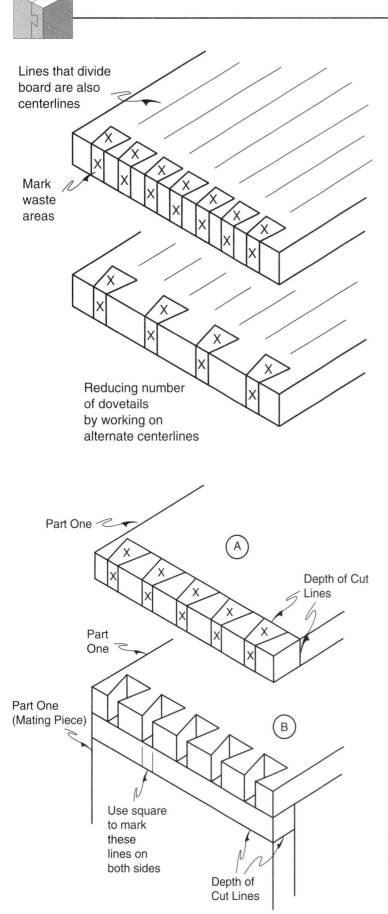

Lines that divide board are also centerlines

Mark waste areas

Reducing number of dovetails by working on alternate centerlines

Part One

A

Part One

Depth of Cut Lines

Part One (Mating Piece)

B

Use square to mark these lines on both sides

Depth of Cut Lines

**9-7 Start a layout for dovetails by dividing the stock into equal spaces.**

for marking the mating part. There does seem to be a preference for doing the pins first but, regardless of the sequence, what counts is how carefully the first step is taken and how accurately the part is used as a pattern.

A good way to start the layout is to divide the stock into X number of spaces to define the number of dovetails you plan to cut (**Fig. 9-7**). The marked lines are the centerlines of the individual dovetails. The initial layout can be drawn full-size on paper if you wish to preview the appearance of the joint. It's easier and neater to make changes on paper than on wood.

The layout on the first part you cut should look like the one shown in **Figure 9-8A**. All slopes are marked, waste areas are indicated, and depth-of-cut lines are shown on surfaces and edges. After the first part is shaped, it is used as a pattern to mark the mating piece as shown in **Figure 9-8B**. Here too, depth-of-cut lines are drawn and vertical cut-lines are carried down from the edge using a square.

Once the slope of the dovetails has been decided, it's a good idea to make a marking template that can be used instead of having to do individual dovetail layouts. **Figure 9-9A** shows how, by cutting a groove through a length of wood, you can produce base stock for dovetail templates of different sizes and with a particular slope angle. **Figure 9-9B** shows examples of templates made by cutting at an angle through the grooved stock.

**9-8 After one part is cut, it is used as a pattern to mark the mating piece. It's a good idea to identify the waste pieces.**

Figure 9-10 shows how a template can be made by first shaping and then bending a piece of thin sheet metal. Although the template will be a specific size, there are still options since the spacing between layouts made with the template can be variable.

Both of the templates discussed so far are made for a particular stock thickness. For greater flexibility, a template can be made like the one being used in **Figure 9-11**. Here, the template is L-shaped instead of being grooved so it can be used on different stock thicknesses.

Finally, as suggested in **Figure 9-12**, the L-shaped template can be substantial in size so it can be clamped in place and used as a guide for the saw. If the template is designed correctly, it can even serve as a depth gauge since the spine on the saw will act as a stop when it hits the top edge of the template.

Secure the component is a vise and make the slope cuts with a dovetail saw (**Fig. 9-13**). Be sure to saw on the waste side of the line. It will be easier to avoid errors if the waste pieces are marked. Don't rush the job. Even a fine-tooth dovetail saw can cause unnecessary feathering and splintering if it is forced. Also, it's easier to be accurate when sawing is done with moderate pressure.

The waste between the saw cuts can be removed by working solely with chisels, but there is no reason why the bulk of it can't be removed with a coping saw (**Fig. 9-14**). Don't, however, attempt to do the complete job with the saw. The joint lines will be much neater and tighter if final dressing is done with sharp chisels (**Fig. 9-15**). Start by making cuts from both sides of the stock, holding the chisel vertically and rapping it smartly with a mallet. Then work with only hand pressure but continue to work from opposite sides. Use care to be sure that the bottom of the waste area is flat and that corners are sharp. Choose chisel sizes that are suitable for the area being worked on.

Often, the area between pins is slightly

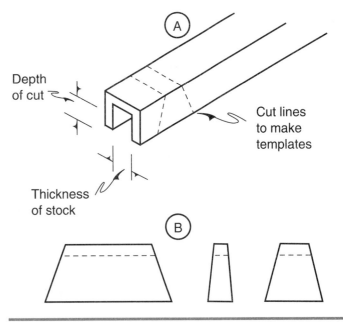

9-9 A length of stock that is grooved to match the thickness of the project material can be cut to form dovetail templates of various sizes.

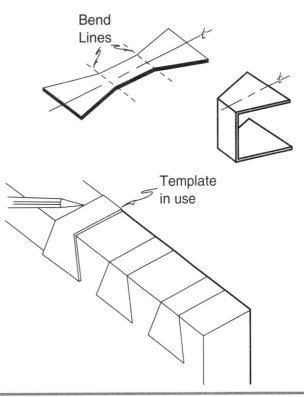

9-10 Another way to make a dovetail template is to shape a piece of thin sheet metal and then bend it over the edge of the stock.

**9-11 A rabbeted template can be used to mark cutlines regardless of the thickness of the stock,**

**9-12 A rabbeted template that is made this way will also act as a guide for sawing.**

**9-13 If the guide is sized correctly, it can also serve as a stop to control the depth of the cuts. The saw can't go deeper when its spine hits the guide.**

**9-14** The bulk of the waste can be removed with a coping saw.

**9-15** Finish the job by working with a chisel. Make cuts from both sides of the stock.

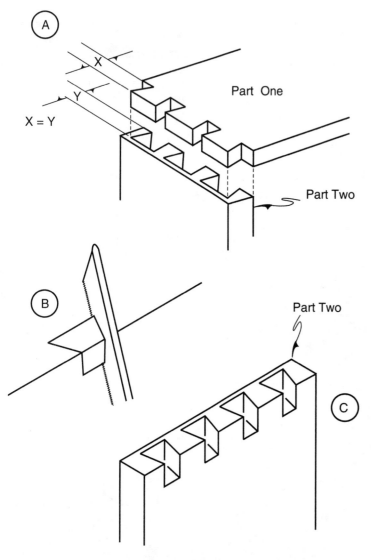

**9-16 The starting cuts for half-blind dovetail pockets are made with the saw held at an angle. The waste between the saw cuts is removed with a chisel.**

## HALF-BLIND DOVETAILS

Half-blind dovetails are often used to join a drawer front to its sides. The joint is visible only when the drawer is pulled out. A tested construction procedure is shown in **Figure 9-16**.

Lay out tails on the side of the drawer working as you would for through dovetails. After the shapes are formed, use the part as a template to mark the front of the drawer. Be sure to have the inside surface of each piece identified.

Draw a line on the end of the drawer to indicate the alignment point of the tails on the drawer side. It is important to maintain this alignment while marking. One way to be sure is to grip the drawer front in a vise so the edge to be marked is flush with the bench top. Place the pattern in position and clamp or weight it down. Use a hard pencil or a knife to transfer the cut-lines. The depth of the pockets will equal the thickness of the drawer side *unless* the drawer front will have a lip. If so, the lip can be formed first by making a rabbet cut and then doing the layout on the shoulder of the rabbet, or by making the pocket cuts deeper than necessary and then doing the rabbet cut to form the lip.

Start cleaning out the waste by making the saw cuts shown in **Figure 9-16B**. Cut on the waste side of the line and be careful not to saw beyond the terminal points. Several saw cuts between the first two will make it easier to remove waste. The job is finished with a chisel, using it alternately from opposite edges of the pocket. Inside corners will not be defined by the saw cuts, so careful work with a chisel of suitable width is necessary. The work is done best by removing small shavings.

The completed parts should fit together snugly. Light taps with a mallet are okay, but the tails should not fit so tightly that they have to forced. Test the results by putting the parts together without glue before doing final assembly.

undercut so parts will fit tightly. The undercutting results in a very slight concave form and is accomplished by tilting the chisel a degree or two when the last vestige of waste is removed.

When the first part is complete, use it as a pattern to mark its mate. Be certain the parts are related correctly and that they are held firmly in position while the marking is done. Identify the waste areas and then follow the same procedures that were used to produce the first component.

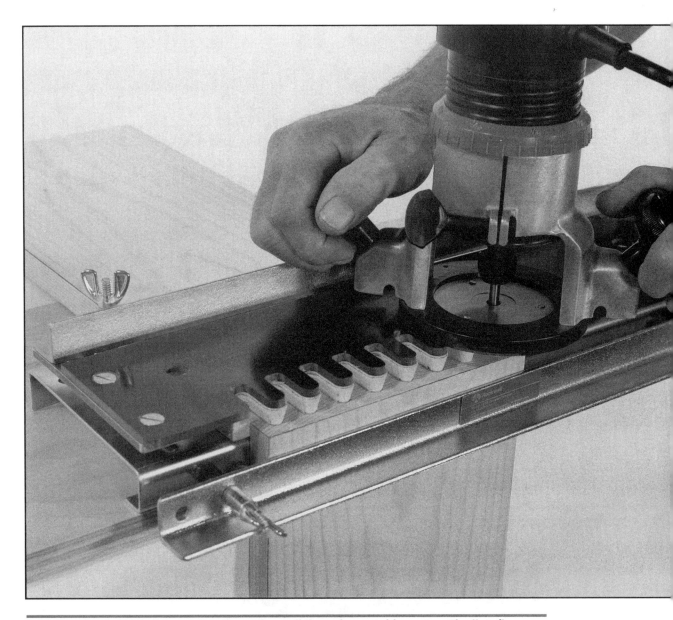

**9-17 Forming half-blind dovetails using a dovetail jig and a portable router. The jig's finger template dictates the size and spacing of the dovetails.**

A quick and accurate way to produce multiple dovetails is to work with a portable router and a special accessory that provides a clamp fixture to hold the components and a finger template that guides the cutter (**Fig. 9-17**). The mating cuts on both parts are formed in one operation, so it's critical that they be placed correctly in the fixture. It's also important never to move the router on or off the template while the tool is running. Any misalignment while the cutter is turning can damage the template, the work, and even the cutter. Most dovetail jigs of this nature work in similar fashion, but there can be some slight differences in how mating pieces are aligned or clamped. Results will be successful if you take time to study the instructions that are supplied with the accessory.

The same type of jig can be used on a drill press if provisions are made so the work

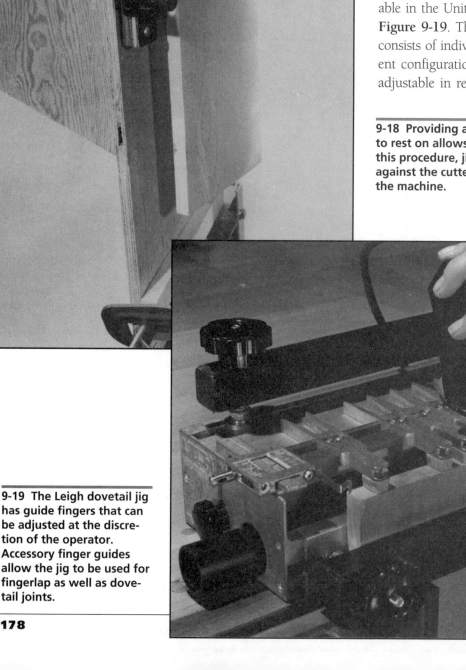

and jig can relate correctly with the cutter (**Fig. 9-18**). In this case, cutting is done by moving jig and work against the dovetail bit that is gripped in the machine's chuck. The highest speed of a drill press will not come near what is available with a portable router, so it's important to feed the work so the bit can cut at its own pace.

Conventional dovetail jigs produce uniformly spaced, half-blind dovetails, but there are other concepts that afford flexibility in spacing and design. One of them, the Leigh jig that is made in Canada but is widely available in the United States, is shown in use in **Figure 9-19**. The guidance system of the jig consists of individual fingers that have different configurations at each end and that are adjustable in relation to each other because

**9-18** Providing a platform for the dovetail jig to rest on allows its use on a drill press. In this procedure, jig and work are moved against the cutter. Use the highest speed of the machine.

**9-19** The Leigh dovetail jig has guide fingers that can be adjusted at the discretion of the operator. Accessory finger guides allow the jig to be used for fingerlap as well as dovetail joints.

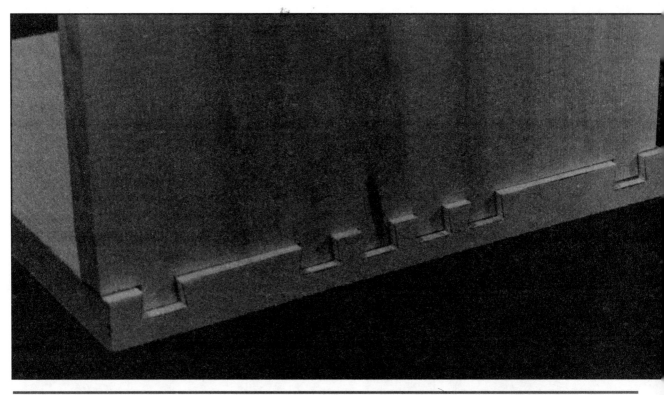

**9-20  A dovetail joint produced on the Leigh jig.  The flexibility of the machine allows original dovetail-joint designs.**

they can be moved along a slide bar. Using the jig professionally takes a little practice, but obeying the detailed instructions that come with it gets you to standard or original dovetails in short order. An example of the type of work that can be done with the Leigh jig is shown in **Figure 9-20**.

## DOVETAILED T-JOINTS

A single through dovetail makes a strong connection that can be used on frame assemblies, furniture rails and aprons, and so on (**Fig. 9-21**). The pin can be shaped with just saw cuts, doing the shoulder cuts first and then sawing down the slopes. The completed pin is used to mark the

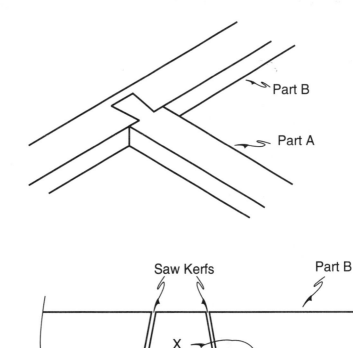

**9-21  A single through dovetail will provide strong frame connections.**

**9-22 Using a formed pocket as a template to mark the mating piece.**

**9-23 The tail can be finished by making light shaving cuts with a chisel. Test for correct fit as you go.**

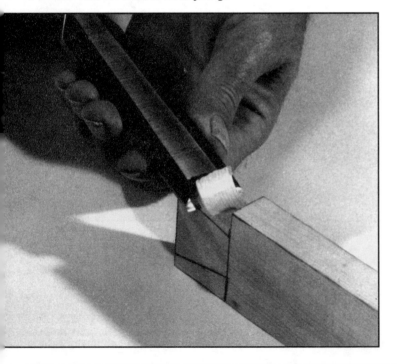

shape of the socket, which is then produced by sawing the slopes and then removing the waste with a chisel. Intermediate saw cuts will make it easier to clear the waste, or the bulk of the waste can be eliminated with a coping saw.

Some workers prefer to form the socket first and then use it as the pattern for the pin (**Fig. 9-22**). The pin is formed with saw cuts, but staying away from the line allows finishing the job with a chisel (**Fig. 9-23**), so that you can test for a snug fit as you go.

**Figure 9-24** shows some variations of the basic joint. Many of the cuts for these joints can be made on power saws if setups are carefully made and the work is firmly supported during the cut. Tails can be cut with the saw blade tilted to the proper angle and with the

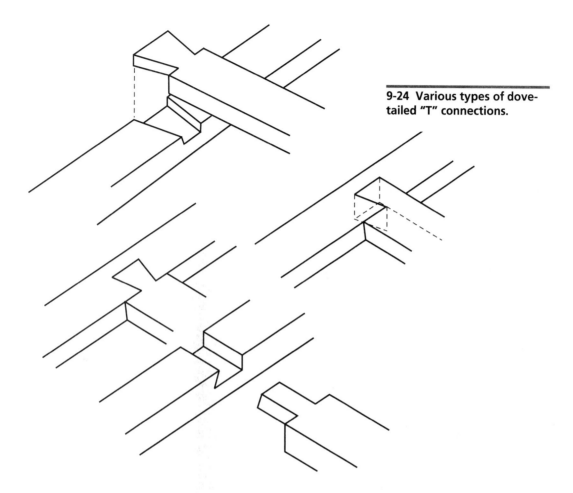

**9-24 Various types of dove-tailed "T" connections.**

work advanced with a tenoning jig. Do the shoulder cuts by advancing the work with the miter gauge. The saw blade is perpendicular, with projection set to meet the base of the slope cut. This can leave a slight imperfection where slope and shoulder cuts meet, but it's not significant unless it is objectionable visually. The imperfection can be eliminated by doing the shoulder cut so it does not quite meet the slope cut and then cleaning out the corner with a file or chisel.

To form sockets, make the outline cuts with the blade tilted to the correct angle and with its projection set for the depth of the socket. Most of the waste between the slope cuts can be removed by making repeat passes with the blade set vertically. What remains can be removed with a chisel or sharp knife.

## DOVETAIL SLOTS

There are many situations where a dovetail slot provides better construction than a simple dado or groove. The sample frame corner shown in **Figure 9-25** makes the point. The joint forms an interlock that will hold regardless of glue conditions. It may seem like excessive attention but the amount of work is a relative factor. Other joints that can be used for the connection involve dowels or a mortise-tenon; and these also require time and care. Another situation where a dovetail groove can be an asset is when joining shelves to case sides (**Fig. 9-26**). The union can be used even without glue or mechanical fasteners.

A good way to form dovetail slots is to work with a portable router. Dovetail bits

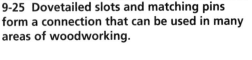

9-25 Dovetailed slots and matching pins form a connection that can be used in many areas of woodworking.

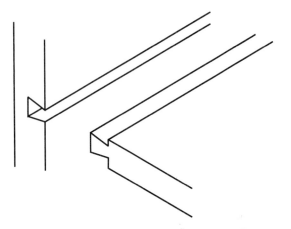

9-26 Shelves that are installed this way can get by without glue or mechanical fasteners. The idea can also be used for sliding shelves.

⁵⁄₁₆″ to ⁷⁄₈″

¼″ to ¾″

9-27 These are the most common sizes of dovetail bits. They are available with ¼-inch or ½-inch shanks.

(Fig. 9-27) come in various sizes so one can be selected to suit the job. Those used most frequently are 1/4- or 1/2-inch. The most common shank size is 1/4-inch so the cutters can be used in any portable router.

A setup for forming a dovetail groove in the edge of a board is shown in **Figure 9-28**. The support blocks that provide extra surface for the base of the router are clamped in place, or the three pieces can be gripped in a vise. The edge guide is positioned so the bit will travel along the center of the board. If the

groove is too difficult to form in a single pass, use the following idea. Use the same setup but make a first pass with a straight bit to remove the bulk of the waste. Then, change to the dovetail bit and make a second pass to complete the shape.

The male part of the joint — the pin — is done the same way, except that two cuts are needed, one on each side of the stock. Each of these cuts is made so the bit is biting into the support blocks as well as the work. Actually, each of the cuts produces a half dovetail.

The width of the dovetail is not limited to the size of the bit. Extra passes, made after adjusting the edge guide, can be used to widen the original cut.

Dovetail slots that are required in surfaces can be produced as shown in **Figure 9-29**. The guide strips, which form a path for the router, are clamped or tack-nailed to the work. Actually, a single strip can serve the purpose, but using two provides extra security.

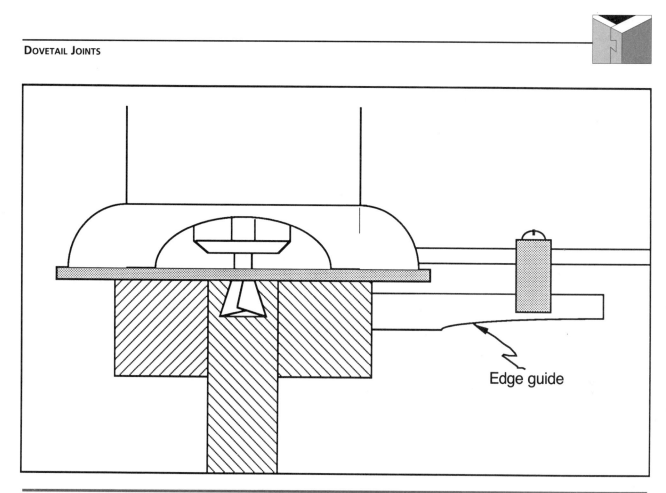

Edge guide

**9-28** Using a portable router to form a dovetail slot in the edge of a workpiece. The work is clamped between blocks that provide sufficient surface for the router to ride on.

**9-29** Forming a dovetail groove in a surface. Twin guide strips, tack-nailed or clamped to the work, provide a trough for the router.

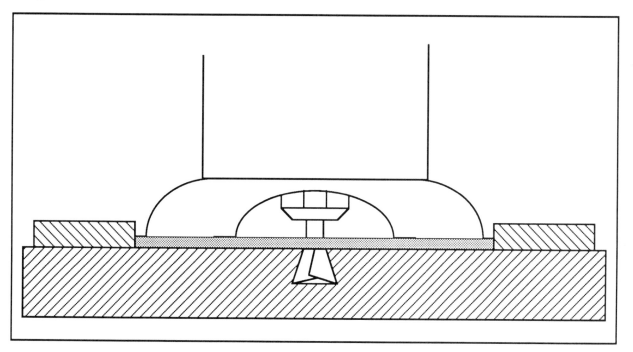

Move work from left to right

"Fence" clamped to table

Table

9-30 Forming dovetail slots on a drill press. Note that the bit is secured in a router chuck instead of the regular 3-jaw device.

Dovetail slots are formed on a drill press by using the setup shown in **Figure 9-30**. If your machine does not have a fence, clamp a straight piece of wood to the table to serve the same purpose. The workpiece is moved from left to right, which is *against* the cutter's direction of rotation, so the action of the bit will help to keep the work against the fence. When stopped grooves are needed, clamp a stop block to the fence to gauge the length of the cut. A stop is especially important if the same cut must be made on many pieces.

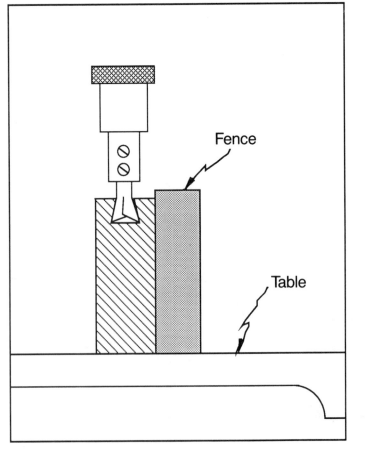

Fence

Table

9-31 Using a drill press to form a dovetail slot in the edge of the stock. Use a high fence to provide support for the work. Move the work, slowly, from left to right.

**9-32 The pins are formed using the same setup. The stock is turned end-for-end for the second cut.**

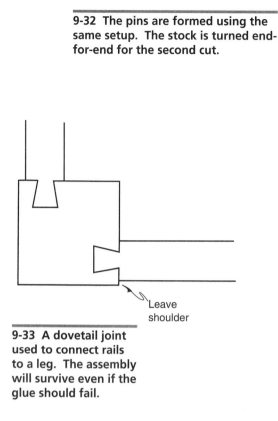

Leave shoulder

**9-33 A dovetail joint used to connect rails to a leg. The assembly will survive even if the glue should fail.**

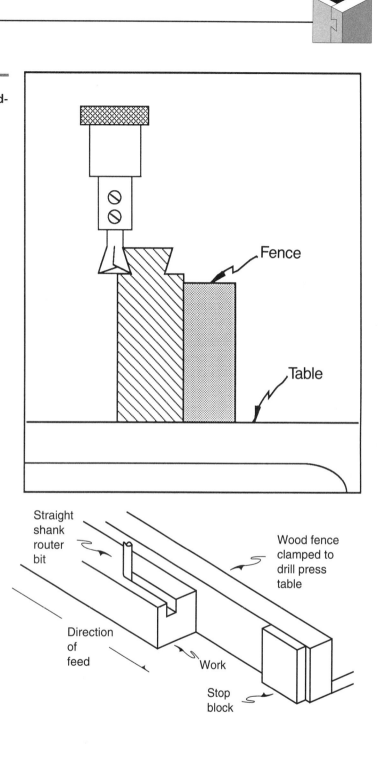

Fence

Table

Straight shank router bit

Wood fence clamped to drill press table

Direction of feed

Work

Stop block

Shape completed with dovetail bit

**9-34 This setup can be used on a drill press to form stopped dovetail grooves.**

**Figure 9-31** demonstrates how a dovetail can be formed in edges by working on a drill press. The work can be done by improvising a tall fence to guide the work. Mating pins are formed in similar fashion by adjusting the position of the work so that helf-dovetails are formed along its edges (**Fig. 9-32**). When you use router bits in a drill press, a special router chuck should be used in place of the regular 3-jaw chuck.

A dovetail is an excellent connection between rails and square legs (**Fig. 9-33**). The stopped dovetail in the legs and the pins on the rails can be formed with a portable router or on a drill press. A good procedure to follow when the slots are formed on a drill press is shown in **Figure 9-34**. A straight-shank bit is used first to remove the bulk of the waste. A second pass with a dovetail bit completes the job. When many pieces are needed, make

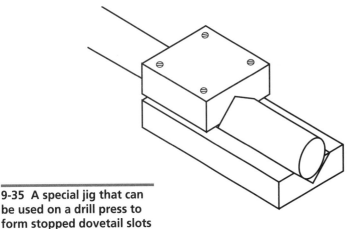

**9-35 A special jig that can be used on a drill press to form stopped dovetail slots in round stock.**

the first pass on all parts before changing to the dovetail bit. It's a good idea to mark the surfaces into which the cuts must be made.

Dovetail slots can be formed in round components, say, a pedestal for a table, by using a drill press with the jig shown in **Figure 9-35**. The jig grips the stock firmly and allows the use of a fence to guide the work into the cutter. Use a stop block on the fence to gauge the length of the cuts. The pins can be installed in one of the ways shown in **Figure 9-36**. Preform flats on the cylinder before the dovetails are cut, or shape the shoulders on the pins to conform with the contact area.

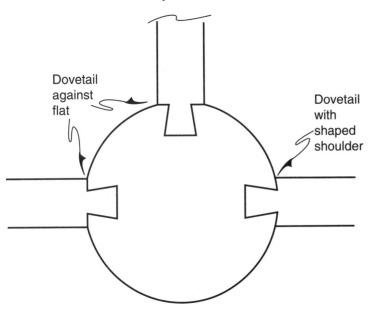

Dovetail against flat

Dovetail with shaped shoulder

The shoulders can be modified on a band saw or by working with files and sandpaper.

## POCKET DOVETAILS

This type of joint, actually a single half-blind dovetail, is often used in quality constructions to join top rails to legs or to sides of cabinets (**Fig. 9-37**). The pockets can be formed fairly easily with a portable router. First use a straight-shank bit to remove the bulk of the waste; then switch to a dovetail bit to flare the sides. The pin is cut by hand with a dovetail saw. In this situation, it is best to form the pocket first and then size the pin to fit.

## DOVETAIL SPLICES

A single through dovetail, sometimes called a *face dovetail*, is an effective way to join two pieces of lumber end-to-end (**Fig. 9-38**). Both parts of the connection can be made by using a dovetail saw and chisels.

**Figure 9-39** suggests a method for working on a table saw. The slope cuts for the tail are made with the blade tilted to the correct angle and with the passes made while the work is secured to a tenoning jig. Make the shoulder cuts by advancing the work with a miter gauge. Note that a slight imperfection results if the blade is set to remove all the waste (**Fig. 9-39B**). To avoid this, use a lower blade projection to remove the bulk of the waste and then clean out the corner that remains with a chisel or file.

**9-36 The pins on legs or rails that connect to a round component can bear against flats formed on the cylinder, or the shoulders of the pins can be shaped to conform to the curve.**

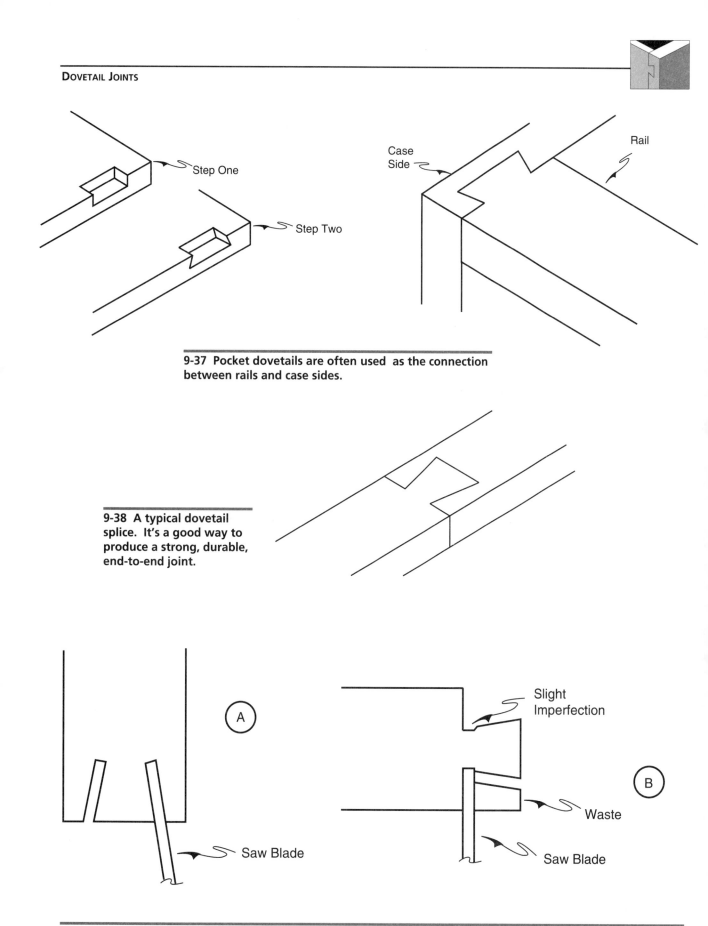

**9-37 Pocket dovetails are often used as the connection between rails and case sides.**

**9-38 A typical dovetail splice. It's a good way to produce a strong, durable, end-to-end joint.**

**9-39 How a table saw can be used to form the tail for an end-to-end dovetail splice. Always work with a tenoning jig when stock must be held on end for sawing**

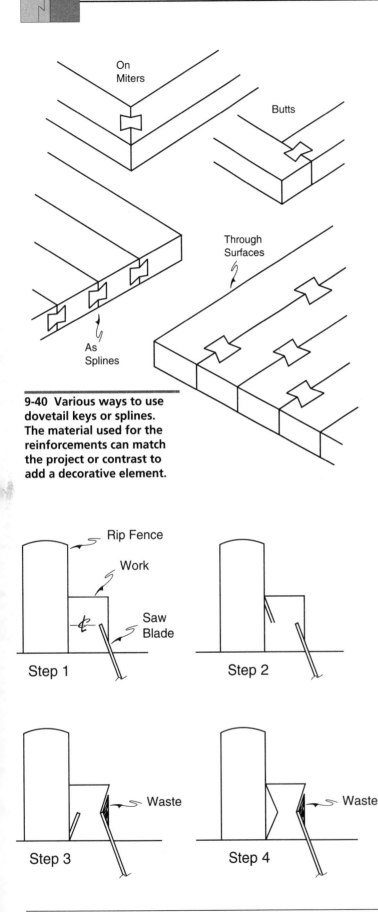

**9-40 Various ways to use dovetail keys or splines. The material used for the reinforcements can match the project or contrast to add a decorative element.**

# DOVETAIL KEYS AND SPLINES

Dovetail keys or splines are, essentially, integral, back-to-back pins (or tails) that can be used as decorative reinforcements in any of the ways suggested in **Figure 9-40**. When the keys or splines are sized correctly, they not only provide an interlock but can also serve to pull parts together.

One method that can be used to produce the base stock for keys or splines on a table saw is outlined in **Figure 9-41**. First, prepare the parent material so its thickness is equal to the widest part of the dovetail and its width is twice the depth of the dovetail slot.

**Step 1** — Tilt the saw blade to match the slope of the dovetail and set its projection so the kerf will end exactly on the stock's centerline. Adjust the rip fence so the blade will be online with the corner of the work. Make the first pass.

**Step 2** — Flip the stock and turn it end for end before making the second pass.

**Step 3** — Repeat the procedure to make the third cut.

**Step 4** — Repeat the procedure once more to finish the job.

Accurate sizing of the base stock and precise adjustment of the saw blade and rip fence are critical. As always, when precision is paramount, make test cuts on scrap stock before working on the project material.

Don't do work of this nature without using a push stick to move the work. It's also a good idea to clamp a thin strip of wood to the table parallel to the rip fence to form a trough for the work to move through. Never work so that scrap pieces will be trapped between the blade and the fence.

**9-41 The procedure to follow when shaping stock for dovetail keys or splines. The shaped piece is then cut into necessary lengths. Always use a push stick when doing this kind of work.**

# 10
# SEGMENTS

Sawing Bevels • Flat Segments • Four-Sided Columns

**10-1 The barrel storage-seat is an example of how segments can be used to form circular projects.**

The technique of cutting and joining segments can be used in many areas of woodworking. Projects can range from table pedestals and lamp bases to posts for a porch. Often, a segmented construction is chosen in place of a solid component because it saves material and reduces the weight of the project. Other times, especially when the project is something like the barrel storage seat shown in **Figure 10-1**, it is the only feasible method.

The mathematics involved in segment cutting has already been discussed in Chapter 1, but to summarize: if flat boards are cut into strips that have beveled edges and then joined edge-to-edge, they will form a circle when the total of the bevel angles equals 360 degrees. The critical consideration when planning and cutting is that the *cut-angle* is one-half of the *joint angle*. The width of the segments is immaterial, although the narrow they are, the closer to a true circle the project will be.

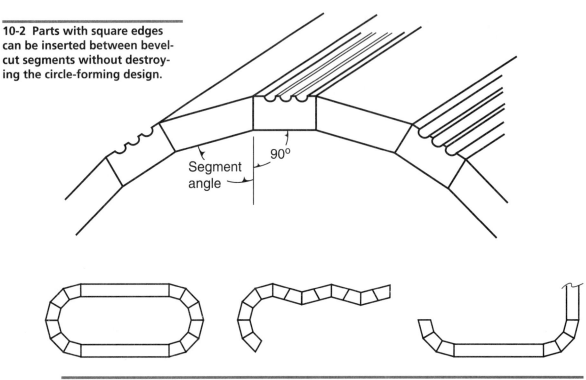

**10-2 Parts with square edges can be inserted between bevel-cut segments without destroying the circle-forming design.**

Segment angle

90°

**10-3 Segments can be assembled to change the direction of a curve, or to form half-round shapes or to turn corners.**

Interesting variations are possible when planning is done along the lines suggested in **Figure 10-2**. The fluted pieces are narrower than adjacent members and are not bevel-cut. Designs of this nature call for careful attention to segment widths if the assembly is to have a selected diameter. It's a good idea to plan the project on a full-size circle drawn on paper. The width of the segments and the cut-angle can be established from the drawing.

**Figure 10-3** shows how you can alter the direction of curves, produce half-round shapes, and form round corners. Ideas like this can be applied to components like aprons, rails, curved backs or arms for chairs and seat frames, and so on. Often, the technique can be used to produce project parts that would otherwise require intricate wood-bending procedures.

The greater the number of segments in the assembly and the narrower they are, the closer the project approaches a true circle, but the circumference will always be a series of flats. However, it doesn't take much effort to bring the project to full-round, especially if a portable belt sander is used. Other tools that can be used are hand planes, spokeshaves, and even scrapers.

## SAWING BEVELS

The easiest way to produce the segments accurately is to work with a power saw (**Fig. 10-4**). Parts can be cut consecutively from a wide board by starting with a bevel-cut on one edge and then flipping the stock and turning it end-for-end for ensuing cuts. The existing bevel always rides against the rip fence. This means that alternate pieces will have opposite face surfaces. For a more consistent grain pattern, do the beveling on a long piece of stock and then separate it into individual segments. It's also possible to

**10-4 Bevel-cutting segments on a table saw. The edge that is already beveled rides against the rip fence.**

bevel-cut pieces that have been precut to length and width; this offers the opportunity to make use of odd lengths of lumber.

Segments can be joined with just glue. Since glue forms the strongest bond when parts abut long grain to long grain, using only glue works best when the grain of the wood is parallel to beveled edges.

Splines can be incorporated to add strength and to facilitate assembly procedures. The spline grooves are cut so they are at a right angle to the bevel cut (**Fig. 10-5**). The grooves in each edge of the segments are formed without changing the initial setup. Be

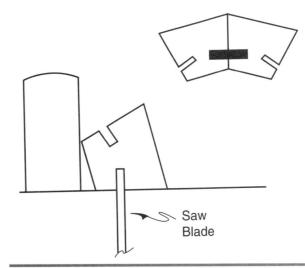

Saw
Blade

**10-5 How to cut spline grooves in beveled segments. Use a push stick, not your hands, to move the work.**

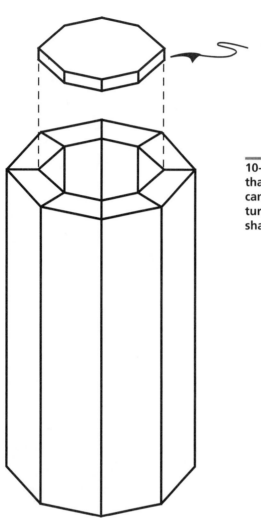

Cap
(both ends)

**10-6 Segmented assemblies that are sealed at each end can be mounted in a lathe for turning to full round or for shaping.**

**10-7 A staved construction to provide stock for a turned lamp base. The openings at each end are plugged so the assembly can be mounted in the lathe.**

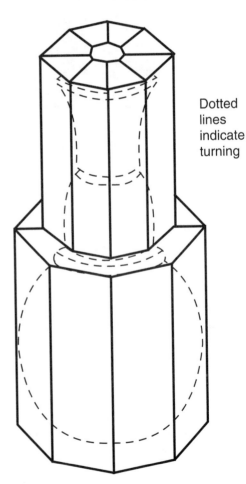

Dotted
lines
indicate
turning

sure, especially when the parts are narrow, that the work is moved with a push stick. If the groove must be wider than the saw's kerf, make a second pass after adjusting the position of the fence or do the cutting with a dadoing tool.

Segmented assemblies are often prepared for turning in a lathe in the manner shown in **Figure 10-6**. When prepared so, the assembly can be turned to a full-round or shaped along its entire length or in particular areas.

A type of segmented assembly, often called *staved construction*, is shown in **Figure 10-7**. A typical application would be a lathe-turned lamp base. The technique offers the following advantages. The project is lighter because of its hollow center. The center void, in the case of the example, provides access for electric wiring. Checks, splits, or shrinkage

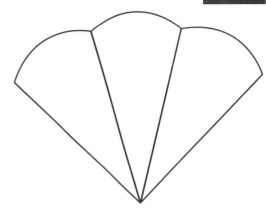

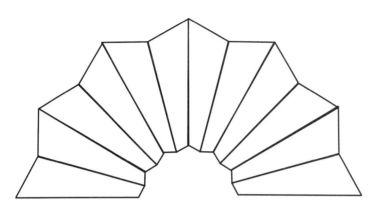

are less likely to occur since flat boards can be seasoned more successfully than large, solid blocks. Projects can be produced with inlay effects by incorporating segments of contrasting wood. Finally, and especially when contrasting wood species are used, there is always the possibility of salvaging material from the scrap bin.

**10-8 Flat segments can be shaped before assembly. Typical applications are surface decorations, arches, and pediments.**

**10-9 Using a taper jig for the angular cuts will ensure that parts will be similar.**

## FLAT SEGMENTS

Segmented pieces can be formed as flat structures as well as cylinders (**Fig. 10-8**). The cut-angle formula applies regardless of whether the segments will form a full or half circle or just part of an arc. An advantage of the technique is that segments can be shaped before assembly. Also, special effects can be created by using contrasting wood or by carefully relating the grain patterns of adjacent pieces.

Flat segments can be cut by using the miter gauge, but a better procedure is to use a taper jig (**Fig. 10-9**). This will ensure the accuracy of the cut-angle and of the width of the components.

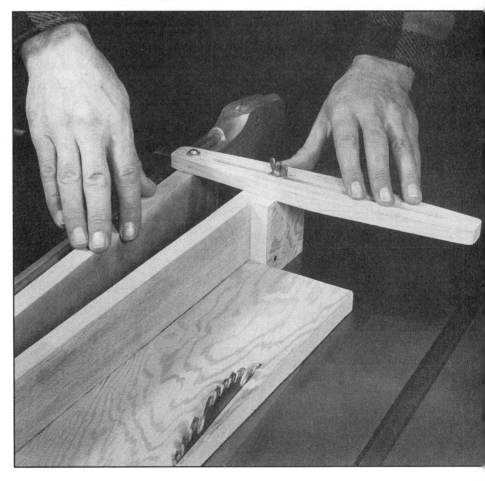

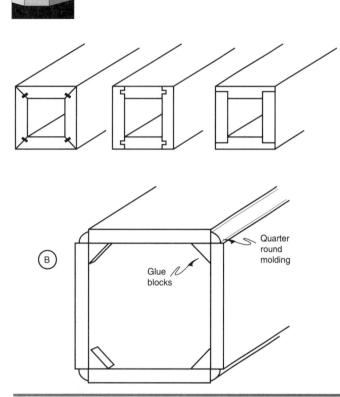

10-10 Several assembly methods for four-sided columns.

of the joint with a spline is an optional consideration. As with any segments, a glue bond between edges that are long grain to long grain is pretty strong so long as the mating edges are accurately cut.

**Figure 10-10** suggests some alternate joint designs. Both the tongue-and-groove and the rabbet joint are strong enough for the use, so the determining factor is how much visible joint line is acceptable.

**Figure 10-10B** shows how to achieve an elaborate effect without complicated cuts. It's best to attach the molding to opposite sides of the column first and then do a final assembly. The drawing shows glue blocks only at the end of the column, but in practice they should be full-length pieces.

**Figure 10-11** shows two other methods that provide decorative effects at corners. The joint in Detail (**A**) is a combination rabbet-dado. The decorative reeds are formed with a shaper or a table-saw molding head before the parts are assembled. An alternate method, when the size of the project permits, is to add the reeds or similar details after parts are put together.

In **Figure 10-11B**, two sides of the column have square edges. The mating pieces are shaped with a shaper cutter or molding head knife that is normally used to produce a cabinet-door lip.

## FOUR-SIDED COLUMNS

This type of construction is often used for components like table legs or pedestals and is considered segmented work even though the number of pieces is minimal. A joint that is used quite often is the simple miter, regardless of whether the cross-section of the column is square or rectangular. Reinforcement

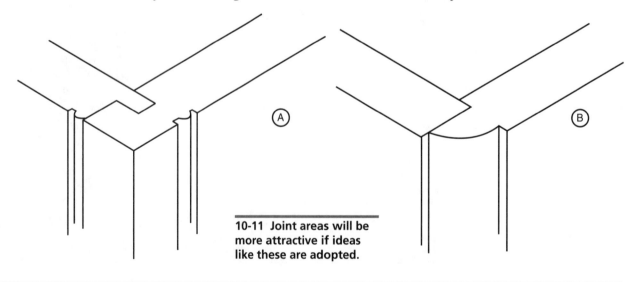

10-11 Joint areas will be more attractive if ideas like these are adopted.

# 11

# JOINTS FOR MOLDING

Typical Molding Applications • Joints • The Coped Joint • Intersections • Splices • Nailing • An Assembly Jig

R eady-made moldings, like those shown in **Figure 11-1**, are classified as *structural* (architectural) or *decorative*. The term relates more to how the moldings are used than to individual designs. A molding might be architectural when used in house construction to cover the gap that exists between a door frame and adjacent walls, but the same molding can be used to embellish the sides of a cabinet or the front of a drawer. Conversely, a decorative molding, like the scalloped design that was used on the project shown in **Figure 11-2**, can be used in an architectural capacity.

Architectural moldings are available in a limited number of woods, especially in a local lumberyard. Typically, they would be available in fir, spruce, or pine. Do-it-yourself centers often carry a line of hardwood or composition-type moldings that fall in the decorative category. Many craftsman catalogs offer a variety of moldings made of wood species like oak, cherry, or walnut. Intricate designs, often pre-finished, are available from suppliers of picture frame moldings.

Manufacturers of cabinets and furniture often create exclusive molding designs for their products. The individual worker can do the same by forming molding on a shaper or with a molding head on a table saw or radial arm saw. Moldings can be made from scratch or a standard design can be modified to suit a particular application.

## TYPICAL MOLDING APPLICATIONS

**Figure 11-3** shows a basic chest that has more visual impact because of the added molding details. The moldings on the front of the drawers can be assembled as a frame and then attached or parts can be added individually. A good procedure for the base is to make the front piece first, mitering the ends so the inside of the cut is exactly in line with the

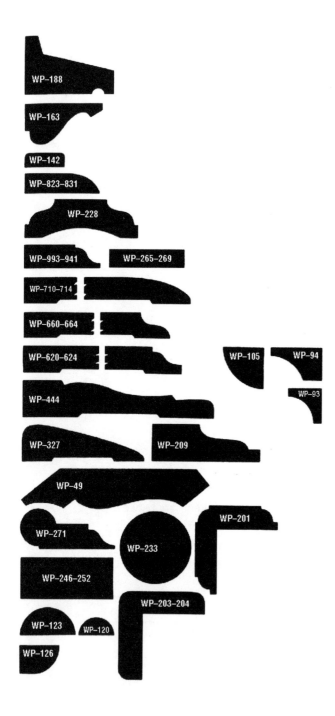

| KEY | |
|---|---|
| **NUMBER** | **NAME** |
| 188 | Drip cap |
| 163 | Cap & brick |
| 142 | Screen |
| 823-831 | Stop |
| 941 | |
| 228 | Batten |
| 265-269 | Lattice |
| 710-714 | |
| 660-664 | Casing |
| 620-624 | & |
| 444 | base |
| 327 | |
| 209 | Shingle |
| 49 | Crown |
| 271 | Picture |
| 233 | Rounds |
| 201 | Corner guard |
| 203-204 | |
| 246-252 | Screen stock |
| 123 | Half round |
| 120 | |
| 126 | Base shoe |
| 105 | Quarter round |
| 94 | Cove |
| 93 | |

**11-1** These are typical structural moldings, but many of them can be used for practical or decorative purposes on cabinets and furniture.

**11-2** The scalloped edges on this project are ready-made moldings that were glued and nailed in place.

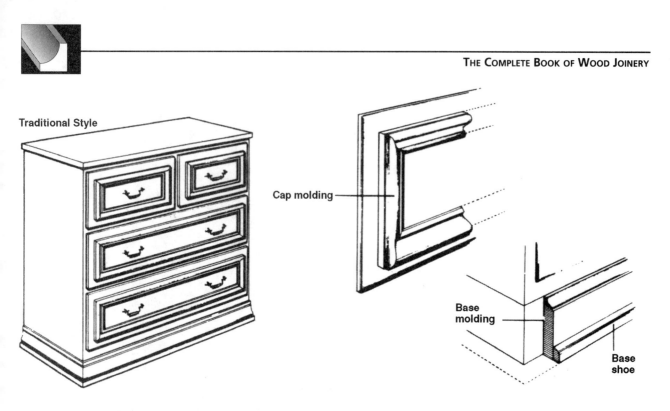

**Traditional Style**

Cap molding

Base molding

Base shoe

11-3  The architectural moldings that were used on this basic chest transform its appearance.

**Spanish Style**

11-4  Shingle moldings  and crown moldings, that are standard, ready-made products, were used to embellish this chest.

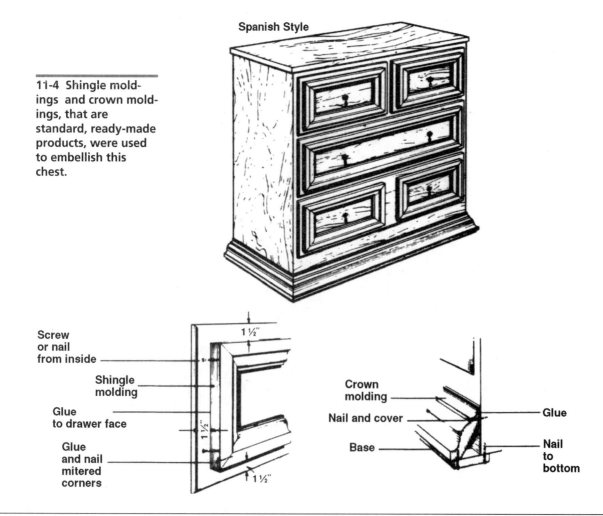

Screw or nail from inside

1 ½"

Shingle molding

Glue to drawer face

Glue and nail mitered corners

1 ½"

1 ½"

Crown molding

Nail and cover

Base

Glue

Nail to bottom

corners of the chest. Cut the side parts a little longer than necessary so they can be trimmed to length after it is certain that the miter joint is tight.

**Figure 11-4** shows a similar chest that has a Spanish motif because of the moldings that are added. The moldings on the drawer fronts can be installed as was described for the first chest. The base treatment is different because of the crown molding that's needed. The corner joint must be a compound angle because the molding has a slope angle. The easiest way to cut it is to situate the molding in a miter box at the slope angle that is needed and then make a simple 45 degree miter cut. Cut the front piece first. Add the side pieces by starting with molding that is longer than necessary and trimming it to length after the compound miter joint has been checked for accuracy.

An alternate method of construction that provides a base assembly with extra strength is shown in **Figure 11-5**. Since the glue blocks can't be added *after* assembly, the base structure must be assembled and added to the chest as a unit. Careful work is required if the subassembly is to fit as it should.

**Figure 11-6** shows how moldings can be functional as well as decorative. The two pieces of cove molding are glued together before they are attached to the drawer front. The base molding, which requires simple miter cuts, is installed by following the usual procedure — that is, the front piece is attached first and then the sides are added.

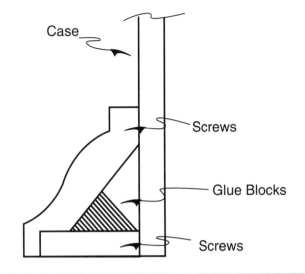

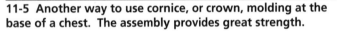

**11-5** Another way to use cornice, or crown, molding at the base of a chest. The assembly provides great strength.

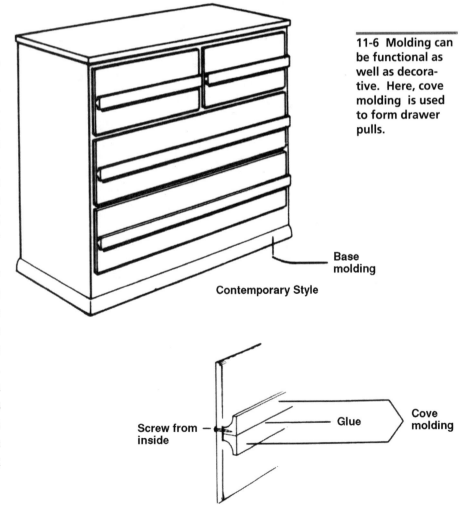

**11-6** Molding can be functional as well as decorative. Here, cove molding is used to form drawer pulls.

Contemporary Style

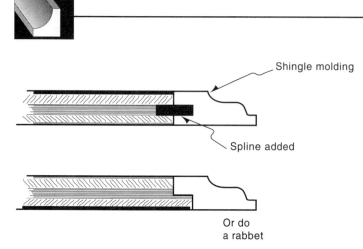

Shingle molding

Spline added

Or do
a rabbet

**11-7 Examples of how ready-made moldings can be used to finish plywood edges.**

Another practical application for ready-made molding is shown in **Figure 11-7**. The molding conceals the plywood edges and adds its own decorative touch. The shingle molding that is shown in the illustration is not the only design that can be used this way. Various types of *stops,* or *quarter-rounds,* or *base shoes,* for example, can be used in similar fashion. If the selected molding is too thick for the panel, it can be attached so only its top surface is flush, in which case it would make the panel look thicker, or it can be made thinner by sawing or planing.

## JOINTS

Moldings that are flat on one surface and that will be surface-mounted are joined with simple miters like any flat material used in a frame (**Fig. 11-8**).

The sawing can be done on a power tool or by hand with a backsaw. When sawing by hand, it's much easier to be accurate by working with a miter box (**Fig. 11-9**). Accuracy on each cut is vital. A small error on each cut adds up to total disaster at assembly time. Nothing is more apparent that a bad miter joint, whether it is the union between major project components or the joints of a simple frame.

Always test tool settings by making cuts on scrap stock. Use fine blades to help avoid splintering and feathering. Many woodworkers cut pieces a bit oversize and then finish by using a belt or disc sander. When the latter method is used, a guide should be set up so the work can be advanced against the abrasive at the exact angle used for sawing.

Some moldings, like *cornice,* or *crown,* moldings, must be cut at a compound angle. The best way to do this accurately is to make a simple 45 degree miter cut but with the work supported at a specific or arbitrary slope angle. A typical procedure, using a miter box, is shown in **Figure 11-10**. The strip of wood that is tack-nailed to the bed of the miter box ensures that each piece will be positioned at the same angle. The stop also serves to secure the work while sawing is being done.

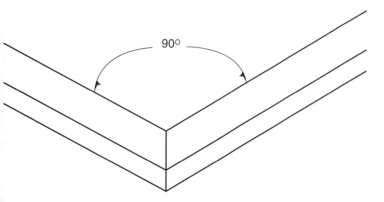

90°

**11-8 Mitered joints must fit tightly, and the corners on square or rectangular frames must make a 90 degree turn.**

**11-9** Working with a miter box when sawing miters is one way to reduce the possibility of human error.

**11-10** A simple 45 degree miter cut will result in a compound angle when the work is braced at the correct slope angle.

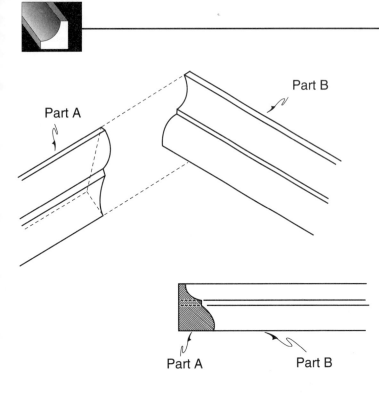

11-11 The basics of the coped joint. One part is cut so it matches the profile of the mating piece.

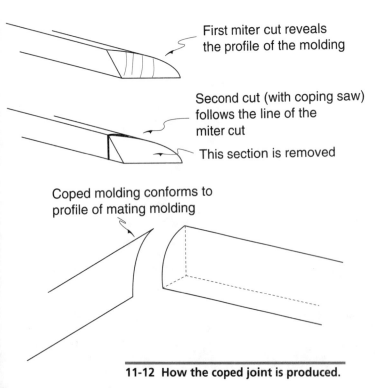

First miter cut reveals the profile of the molding

Second cut (with coping saw) follows the line of the miter cut

This section is removed

Coped molding conforms to profile of mating molding

11-12 How the coped joint is produced.

## THE COPED JOINT

A *coped joint* is made by cutting the reverse profile of one component in the end of the mating part (**Fig. 11-11**). It differs from a miter joint in which both pieces are cut at the same angle. Visually, a coped joint will still be a miter, but it has the advantage of obscuring any separation that might occur after the parts have been installed. The coped joint is more common on trim work in house constructions but it can be useful on furniture and cabinetwork also. It is used only where moldings meet at an inside corner.

There are two ways to form a coped joint. The simplest method is to transfer the profile of one part to the end of the mating piece by using a compass and then making the cut with a coping saw. The system works best on flat molding and when the pattern design is not extreme.

The first step for the second method is to saw a routine 45 degree miter in the part that will be coped. It's important to bear in mind how the molding will be placed. Be aware of what will be the back and the base of the molding before making the miter cut.

The cope cut (**Fig. 11-12**) is made by following the line of the miter cut with a coping saw. Make the cut so it is perpendicular to the back surface of the molding, or undercut it just a bit so there will be a tight fit at the visible edge of the joint. The critical part of the job is following the miter cut precisely. A coping saw blade with very fine teeth will produce a smooth cut and will make the cut easier to control. The edge will be easier to follow if it is darkened a bit with a pencil after the initial miter cut is made.

## INTERSECTIONS

When moldings are symmetrical, a T-joint is produced by shaping a point on the end of one piece and then using it as a pattern to mark the mate (**Fig. 11-13**). Saw the "V" with a backsaw or dovetail saw, staying on the waste side just a bit so finishing can be done with sandpaper or a file. If the surfaces are not flush — there might be some irregularity in the moldings — blend them by using fine sandpaper.

Coped joints can be used when, for example, half-round moldings form a "T" or cross joint (**Fig. 11-14**). In either case, one strip of molding is continuous and the one or the two that abut it are coped. Cope cuts on molding like half-rounds will be precise if they are smoothed with a drum sander or sandpaper wrapped around a suitably-sized dowel, after they have been sawed.

A transition piece, often called a *butt block*, can be used where dissimilar moldings meet or cross (**Fig. 11-15**). The block itself can be a decorative element, especially if it is carved or embossed in some fashion.

## SPLICES

The connection that should be used when moldings are joined to make a continuous run is called a *scarf joint*. Opposing 45 degree miter cuts are made where the parts will connect so they can come together as shown in **Figure 11-16**. The joint, as opposed to a simple butt, is not likely to show a gap. A slight undercut is desirable since it will ensure that the visible joint line will be tight.

Use cut molding as pattern

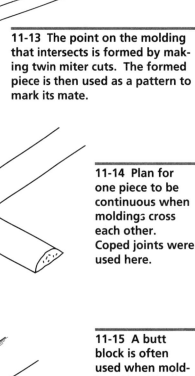

**11-13 The point on the molding that intersects is formed by making twin miter cuts. The formed piece is then used as a pattern to mark its mate.**

**11-14 Plan for one piece to be continuous when moldings cross each other. Coped joints were used here.**

**11-15 A butt block is often used when moldings intersect. The block can be plain or it can be embellished by carving or embossing.**

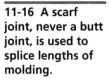

**11-16 A scarf joint, never a butt joint, is used to splice lengths of molding.**

**11-17 Drive nails into corners of profiles whenever possible. They will be easier to conceal.**

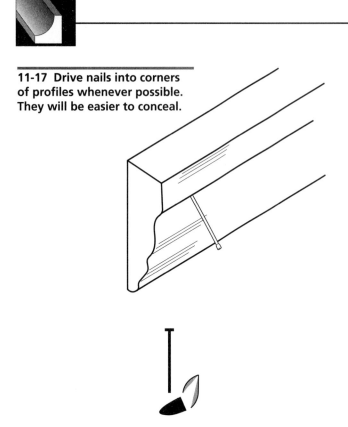

## NAILING

Most moldings are attached with glue and reinforced with finishing or casing nails. Driving the nails into corners of profiles when possible will make it easier to conceal them (**Fig. 11-17**). Use a nail set to sink the nails a bit and then fill the cavity with wood dough.

A professional way to conceal nails when they are driven into surfaces is shown in **Figure 11-18**. Use a small, sharp chisel to lift a sliver of wood where the nail will be driven. Drive the nail into the depression and set it so its head will be flush. Then glue the sliver back into place using a piece of tape to hold it down. After the area is smoothed with sandpaper, even a discerning eye will not discover how the job was done. The method is especially appropriate when the project will have a clear finish.

**11-18 This clever trick is routine with professionals. Lift a sliver of wood and drive the nail into the dent. Glue the sliver back into place and there is no evidence of a nail.**

## AN ASSEMBLY JIG

Moldings are often put together as a frame before they are added to a project. An accurate way to work, especially when several similar units are needed, is to set up an assembly jig like the example in **Figure 11-19**. Use thin plywood for the jig so it won't be in the way if nails are used in addition to glue to join the parts.

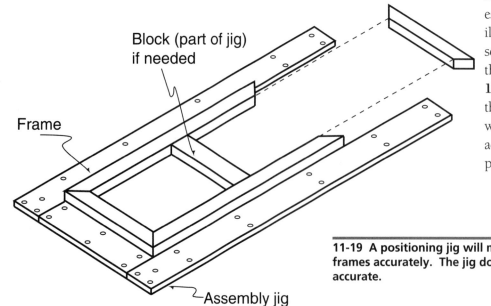

Block (part of jig) if needed

Frame

Assembly jig

**11-19 A positioning jig will make it easier to assemble frames accurately. The jig doesn't have to fancy — just accurate.**

# 12

# SPECIAL BEVEL-JOINT TECHNIQUES

Typical Applications • Cutting on a Scroll Saw • Cutting on a Band Saw • Variations

This chapter deals with a special way to cut bevels so that, for one thing, bowl-type projects, like that shown in **Figure 12-1**, can be produced from a flat board. The ideal tool to use for this kind of work is a scroll saw although, with some changes in procedure, it's possible to work with a band saw. The illustration in **Figure 12-2** depicts the concept.

If a scroll saw is used with its blade in normal position to cut out a disc from the center of a board (**A**), the disc will fall through (**B**). But, if the table is tilted so the cut is a bevel (**C**), the disc will jam tightly in the part it was cut from (**D**). If you cut a series of concentric rings instead of a single disk, each ring will fit

12-1 Special bevel-cutting techniques make it possible to produce deep, bowl-type projects from a flat board.

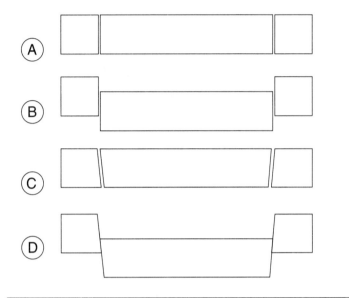

12-2 Internal disks cut normally will fall through the part they were cut from. If the saw's table is tilted so the cut is a bevel, the cutout will jam into place.

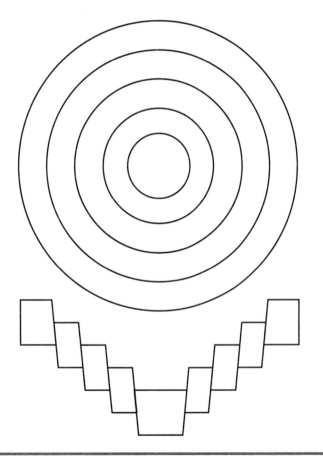

12-3 The more rings that are cut, the deeper the project will be. Ideally, the bevel angle that is used should result in ample projection while providing sufficient contact area between rings.

tightly inside its neighbor and the result will be a cone shape (**Fig. 12-3**). The more rings that are cut, the deeper the cone will be. How much each ring will project depends on the bevel angle, the thickness of the stock, and the width of the kerf made by the blade.

The bevel angle is chosen in relation to the kerf's width and the stock's thickness. The smallest bevel angle will result in the greatest projection but the least amount of contact area between rings. Extreme bevel angles will result in a lot of contact area but little projection. A bevel-angle range of two to five degrees works well in materials from 1/4-inch to 3/4-inch thick.

A scroll saw blade that is 0.020-inch thick by 0.110 inch wide and has fifteen teeth per inch works okay on many jobs, but heavier blades can be used on thick stock and lighter ones on thin material. Decisions can't be made arbitrarily; it's best to decide on how to proceed by making test cuts in scrap material. The amount of projection should not be the prime factor. It's important to have enough contact area where the rings abut so the joint will have strength. The degree of contact also determines the cross-sectional thickness of the project through the joint areas. This is very important when the technique is used to provide a blank that will require further treatment.

## TYPICAL APPLICATIONS

**Figure 12-4** shows a bowl being lathe-turned from a blank that was produced using the bevel cutting process. This is one situation where the thickness of the parts in the joint area is critical. Since several factors determine the wall thickness, it's best to plan for projects like this by drawing a full-size, cross-sectional plan on paper before doing the bevel cutting.

Deep projects are not the only possibility. Trays and plates with raised lips (**Fig. 12-5**) require but a single bevel cut. Projects of this

**12-4** A built-up blank, produced by bevel sawing, makes good stock for lathe turnings. The wall thickness of the blank is critical on work like this. For an inlay effect, bevel cut blanks of contrasting wood and then interchange layers.

**12-5** A single bevel cut can be used to provide a lip for trays and plates. The technique can also be used on square or rectangular projects.

nature can be finished by hand with files and sandpaper or they can be mounted on a faceplate for finishing with a lathe.

The model boat hull shown in **Figure 12-6** serves as an example of what can be done by varying the contours of the cut. This is another type of project where it pays to make a full-size profile and top view of what is needed before marking stock for the cuts.

An assembly of bevel-cut components does not require clamping. The contact areas come together tightly enough when the pieces are jammed into place. Be generous with glue but be sure to quickly remove the excess that is squeezed out with a damp

**12-6 Projects like this hollow model boat hull can be produced by bevel sawing.**

cloth. Be sure, when assembling, that each section is on a horizontal plane.

## CUTTING ON A SCROLL SAW

Use a compass to lay out the concentric rings on the surface of the stock and then drill a blade-insertion hole for each ring. Insertion holes are necessary since the blade must be passed through the stock before it is secured in the tool's chucks. This is, essentially, *piercing*, the scroll saw technique that allows internal cutting without a lead-in cut from an edge of the material. Drill insertion holes at the same angle as the bevel cuts and size them so

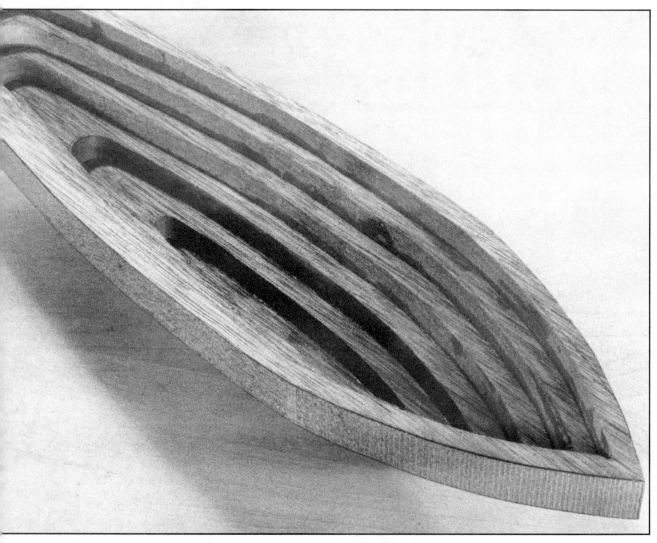

**12-7** A blade-insertion hole is required for each cut when the work is done on a scroll saw. Feed the stock so that the inside ring or cutout is always on the down side of the table. If this isn't done, the cutouts will not mesh.

they barely allow the blade to pass through. The smaller they are, the less attention they will need when the project is finished.

A critical factor when sawing — *always* keep the work on the same side of the blade (**Fig. 12-7**). If this is not adhered to, the slope-direction of the bevel will change and

the parts will not conform as they should. Usually, it's best to cut so that the inside piece is on the lower area of the table.

Remember that the cut edges cannot be sanded, so it's important to work slowly and with a blade that will produce the smoothest cuts.

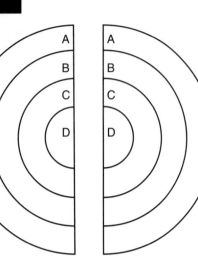

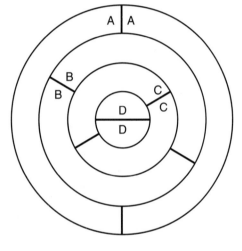

**12-8 Circular work on a band saw is done by doing the bevel cutting on half sections. The parts are put together with staggered joints.**

**12-9 This is one way to handle bevel cutting on a band saw when projects are not circular. Pieces are cut longer than necessary and then trimmed so joints can be staggered.**

## CUTTING ON A BAND SAW

Bevel joints can be made on a band saw but only with a major change in the technique. Internal cuts without a lead-in cut can be made on a scroll saw because the blade can be passed through a hole in the work before cutting starts. A band saw blade is a continuous loop so it can't be inserted through a starting hole, unless the shop is equipped so the blade can be broken and then welded. A feasible approach is to saw the stock in half and do the bevel cutting on the half sections, which can then be assembled with staggered joints as shown in **Figure 12-8**.

Figure 12-9 suggests how to approach bevel sawing on a band saw when the project is not circular. The sections are cut longer than necessary and then trimmed so they can be put together with staggered joints. **Figure 12-10** shows a half section of a project that was produced with band-sawed bevel cuts.

**12-10** Half-section of a project that was produced by bevel cutting on a band saw.

## VARIATIONS

Figures 12-11 and 12-12 demonstrate a variation of the bevel joint technique that can be done on a scroll saw or band saw by sawing a continuous spiral line. The technique provides for the same kind of projection that results with concentric rings. An advantage is that blade-insertion holes are not needed when working on a scroll saw, and it's not necessary to produce

**12-11** A single continuous spiral cut can be done instead of concentric rings. This can be done on a scroll saw or band saw.

half sections when a band saw is the tool. A disadvantage is that the gluing procedure is a little more difficult. Small brads, however, can be used to hold the layers in projected form until the glue dries. Small C-clamps or spring clamps, placed strategically, can also be used.

**12-12** A spirally cut project will project just like one that was cut concentrically. Spreading the project is easier if it is placed on a cylinder.

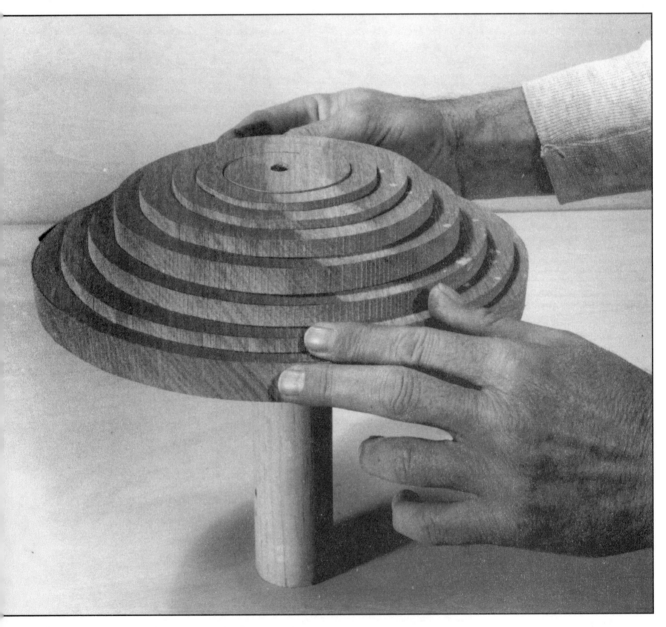

# 13
# PLATE JOINERY

13-1 Most plate, or biscuit, joint portable tools work in similar fashion, but they can have unique configurations and adjustment methods. Porter-Cable's version has an upright motor and a belt-drive system that contributes to smooth, quiet operation.

**P**late joinery has been around for some time in industry, but it has only recently come into the realm of the home woodworker, mostly because of the ease with which the technique can be used and because of the introduction of reasonably priced portable tools like those shown in **Figures 13-1** and **13-2**. The most common use of the technique, especially in commercial shops, is for joining panel materials like plywood and particleboard. Those who have the appropriate tool will quickly shun the common practice of edge-joining boards with dowels, substituting the *biscuits* (often called *plates, wafers, or splines*) that the machine is designed to work with.

The power tool functions with a horizontally positioned carbide-

**13-2 Freud's machine has a horizontal design. Cutting with any of the tools is accomplished by pressing the tool against the work, so it is important to keep the work firmly clamped.**

tipped cutter that forms a half-ellipse cut in the edge of the work. The cutter is behind a fence and comes into play only when the worker, with the machine braced firmly against the work, exerts forward pressure: the fence retracts and the blade makes the cut. The cut, which can be adjusted to suit the various biscuit sizes listed in **Figure 13-3**, is a bit deeper and wider than necessary to allow room for excess glue and a degree of freedom when aligning the components. This is a plus factor when the technique is compared with

dowel joinery, which requires a more precise approach so holes will align perfectly.

The biscuits, being under compression, absorb moisture from common carpenter's glue and expand enough to make a tight joint. That's the reason some workers will apply glue only in the biscuit areas, but it's an optional consideration. The use of biscuits doesn't preclude coating the entire seam with glue.

While biscuits are most commonly used in edge-to-edge systems, there is enough flex-

## BISCUITS

**DIE-CUT, COMPRESSED BEECHWOOD DIAGONAL GRAIN PATTERN**

| SIZES | |
|---|---|
| "0" | = 5/32 x 5/8" x 1-3/4" |
| "10" | = 5/32 x 3/4" x 2-1/8" |
| "20" | = 5/32 x 1" x 2-3/8" |

**13-3 The biscuits are available in several standard sizes.**

ibility in plate or biscuit joinery so that the technique can be used in any of the common joints shown in **Figure 13-4**, including miter and butt joints. Making layouts for accurate cutting is a simple procedure. Butt the mating parts together and draw a common centerline across them (**Fig. 13-5**). Then, position the tool so that its engraved centerline is aligned with the mark on the work before pressure is applied for the cut.

All the tools that are now available work in similar fashion, but there can be unique features and adjustment procedures so it's critical to study the instructions that are supplied by the manufacturer.

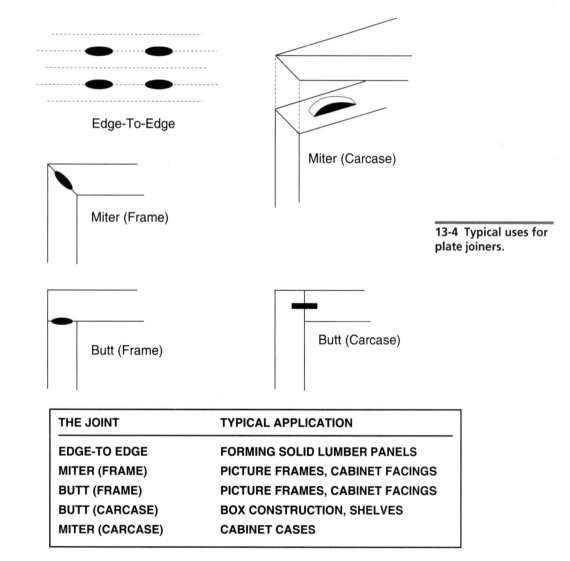

Edge-To-Edge

Miter (Carcase)

Miter (Frame)

Butt (Frame)

Butt (Carcase)

**13-4 Typical uses for plate joiners.**

| THE JOINT | TYPICAL APPLICATION |
|---|---|
| EDGE-TO EDGE | FORMING SOLID LUMBER PANELS |
| MITER (FRAME) | PICTURE FRAMES, CABINET FACINGS |
| BUTT (FRAME) | PICTURE FRAMES, CABINET FACINGS |
| BUTT (CARCASE) | BOX CONSTRUCTION, SHELVES |
| MITER (CARCASE) | CABINET CASES |

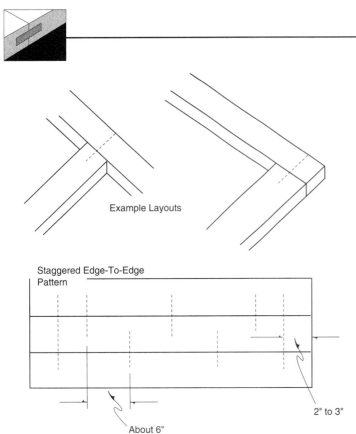

Example Layouts

Staggered Edge-To-Edge
Pattern

2" to 3"

About 6"

A stationary plate joinery tool is offered by Delta (**Fig. 13-6**). This is a bench-mounted tool that allows the work to be applied to the tool instead of the tool being used on the work. This can be a convenience on many operations. Other features include hold-downs and an angle guide so work can be positioned and secured before cuts are made (**Figs. 13-7** and **13-8**).

**13-5** The best way to do layout is to mark a common centerline across the components. Then, align an engraved mark on the tool with the mark on the work.

**13-6** Delta's offering in the field of plate joinery is actually a stationary tool. It is clamped or bolted to a workbench or other sturdy surface. The table is adjustable vertically, which provides for flexibility in terms of edge distance for cuts.

13-7 The hold-downs that are supplied can be used vertically, as shown, or horizontally.

13-8 An angle guide, some-thing like a miter gauge, is used to position angular cuts.

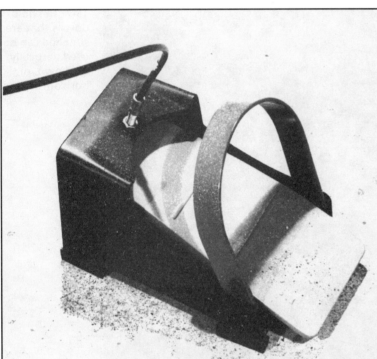

The stationary machine is turned on with a common switch, but the cutter is advanced by means of a foot pedal (**Fig. 13-9**). Thus, the hands are free to help control the work.

The machine can be used not only to make elliptical cuts but also to form grooves for conventional spline joints (**Fig. 13-10**).

**13-9  Hands are free when using the Delta tool since a foot pedal attached to the machine by a flexible cable is used to advanced the cutter.**

CAUTION
ROTATING BLADE

**13-10  Forming grooves is one off-beat use for the stationary plate joiner. Edge distance is controlled by the height of the table.**

# 14

# MISCELLANEOUS JOINTS AND TREATMENTS

Drop Leaf Table Joint • Lock Corner Joint • Combination Dado Rabbet • The Waterfall Joint • Milled Drawer Joint • Door Joints • Cogged Joint • Round Corner Joints • Square Rail to Round Leg • Rounds to Flats • Two Special Slab Joints • Methods for Locking Joints

## DROP LEAF TABLE JOINT

**A** drop leaf can be installed in simple fashion by leaving square edges on both the table and the leaf and using plain butt hinges or a full-length piano hinge as the pivot mechanism. The *true drop leaf joint*, or *rule joint*, as it is often called, is more professional and neater in appearance (**Fig. 14-1A**). When formed traditionally, it is a design feature found on many pieces of modern and traditional furniture.

The shapes required can be produced on a shaper or by using a molding head on a table or radial arm saw. **Figure 14-1B** suggests how standard cutters can be used to form both the table edge and the leaf. The cutter used on the table is a *quarter-round* cutter. The mating cut on the leaf is done with a *combination quarter-round* and *cove cutter.* The

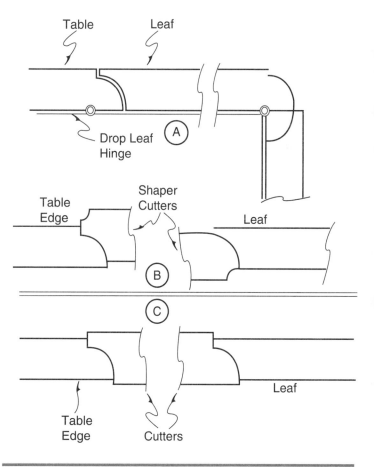

**14-1 The edges needed for a drop leaf table joint can be produced in different ways.**

radius of the cuts must match and the setup must be made so that the parts have equal shoulders. It's also possible to use sets of cutters that are designed specifically for the drop leaf joint (**Fig. 14-1C**). Their use, however, is not limited to this single application. If you view them as individual tools, you will see that they are basically *quarter-round* and *cove* cutters, and as such, they can be used to shape any edge and to form moldings.

A common hinge for the drop leaf is a *back flap*. It is installed so its knuckle seats in a shallow groove cut into the wood. The center of the knuckle and the center of the cut's radius must be the same. A similar hinge is designed with one leaf slightly bent so it can be installed without a special groove for the knuckle. Ordinary *hasp hinges* will also work. Whatever you use, be sure to provide a slight clearance between the shaped edges so they don't rub against each other. A simple way to provide the clearance is to place a piece of heavy paper between the edges of the components when you are assembling.

## LOCK CORNER JOINT

A *lock corner joint* is often used in drawer and box constructions and is frequently found at corners of chest projects. It's a strong joint with a good interlock, and it isn't difficult to make even though it calls for very careful cutting (**Fig. 14-2**). On a table saw, set a dadoing tool for cutting a 1/4-inch groove and then start cutting on one part as shown in **Figure 14-2A**. Make the first cut with the stock on edge and with the dado projecting 1-inch (for 1-inch thick stock). Make the second cut using the miter gauge and with the stock flat on the table.

The cuts for the mating piece are shown in **Figure 14-2B**. Notice that the only change is the dado's projection; the width of the cut remains the same. Accuracy is all important, so be sure the work is positioned correctly for each cut.

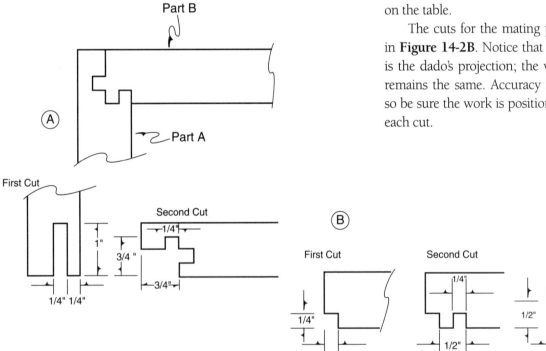

**14-2 The cutting procedure to follow when forming the components for the lock corner joint.**

## COMBINATION DADO RABBET

The combination *dado-rabbet joint* is similar to the lock corner joint (**Fig. 14-3**). It does not have the same degree of interlock, but it's a strong joint with many applications, one of them being the connection between a drawer front and its sides.

The cuts needed in both pieces are detailed in **Figure 14-3A**. They can be made with a dadoing tool that is set for the width of the cut. The second cut on part "A" can be made with the dadoing tool, but you can switch to a regular saw blade to remove the waste *after* all dadoing is done (**Fig. 14-4**). Design the joint as indicated in **Figure 14-3B** if you wish the drawer front to have a lip. The only change in the procedure occurs on the first cut of part "A". The groove must be deeper to provide for the lip.

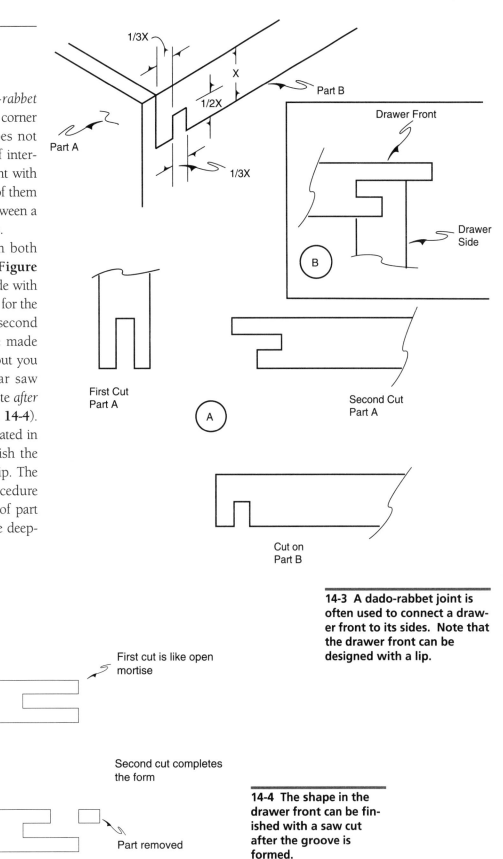

First Cut
Part A

Second Cut
Part A

Cut on
Part B

**14-3** A dado-rabbet joint is often used to connect a drawer front to its sides. Note that the drawer front can be designed with a lip.

First cut is like open mortise

Second cut completes the form

Part removed

**14-4** The shape in the drawer front can be finished with a saw cut after the groove is formed.

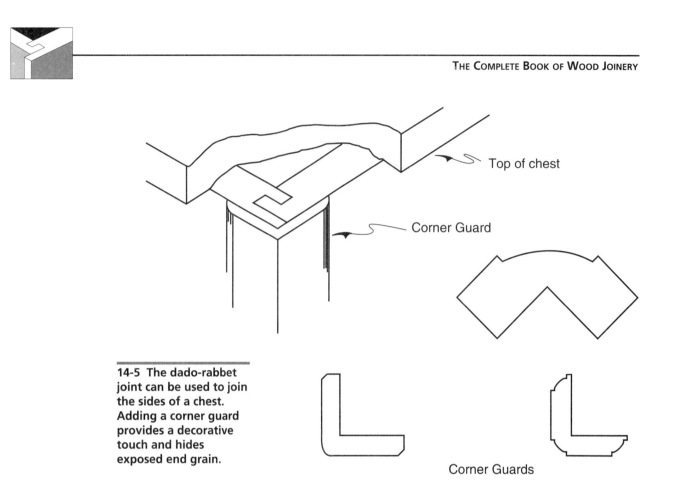

**14-5** The dado-rabbet joint can be used to join the sides of a chest. Adding a corner guard provides a decorative touch and hides exposed end grain.

Top of chest

Corner Guard

Corner Guards

The dado-rabbet joint can also be used on corners of boxes and case constructions. If the visible end-grain is objectionable and the design of the project permits, you can add *corner guards* as shown in **Figure 14-5**.

## THE WATERFALL JOINT

The *waterfall joint*, as we have mentioned earlier, is an exceptionally good joint to use on plywood since it hides objectionable edges and allows the surface grain pattern to flow neatly over the edge (**Fig. 14-6**). There is no reason, however, why it can't be used on solid stock as well.

The cutting procedures, as they would be done on a table saw, are outlined in **Figure 14-7**. To form the joint, remove a wedge of material, in essence, allowing one part to fold down against the other with minimum disruption of the surface grain pattern. It's necessary for the second cut to be made so the kerf will

meet exactly with the top corner of the part. Something will be lost simply because the kerf has width, but the appearance will still be far superior to what occurs when two strange pieces of wood are matched. Working with a good, thin-kerf blade is an asset.

## MILLED DRAWER JOINT

The same cutter used to form the milled edge-to-edge joint, or *glue joint*, can be used as shown in **Figure 14-8** to make a good connection between a drawer front and its sides. The drawer front can be flush with its sides or it can have a lip. In either case, the shaping operation will be easier to do if a conventional rabbet is cut first to remove the bulk of the waste.

Be very careful, regardless of whether the work is done on a shaper or with a molding head, to be sure the relationship between work and cutter is correct. Making test cuts on scrap stock is a good procedure.

**14-6** The waterfall joint lets surface grain patterns flow neatly over the edge.

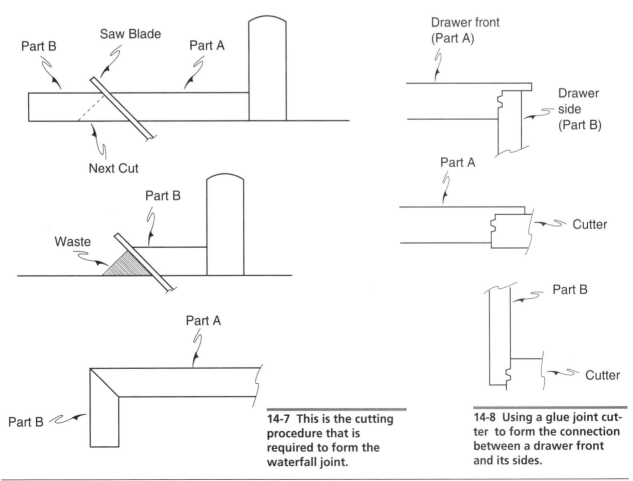

**14-7** This is the cutting procedure that is required to form the waterfall joint.

**14-8** Using a glue joint cutter to form the connection between a drawer front and its sides.

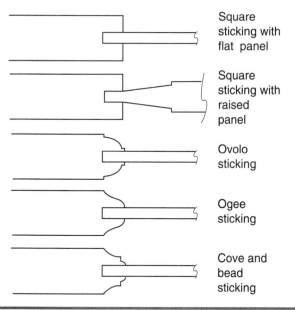

Square sticking with flat panel

Square sticking with raised panel

Ovolo sticking

Ogee sticking

Cove and bead sticking

**14-9 Examples of standard sticking that are used on frame-panel assemblies.**

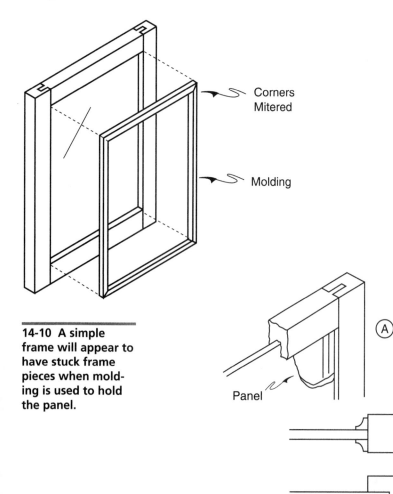

Corners Mitered

Molding

**14-10 A simple frame will appear to have stuck frame pieces when molding is used to hold the panel.**

Panel

Ⓐ

Ⓑ

Ⓒ

# DOOR JOINTS

Door assemblies on quality furniture and cabinets often consist of panels that are framed with solid wood. The frame is usually four pieces—two vertical *stiles* and two horizontal *rails*. If an extra member is introduced either vertically or horizontally, it is called a *cross-rail* or a *cross-stile*.

*Sticking* is a term used to describe the treatment of the inside edges of the frame members. As shown in **Figure 14-9**, the sticking can be square or it can be shaped. The *ovolo, ogee,* and *cove and bead* are standard molding forms that are used when sticking is shaped, but other treatments are possible. For example, edges can simply be beveled or chamfered. Commercially made frames are formed on a machine called a *sticker,* but the same work can be done in a small shop with a shaper or a router and sometimes with a molding head used on a table or radial arm saw.

A very basic square-stuck frame is shown in **Figure 14-10**. Inside edges are flat so the panel is held in place with molding that is used on the back and front surfaces. The appearance is of shaped sticking, but no elaborate equipment is needed to do the job. The corner joint does not have to be tenoned as shown. Options include a splined joint, a doweled miter, or even a dowel butt joint.

In **Figure 14-11**, the basic idea is taken a

**14-11 Other methods to use to simulate sticking These are designs that can be used when equipment to do sticking in regular fashion is not available.**

step further by including the panel groove that is shown in the detail (**A**). In this case, the length and thickness of the tenon on the rail matches the dimensions of the groove. (**B**) is a cross-section of square sticking without a groove. The panel is secured with an add-on frame of molding. (**C**) shows a cross-section through rabbeted rails and stiles so the panel can be secured with an add-on frame on only one side. In this case, the corner joints can be simple half-laps.

Rabbeted frames can also be handled as shown in **Figure 14-12**. A good procedure to follow is to shape the edges of the frame stock before making the rabbet cut. The frame parts do not require further attention if they will be joined with a miter. If, however, the corner joints are doweled butts or have a tenon design, then the ends of the rails must be *coped* so shaped edges will mate (**Fig. 14-13**).

The cope cuts are no different from those that were described for joining moldings. In this application, the cope cuts are formed by machine, instead of by hand, using a cutter whose profile is the reverse of the shape on the stile (**Fig. 14-14**). Standard cutters can be used in routine fashion in many situations but often, especially when the corner joint involves a tenon, a special cope cutter, mounted in the shaper on a *stub spindle*, is

**14-12 Frame stock can be edge-shaped and then rabbeted to provide a seat for a panel. If a miter joint is used, there is no need for a cope cut.**

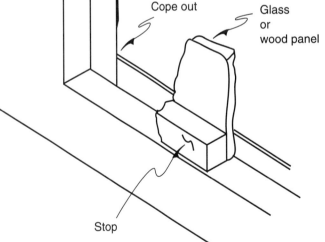

**14-13 Frame assemblies that are butted must have coped rails.**

Cope out

Glass or wood panel

Stop

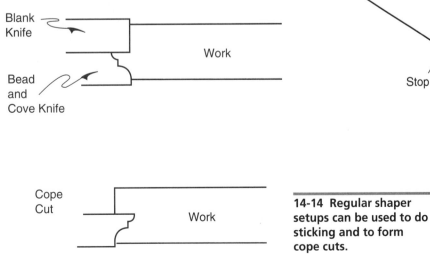

Blank Knife

Work

Bead and Cove Knife

Cope Cut

Work

**14-14 Regular shaper setups can be used to do sticking and to form cope cuts.**

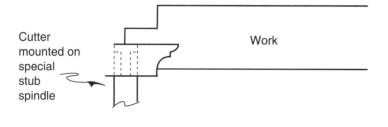

Cutter mounted on special stub spindle

Work

**14-15 Cope cuts on tenoned joints are done on a shaper by mounting the cutter on a stub spindle.**

used (**Fig. 14-15**). This setup allows cuts to be made regardless of how far over the spindle the work extends.

A common joint between rails and stiles that involves a cope cut is shown in **Figure 14-16**. With appropriate cutters used on a shaper, both rails and stiles can be formed in a single pass. In addition to the necessary

shaped edges and cope cuts, the cutters will provide a groove for panels and a tenon or tongue for the connection (**Fig. 14-17**).

The cutter arrangement for a shaper is shown in **Figure 14-18**. For the edge shaping, the cutters are mounted with a blank knife between them as shown in (**A**). The result, in this case, will be cove and bead sticking with a groove for the panel. The setup for the cope cut is shown in (**B**). Reverse cove and bead cutters are used, separated by a *collar* whose thickness and diameter produces a tenon that fits the groove formed in the first operation.

Other types of coped joints that are used on door frames are shown in **Figures 14-19** and **14-20**. Cope cuts are required when stuck rails and stiles are butted. Using a miter joint eliminates the need for a cope cut.

**14-16 A common cabinet door assembly that involves sticking and cope cuts.**

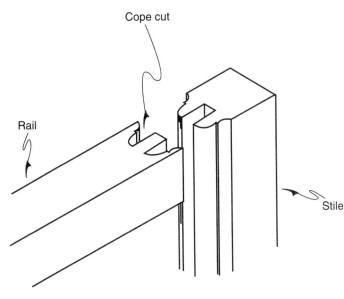

Cope cut

Rail

Stile

14-17 How stiles and rails fit together. The cope cut is just a reverse profile of the shape on the stile.

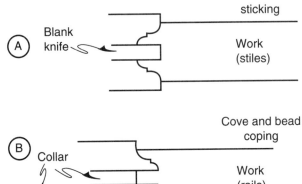

Cove and bead sticking

(A) Blank knife

Work (stiles)

Cove and bead coping

(B) Collar

Work (rails)

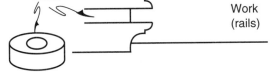

14-18 This is the setup that was used to form the joint parts that were shown in Figure 14-17.

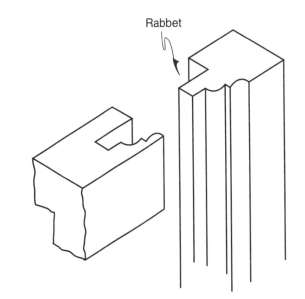

Rabbet

14-19 Sticking can be done on only one side if the back of the frame is rabbeted to receive the panel.

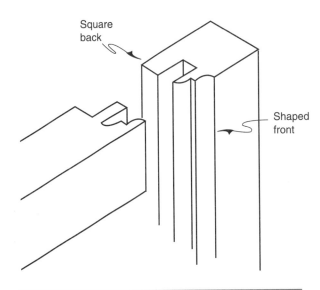

Square back

Shaped front

14-20 The design shown in the previous illustration with a groove for the panel added.

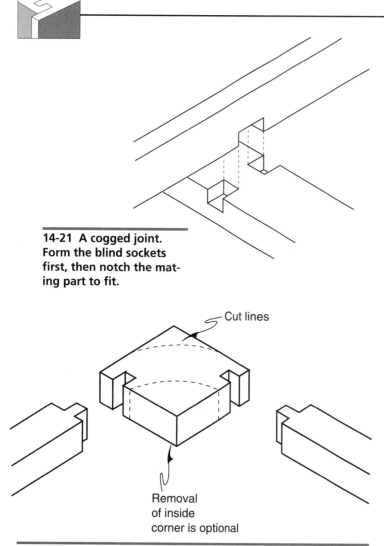

**14-21 A cogged joint. Form the blind sockets first, then notch the mating part to fit.**

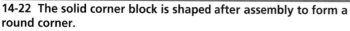

Cut lines

Removal
of inside
corner is optional

**14-22 The solid corner block is shaped after assembly to form a round corner.**

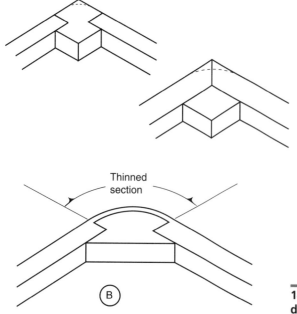

Thinned
section

(B)

## COGGED JOINT

A *cogged joint* makes a good connection between an on-edge piece and the part it must cross (**Fig. 14-21**). Do the stopped sockets first. If only a few are needed, they can be formed by working with a backsaw as if they were blind dovetail sockets. That is, make angled saw cuts and then clean out the waste with a chisel. If many are needed, the parts can be clamped together and the sockets formed by working with mortising bits and chisels on a drill press. The notch in the crossing piece can be formed with a dadoing tool or by using a backsaw for the shoulder cuts and a chisel to remove the waste.

## ROUND CORNER JOINTS

There are several techniques for making round corners that may, for example, be added on a frame for a padded seat or a rail or apron assembly.

**Figure 14-22** demonstrates one method. A solid corner block is attached to rails with mortise-tenon joints. The block is shaped to conform with the rail after the parts are assembled.

**Figure 14-23** shows two other methods for blocked corners and a special technique (**B**) that does the job without visible joint lines. The corner section can be thinned out by cutting on a band saw, or on a scroll saw, or by making a series of overlapping cuts with a dadoing tool. The section should be thinned only enough so the area can bend without cracking. Soaking the wood in hot water or steaming it over a kettle will make it more pliable. It's wise to do some testing first since some wood species bend more easily than others. Cut the filler block after the bend is made so it will fit exactly.

**14-23 Other methods to use to turn corners. The design in (B) provides a continuous grain pattern.**

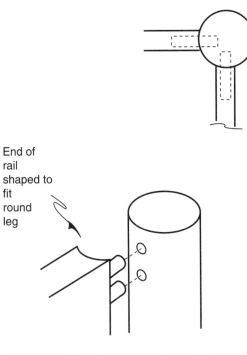

End of rail shaped to fit round leg

**14-24 Square-end rails must be shaped to conform when they are attached to a round component.**

## SQUARE RAIL TO ROUND LEG

The major consideration when a square-end rail is attached to a round leg is in shaping the rail to conform with the contour of the leg. This is true whether the connection will be made with dowels (**Fig. 14-24**) or with some other design. The concave shape on the rail can be formed with drum sanders chucked in a drill, press or portable drill or they can be formed by hand with round files and sandpaper wrapped around a cylinder. If the rail is tenoned, the shoulders can be shaped on a band saw or by hand with files.

## ROUNDS TO FLATS

Practical methods for joining round components like chair rungs to flat areas are shown in **Figure 14-25**. It's important that the hole drilled for the insert permits a slip fit; the part

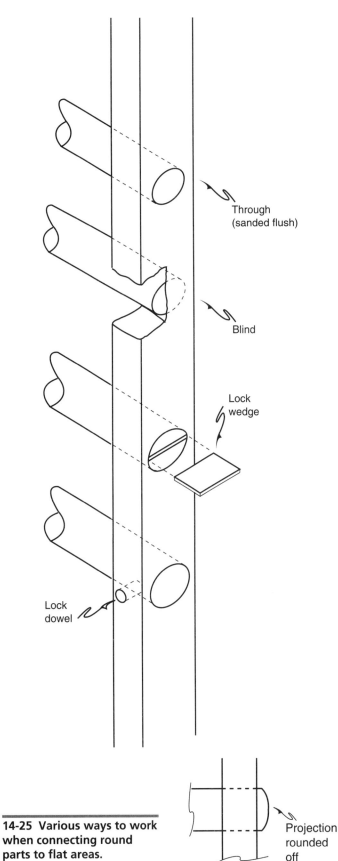

Through (sanded flush)

Blind

Lock wedge

Lock dowel

**14-25 Various ways to work when connecting round parts to flat areas.**

Projection rounded off

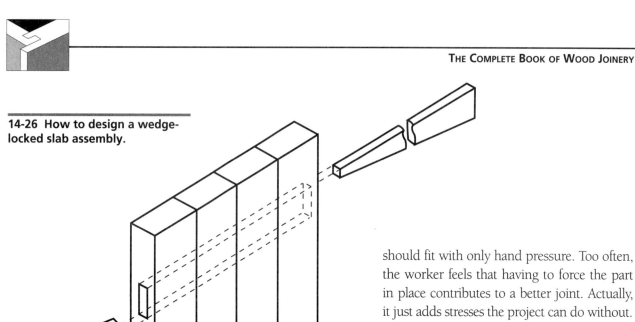

**14-26 How to design a wedge-locked slab assembly.**

should fit with only hand pressure. Too often, the worker feels that having to force the part in place contributes to a better joint. Actually, it just adds stresses the project can do without.

This is also true for a lock wedge. Don't form the wedge so thick that it must be smashed into place. Also, drive the wedge so it is across the grain of the component the round part enters. A wedge driven parallel to the grain will produce tension that can cause splitting.

A wedge can also be used when the insert seats in a blind hole. The wedge is sized so it will do its job without preventing the insert from bottoming in the hole.

A lock dowel can be used whether the insert is installed in a through or blind hole.

## TWO SPECIAL SLAB JOINTS

A locking arrangement that is the result of long wedges in shown in **Figure 14-26**. The rectangular openings in the slab pieces can be formed by mortising on a drill press. Cut the wedges after the mortising is done; then size them to fit. Cut them longer than necessary so they can be trimmed and sanded flush after the assembly is complete. Install the wedges loosely at first and then tap them in slowly with a mallet while applying clamp pressure to adjacent areas.

**Figure 14-27** shows how a dovetail can be used in a slab assembly. In (**B**), the added component is sized to serve as a rail or apron in addition to reinforcing the slab. In designs like this, the slab parts should be joined in

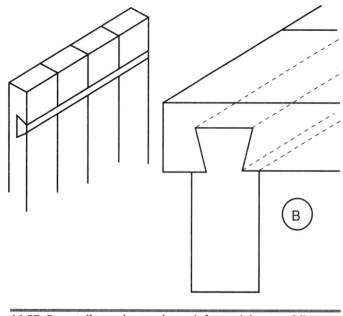

**14-27 Dovetails can be used to reinforce slab assemblies or to add a decorative detail. (B) shows an integral rail design.**

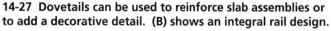

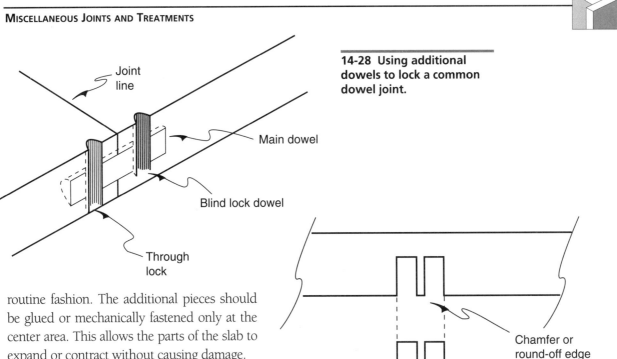

**14-28  Using additional dowels to lock a common dowel joint.**

routine fashion. The additional pieces should be glued or mechanically fastened only at the center area. This allows the parts of the slab to expand or contract without causing damage.

## METHODS FOR LOCKING JOINTS

Most joints can be locked either by designing the connection in a special way or by introducing an additional component like a dowel or spline.

A doweled butt joint is locked when additional dowels are installed as suggested in **Figure 14-28**. Drill the holes for the lock dowels while the joint is under clamp pressure. The diameter of the lock dowel should not be greater than half the diameter of the primary joint dowels.

**Figure 14-29** shows how to lock a part that might ordinarily be set in a simple dado. The cut in one piece can be viewed as twin dadoes, with material left between them as a wedge that will fit a groove formed in the insert. The thickness of the wedge should be just a fraction greater than the width of the groove

**Figure 14-30** shows a way to use a spline to lock a part that is installed in a conventional dado. The width of the dado will affect the cut-angle needed for the spline. Note how the spline groove is formed in the insert piece.

**14-29  An integral wedge is provided by cutting twin dadoes.**

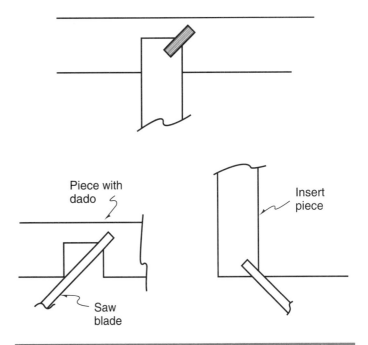

**14-30  How to include a spline in a dado joint.  The spline is installed after the main components are together.**

**14-31** A spline used this way in a mortise-tenon joint provides a lock in only one direction. Using a contrasting material for the spline provides a decorative detail.

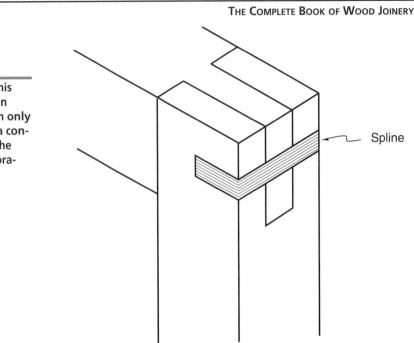

Spline

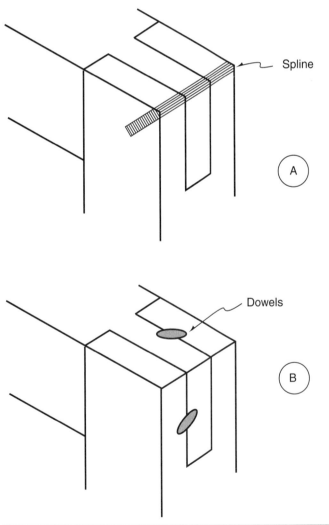

Spline

(A)

Dowels

(B)

**14-32** Splines or dowels used this way provide a locking factor in either direction. Cut the locking pieces oversize so they can be trimmed and sanded flush after assembly.

The cut can be made freehand if the stock is wide enough for safe handling. Always use a tenoning jig when cuts like this are needed on narrow stock.

A spline can be installed in an open mortise-tenon joint as shown in **Figure 14-31**. Be careful not to make the spline so thick that it can cause splitting. The spline will contribute a decorative detail if it is made from a contrasting material. A spline installed this way locks the joint in only one direction. In **Figure 14-32A**, the spline supplies a lock-factor in two directions.

The design in **Figure 14-32B** is similar, but dowels are used in place of a spline. The design shown supplies a locking factor in two directions. It's a good idea to form the lock component wider or longer, as the case may be, so it can be trimmed and sanded flush after assembly is complete.

Joints that involve three members can be designed so they will have integral strength *plus* an interlock. A basic design that is adapt-

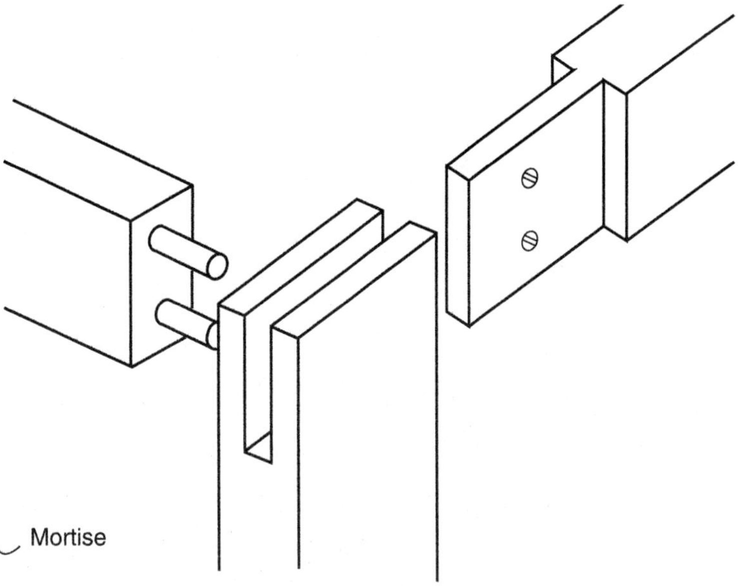

**14-33 A three-way lock joint that can be used for chair frames, table and bench substructures, and other projects.**

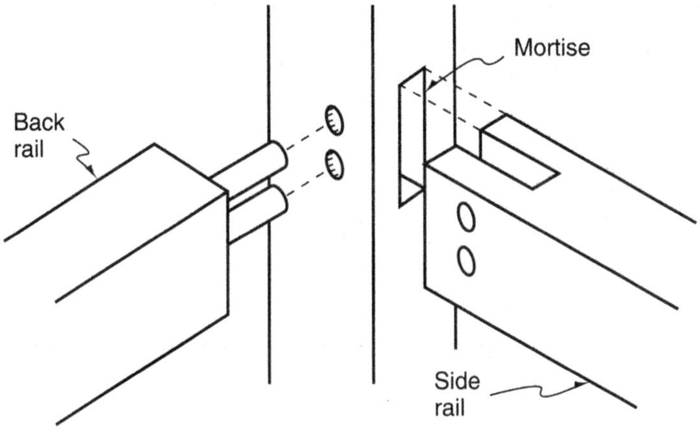

Back rail

Mortise

**14-34 This three-way joint design makes a very strong connection between rails and the leg of a chair.**

Side rail

Cross lap joint

Cross slots

Leg-and-rail joint

able for many applications is shown in **Figure 14-33**. The best procedure is to hold the mortise-tenon parts together with clamps while drilling the holes for the dowels. The dowels can be through or blind.

A similar procedure is shown in **Figure 14-34** in a three-part joint that involves the rails and back leg of a chair. Here too, the holes for the dowels should be drilled in the side rail and leg while they are held together with clamps.

**Figure 14-35** illustrates a three-way joint

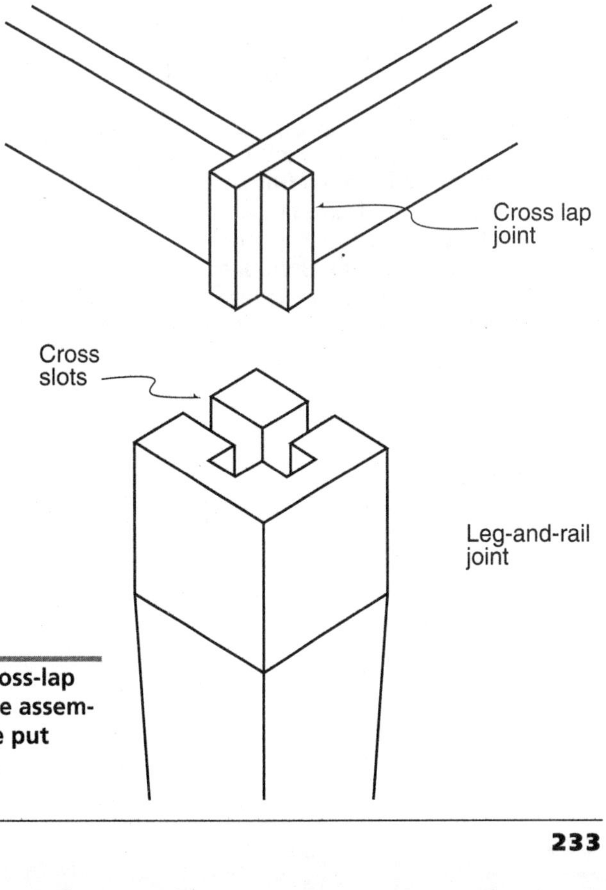

**14-35 In this design, the cross-lap can be viewed as a separate assembly or all three parts can be put together at the same time.**

that is a strong design for the substructure of, for example, a table. **Figure 14-36** suggests a three-way connection that is good to use on open framework or on a skeleton frame that will be sheathed with a panel material. In this case, all three components should be held in correct position while the hole for the dowel is drilled.

The joint assembly shown in **Figure 14-37** calls for very precise layout and cutting. It is, however, typical of the kind of attention that contributes to quality construction and durable projects.

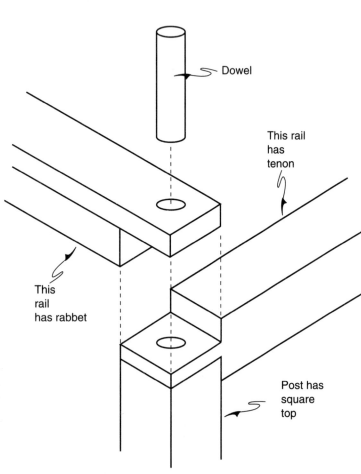

**14-36** This three-way joint is a good choice for open frames or for skeleton frames that will be sheathed with a panel material. On large assemblies, intermediate rails can be introduced.

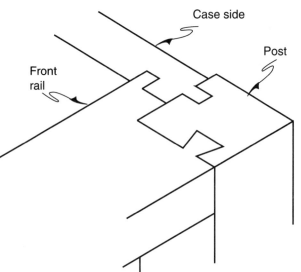

**14-37** Connections like this require precise cutting, and they do take time to execute, but their contribution to durability is obvious.

# 15

# SCULPTURED JOINTS

- Transition Pieces

**T**he difference between a sculptured joint and conventional designs is the difference between a tree limb and a dowel glued in a post. Whether the limb is attached by a joint at all is a moot point, but the important thing is that the natural-appearing melding of limb and trunk is what the woodworker imitates when he or she sculptures a joint (Figs. **15-1** and **15-2**).

A sculptured joint is not a specific connection, but a *design method* for treating *any* joint so lines will flow naturally together instead of meeting at sharp angles (**Fig. 15-3**). In essence, sculpturing is successful when the parts blend for maximum concealment of joint lines. This isn't difficult to accomplish, but

**15-1 Nature's sculptured joints**

**15-2** A woodworker's sculptured joints.

**15-3** Sculpturing means a melding of parts so there is a smooth flow at joint lines instead of square corners and edges.

since any slight separations that may eventually occur because of shrinkage in connected pieces are even more obvious on a sculptured joint than they are on a conventionally executed joint, maximum attention to the strength and durability of the joint itself is a primary consideration when sculpturing.

Of course, any joint should be as strong and stable as possible. Conventional treatments often include features like the slight setback that is recommended where a rail joins a leg so that a slight separation will not be obvious. This is not done when sculpturing, so whatever can be done to reinforce and to lock the joint will work in your favor.

It can be said that sculpturing itself is contrary to the nature of wood — the lines of the joint might flow but the grain pattern will not. This criticism, however, applies to any joint, so it's a minor argument against the concept.

Many commercial pieces are often sculptured in limited areas. The joints that connect the arms, rails, and legs of the chair that was shown in **Figure 15-2** are sculptured. Other joints are not, but it doesn't affect the overall appearance of the project, especially when all components are shaped to flow nicely.

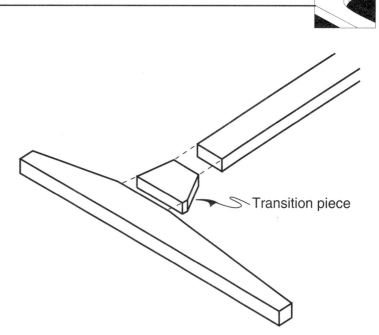

Transition piece

**15-4** Transitions can be accomplished by using extra pieces in the joints. The idea saves material but introduces other problems, like additional joint lines.

## TRANSITION PIECES

Parts must often be bulked out in the joint area so there will be sufficient material for sculpturing. The most economical way to do this is to add an extra part as shown in **Figure 15-4**. This will work okay, but it adds to the number of glue lines to worry about. To minimize glue lines, you can work with a piece that is wider than needed so it can be preshaped to provide an integral transition area as shown in **Figure 15-5**.

**15-5** A better method is to start with wide stock that can be cut to provide an integral transition area. This minimizes joint lines.

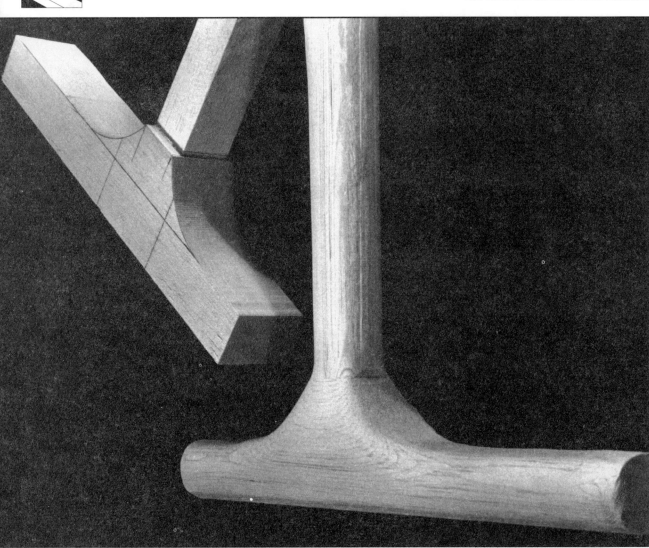

15-6 Components with round or oval cross-sections can be handled this way. The assembly in the foreground is rough shaped; final smoothing has yet to be done.

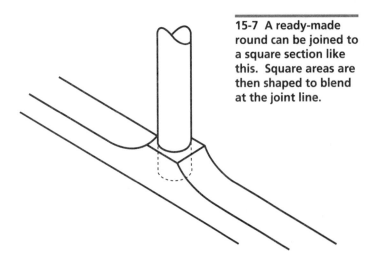

15-7 A ready-made round can be joined to a square section like this. Square areas are then shaped to blend at the joint line.

The same method will work when the components will have a circular cross-section (**Fig. 15-6**). It's often possible on this type of work to save time and effort by using a ready-made part, for example, a large round or dowel (**Fig. 15-7**). However, the joint line between the dowel and the flat area will not be as easy to meld as it would be if the initial components were square.

Transitions can also be made from round or oval shapes to components which have a basically flat form by making the initial connection as suggested in **Figure 15-8**. **Figure 15-9** shows one method that can be

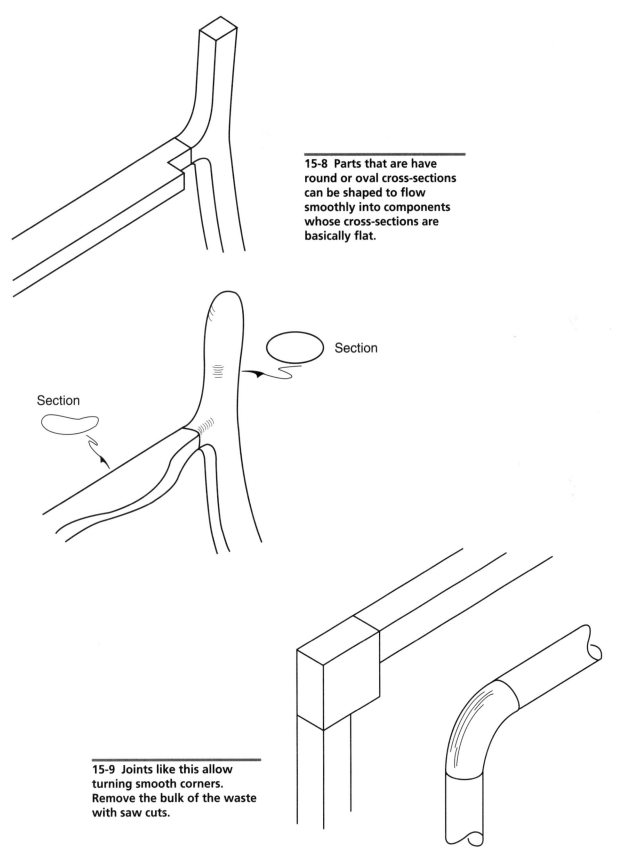

**15-8 Parts that are have round or oval cross-sections can be shaped to flow smoothly into components whose cross-sections are basically flat.**

Section

Section

**15-9 Joints like this allow turning smooth corners. Remove the bulk of the waste with saw cuts.**

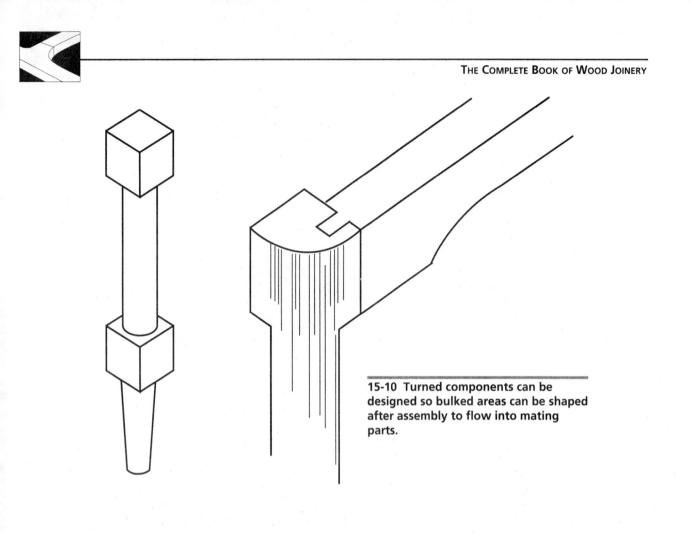

**15-10** Turned components can be designed so bulked areas can be shaped after assembly to flow into mating parts.

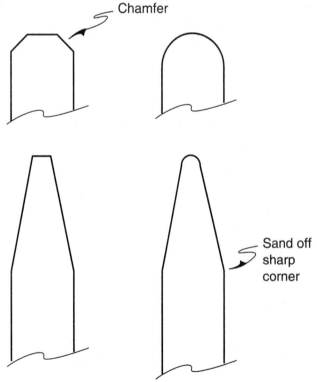

Chamfer

Sand off sharp corner

**15-11** Edges of tables, seats, shelves, and other components should be shaped to conform to the overall sculptured effect.

used to execute a round corner. The outside and inside edges of the block can be removed by sawing before the final shaping is done.

Legs and similar components that are shaped in a lathe can have bulked sections for use as transition pieces when they are assembled to mating pieces (**Fig. 15-10**). Turnings are done in a conventional manner when the bulked section is on a true longitudinal centerline. Offset turning techniques are used if the bulked area must provide more transitional material in a particular direction. In many cases, most of the turning can be done with the work mounted on true centers, with a shift made to off-centers for the bulked areas. Experienced lathe turners know that off-center work will be out of balance, which causes a vibration problem. Also, the turning diameter of the bulk areas will be greater than that of the section that was turned on true centers. Work at reduced speeds, take slight

**15-12** A half-round rasp or a Surform tool can be used initially to remove much of the waste material. Finishing is done with various grits of sandpaper.

cuts, and be sure the tool rest is clear of the work's turning diameter where you are applying the cutting tools. If this is a new experience, do some practicing on small pieces of softwood.

Sculpturing can be done on the edges of components as well as joint areas. Compatible edges on shelves, or table tops, or whatever, are essential to the overall feeling (**Fig. 15-11**). Most times, the work will be easier to do if the bulk of the waste is removed by sawing.

Some preshaping of parts on power tools is possible, but since the final forms are com-

pound contours and fillets, final work is always done with hand tools. A good argument against too much preshaping is the fact that parts do have to be clamped, and it's much easier to apply clamps against square edges.

**Figures 15-12** through **15-16** shows various tools and methods that can be used when sculpturing. The basic approach is to use a tool that will help remove the bulk of the waste quickly. Final touches are accomplished with smooth woodworker's files and various grits of sandpaper.

15-13 A spokeshave is another good tool to use. Cuts can be heavy or light depending on how much projection you set on the blade. Stroke with the grain of the wood.

15-14 Surform tools (by Stanley) are available in many shapes and sizes and are very useful when doing sculptured joints.

15-15 Sometimes it's possible to use a power tool for some preliminary shaping after parts are assembled. Here, corners are being rounded off on a shaper; the same job can be done with a portable router. Final melding will be done with sandpaper.

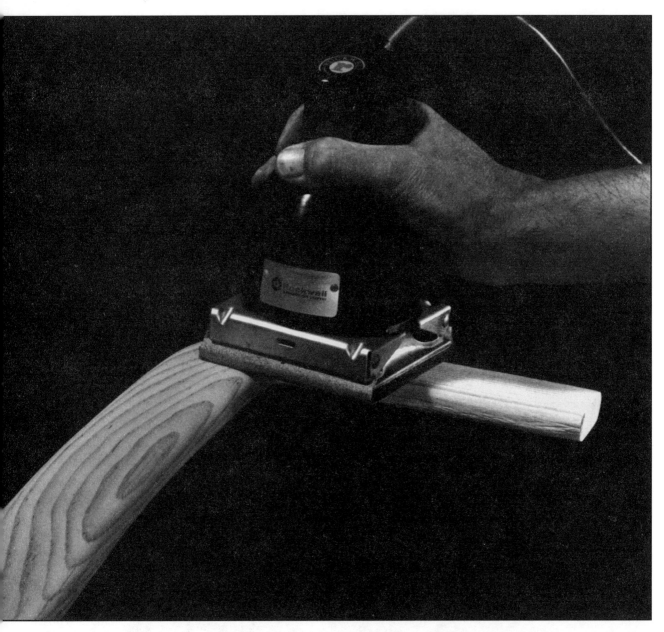

15-16 A good, palm-size pad sander is an excellent tool for doing the final shaping and smoothing of sculptured joints. This is a critical step and must not be rushed. Surfaces must be satiny smooth.

# 16

# CHEST OR CASE CONSTRUCTIONS

There are many joint designs and many variations of basic joints. Which one to use for a particular connection will not be a problem if you study, as we have suggested, the type of stresses imposed on a joint area, and consider where and how the project will be used. When more than one joint design can be used, base a choice on the one that is easiest to do or that you can do most efficiently with the tools you have.

There are practical considerations and there are personal preferences in joint selection. If the intention is for the project to have permanence, select joints accordingly. If putting things together adequately and quickly is a prime factor, then avoid the elaborate connections that require time and patience. There *are* times when a dado or a rabbet or even a butt joint makes more sense than a dovetail joint.

Whatever the decision, whether the joint is complex or simple, it will do its job as efficiently as you do yours. A sloppy dovetail is *not* better than doing without a dovetail. A butt joint will not look as good as it might, or hold as well as it can, if the mating surfaces are not square and do not make maximum contact.

Shown in this chapter are some typical and some not so typical joint applications. Browse through the illustrations before designing a project to find ideas that you can put to use.

## CHEST OR CASE CONSTRUCTIONS

Figures 16-1 through 16-3

A    Frame assembly

B    Case sides

C    Tenon

D    Groove

E    Dust panels of plywood, hardboard or particleboard (dust panel is not required in top frame since it will be covered by the top of the case)

F    Tenons (or dowels) into sides

G    Screws can be used to secure the top

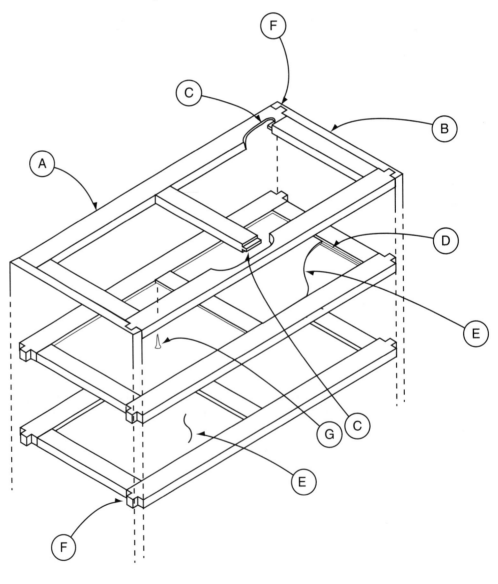

16-1 A case construction utilizing solid sides and web frames. Units that are designed this way will have good dimensional stability. Humidity variations will cause minimal changes.

16-2 The components running between the front and back rails of the web frames are drawer guides. The bottoms of the drawers will have a grooved strip that will ride on the guides.

16-3 The sides of the chest shown in the previous illustration are a frame-panel construction. The inserted panels are not glued in place so they can change dimensionally without splitting.

## WEB FRAMES
Figures 16-4 through 16-6

**A**  Frame assembly (often called "web frame")

**B**  Front and back rails

**C**  End rails

**D**  Drawer guide

**E**  Groove (for dust panels)

**F**  Dust panels

**G**  Integral tenon fits stopped dado in case side

**H**  End rails have a groove on one side, tongue
(tenon) on the other

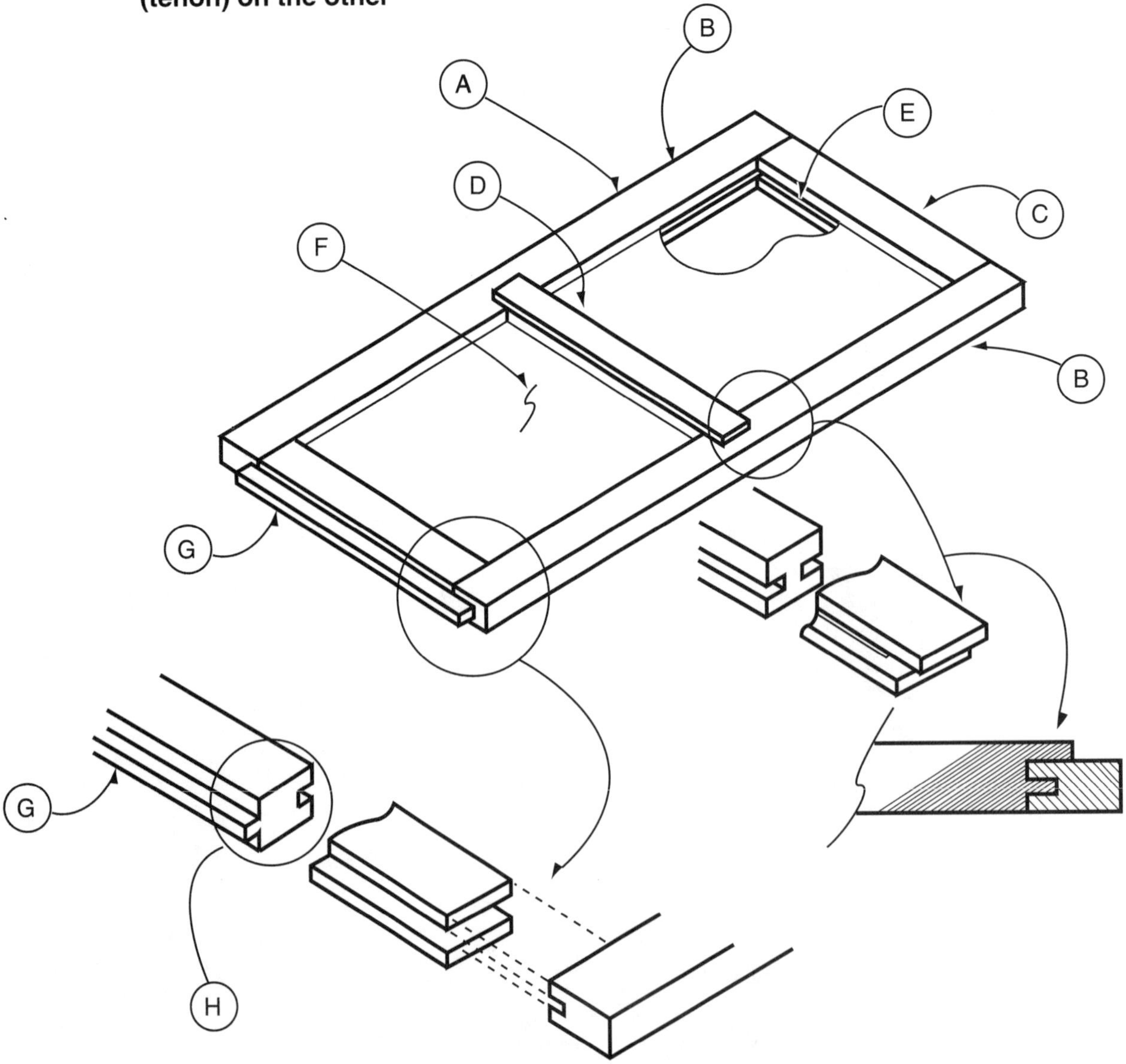

**16-4** The basics of a web frame. Note how the end rails are formed to provide a tenon (or tongue) that will mate with a groove formed in the sides of the case. This is a strong construction but the joints that are shown are not the only ones that can be used.

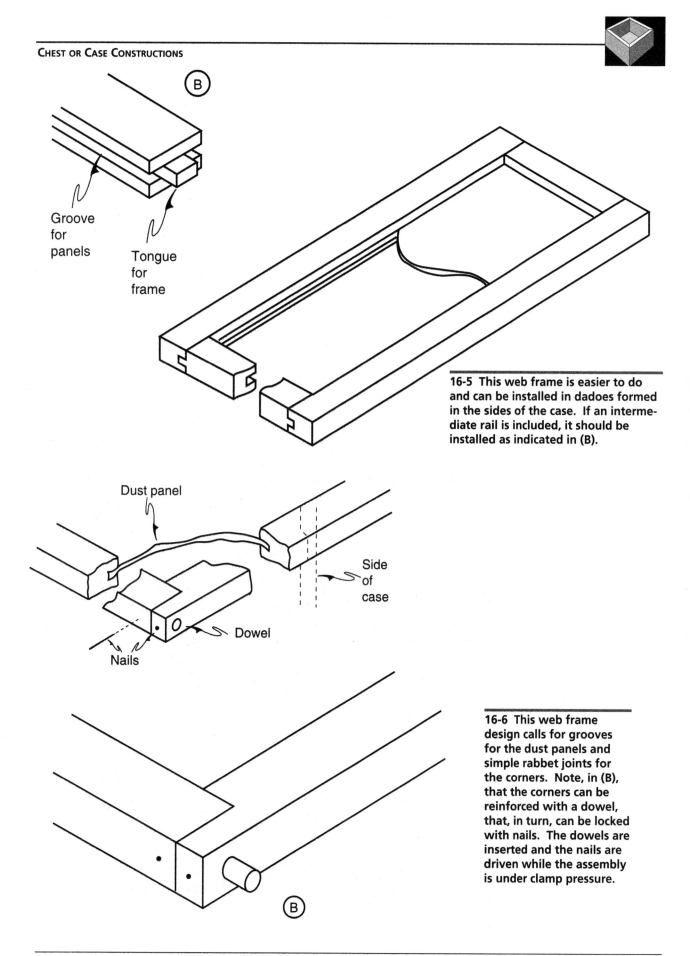

B

Groove
for
panels

Tongue
for
frame

**16-5** This web frame is easier to do and can be installed in dadoes formed in the sides of the case. If an intermediate rail is included, it should be installed as indicated in (B).

Dust panel

Side
of
case

Dowel

Nails

**16-6** This web frame design calls for grooves for the dust panels and simple rabbet joints for the corners. Note, in (B), that the corners can be reinforced with a dowel, that, in turn, can be locked with nails. The dowels are inserted and the nails are driven while the assembly is under clamp pressure.

B

## CABINET BASE
Figure 16-7

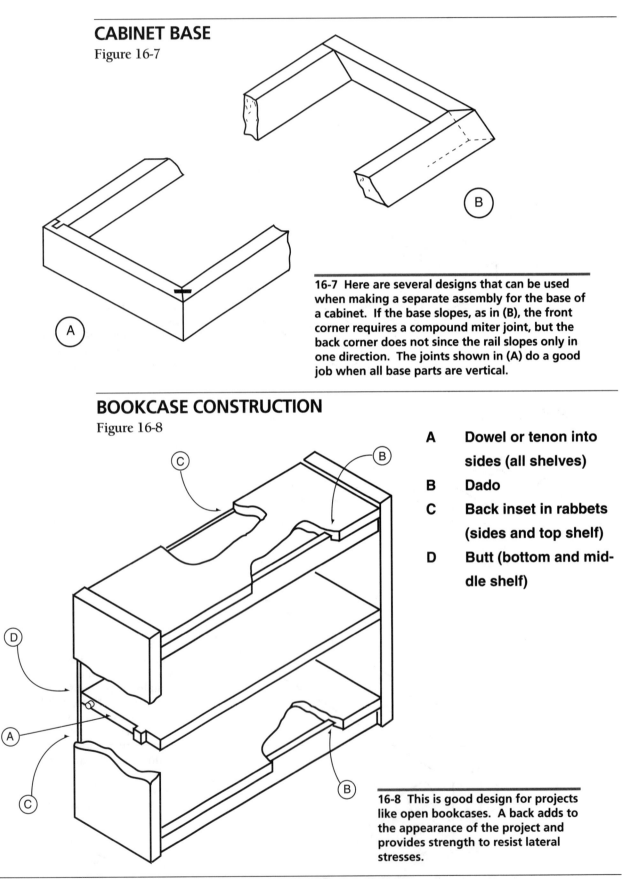

16-7 Here are several designs that can be used when making a separate assembly for the base of a cabinet. If the base slopes, as in (B), the front corner requires a compound miter joint, but the back corner does not since the rail slopes only in one direction. The joints shown in (A) do a good job when all base parts are vertical.

## BOOKCASE CONSTRUCTION
Figure 16-8

**A** Dowel or tenon into sides (all shelves)

**B** Dado

**C** Back inset in rabbets (sides and top shelf)

**D** Butt (bottom and middle shelf)

16-8 This is good design for projects like open bookcases. A back adds to the appearance of the project and provides strength to resist lateral stresses.

## KITCHEN BASE CABINET
Figure 16-9

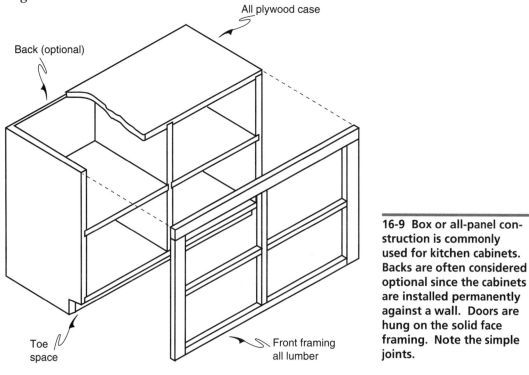

All plywood case

Back (optional)

Toe space

Front framing all lumber

**16-9** Box or all-panel construction is commonly used for kitchen cabinets. Backs are often considered optional since the cabinets are installed permanently against a wall. Doors are hung on the solid face framing. Note the simple joints.

## DRAWERS
Figures 16-10 through 16-12

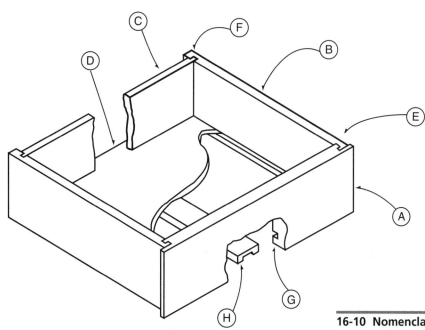

| | |
|---|---|
| **A** | **Drawer front** |
| **B** | **Drawer sides** |
| **C** | **Drawer back** |
| **D** | **Drawer bottom (let into grooves in front and sides)** |
| **E** | **Combination dado and rabbet joint** |
| **F** | **Dado in sides; rabbet in back** |
| **G** | **Grooves** |
| **H** | **Centered drawer guide** |

**16-10** Nomenclature of a typical drawer. Bottoms, usually let into grooves, are not glued. Many types of ready-made metal drawer guides are available.

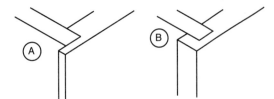

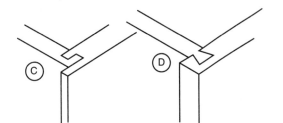

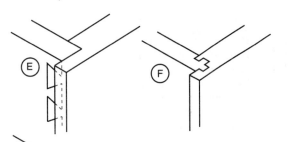

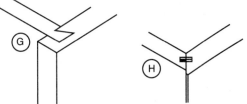

16-11 There are many joints that can be used to connect a drawer front to its sides. Important factors to consider include the overall appearance of the project and what the drawer will contain. A drawer for postage stamps, for example, does not require the strength called for if the drawer will be used for storing tools.

A    Rabbet

B    Dado

C    Combination of rabbet and dado

D    Single dovetail

E    Multiple dovetail

F    Special lock joint

G    Half dovetail

H    Miter reinforced with spline

I    Fingerlap for special effect

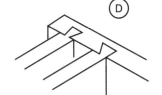

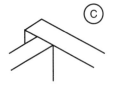

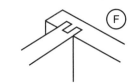

A    Dado

B    Dado in drawer side; rabbet in drawer back

C    Butt

16-12 These are joints that can be used to install the back of a drawer. The comments made in relation to drawer-front joints also apply here.

D    Single dovetail or half dovetail

E    Dado in drawer side; tongue in drawer back

F    Double dado in drawer side; single dado in drawer back

## LEG AND RAIL ASSEMBLY
Figures 16-13 through 16-15

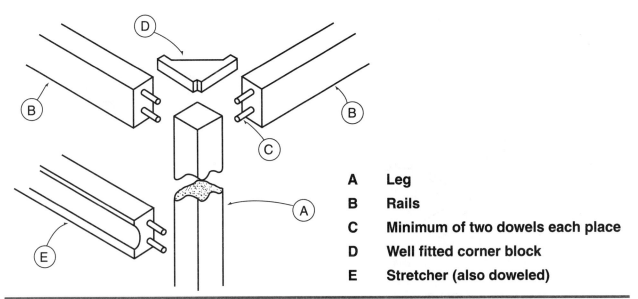

A     Leg

B     Rails

C     Minimum of two dowels each place

D     Well fitted corner block

E     Stretcher (also doweled)

**16-13  A typical leg-rail-stretcher assembly.  Two dowels are used in the joints to resist twisting tresses.  Corner blocks must be formed to fit snugly.**

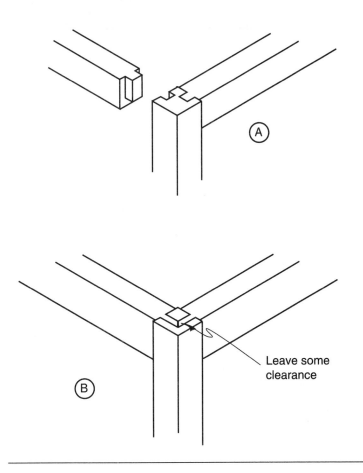

Leave some clearance

**16-14  Two other joints that can be used for a leg-rail connection.  Using a miter (B) makes it possible to use a longer tenon  on the rails.**

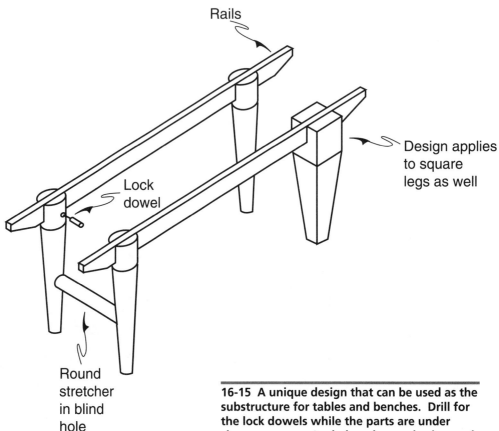

Rails

Design applies
to square
legs as well

Lock
dowel

Round
stretcher
in blind
hole

**16-15** A unique design that can be used as the substructure for tables and benches. Drill for the lock dowels while the parts are under clamp pressure. Lock dowels can also be used in the stretchers.

## LEGS TO SLABS
Figure 16-16

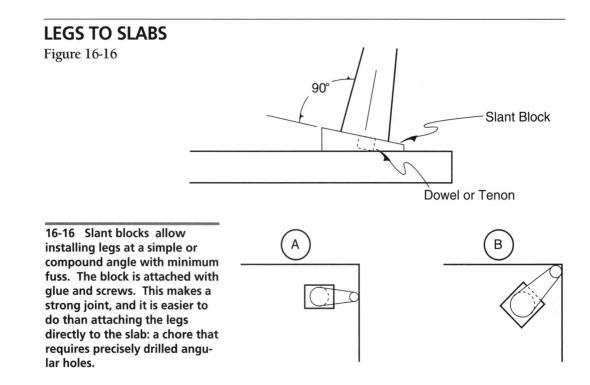

90°

Slant Block

Dowel or Tenon

**16-16** Slant blocks allow installing legs at a simple or compound angle with minimum fuss. The block is attached with glue and screws. This makes a strong joint, and it is easier to do than attaching the legs directly to the slab: a chore that requires precisely drilled angular holes.

A

B

## TRESTLE TABLE
Figure 16-17

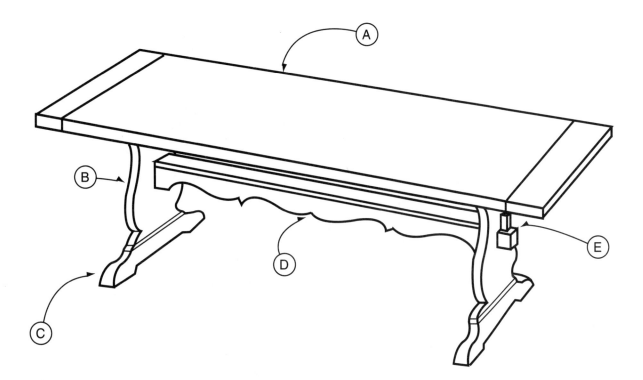

| | |
|---|---|
| A | Slab made of narrow boards, edge-joined and with end boards |
| B | Legs also of glued-up boards with wide tenons formed at each end before curves are cut |
| C | Base mortised to receive leg tenon |
| D | Heavy stretcher with tenon at each end to pass through legs |
| E | Tenon tusked |

Note: Bottom of slab is mortised to receive tenon in top of legs

16-17  A typical trestle table design and suggestions for strong joints that suit the project's style.  The same design can be adopted for coffee, cocktail, and dining tables, and even for benches.

## ATTACHING TABLE TOPS
Figures 16-18

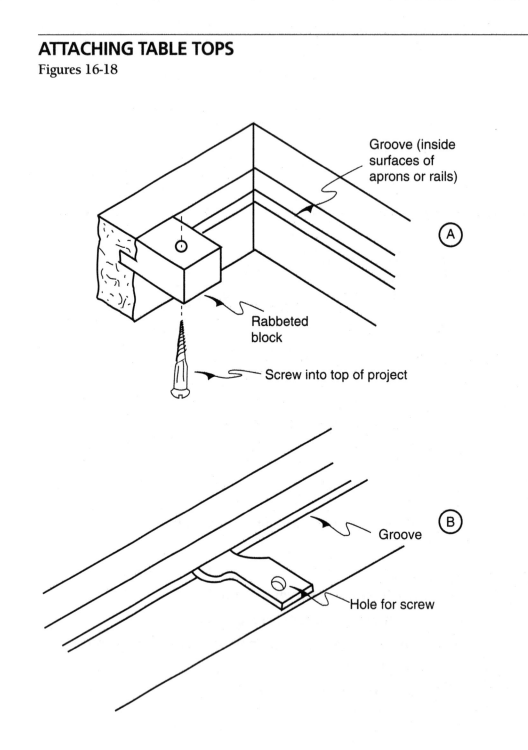

Groove (inside surfaces of aprons or rails)

(A)

Rabbeted block

Screw into top of project

Groove (B)

Hole for screw

16-18 Solid lumber tops should be attached so they can expand or contract without splitting or separating at joint lines. (A) shows a block design that can be made in the shop. (B) shows a ready-made table-top clip. Usual spacing for the fasteners is about 12 inches.

## PEDESTAL TABLE
Figure 16-19

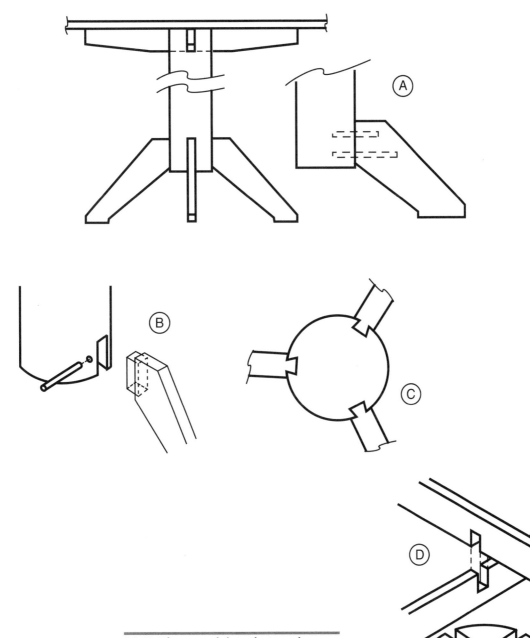

16-19 These are joints that can be used on a pedestal table — (A) dowels, with a longer one at the point of greatest stress; (B) mortise-tenon with a lock dowel; (C) dovetails to supply maximum strength; (D) edge-lapped rails to fit grooves cut into the pedestal.

# FRAMED PANELS
Figures 16-20 through 16-26

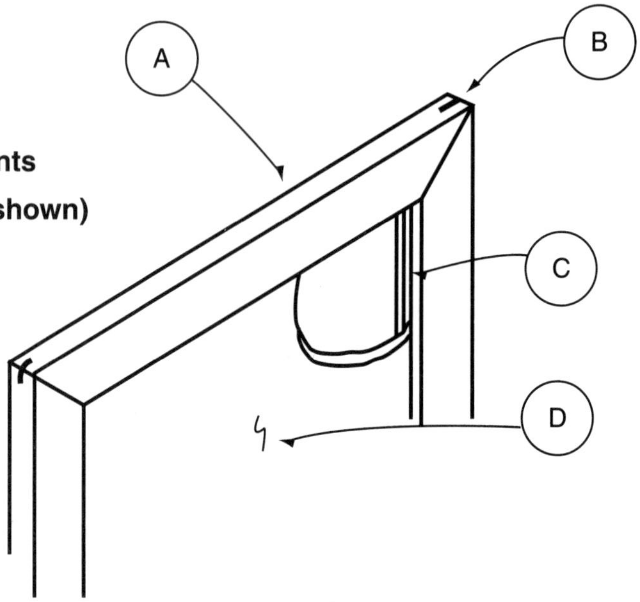

A      Frame with mitered joints

B      Reinforcement (spline shown)

C      Groove

D      Panel

E      Flush panel has a groove in the frame and a rabbet in the panel. This design is often used for the sides of case goods as well as for doors

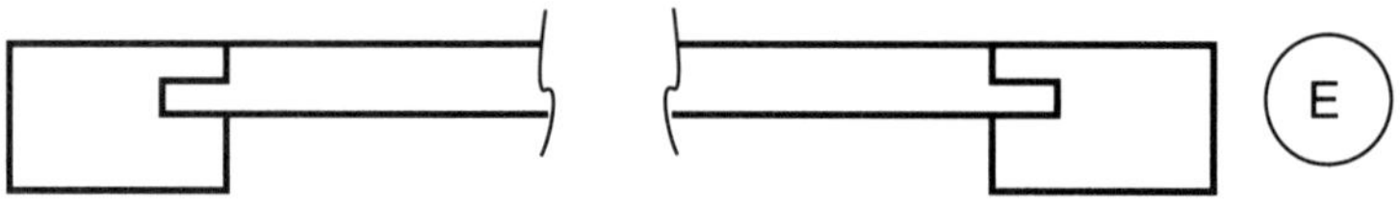

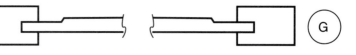

F      Elevated panel uses grooves in both the frame and the panel

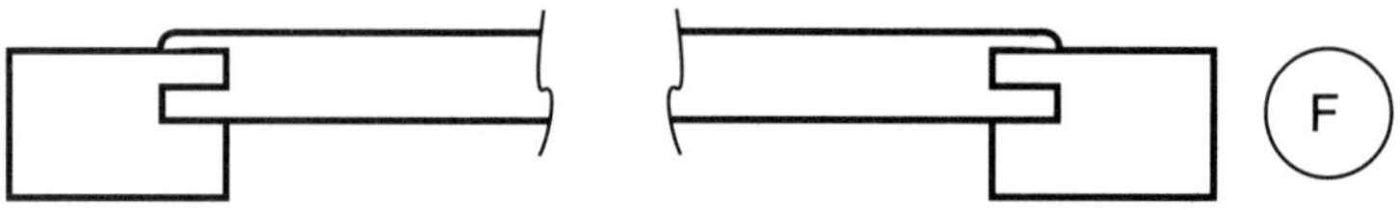

G      Panel raised on one side but with square shoulders

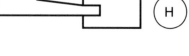

H      Panel raised on one side but with beveled shoulders

I      Rabbeted frame for a thin panel or glass insert. Wood stops are used to secure the panel

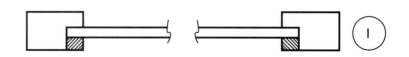

16-20 Various ways to insert panels in a frame. All the ideas can be used for doors and for sides of cabinets.

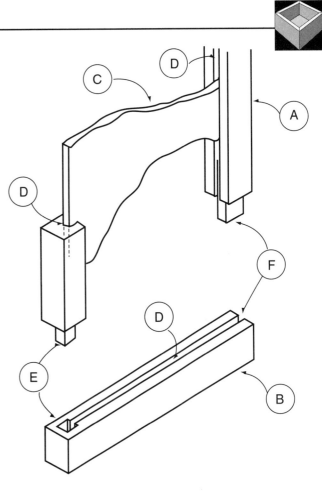

A    Stile

B    Rail

C    Panel

D    Grooves

E    Blind mortise-tenon

F    Open or stub mortise-tenon

**16-21** This is a basic frame-panel construction with parts identified and suggestions for two corner-joint designs.

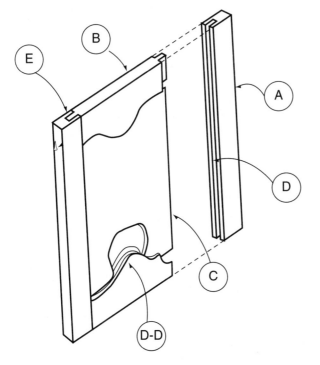

A    Stile

B    Shaped rail

C    Panel cut to fit

D    Groove

D-D   Groove in shaped rails done on a shaper

E    Tenon

**16-22** Frames can be made fancier by working along the lines shown here. Curved rails can be grooved on a shaper or with a portable router. Square sticking is shown, but edges can, of course, be shaped.

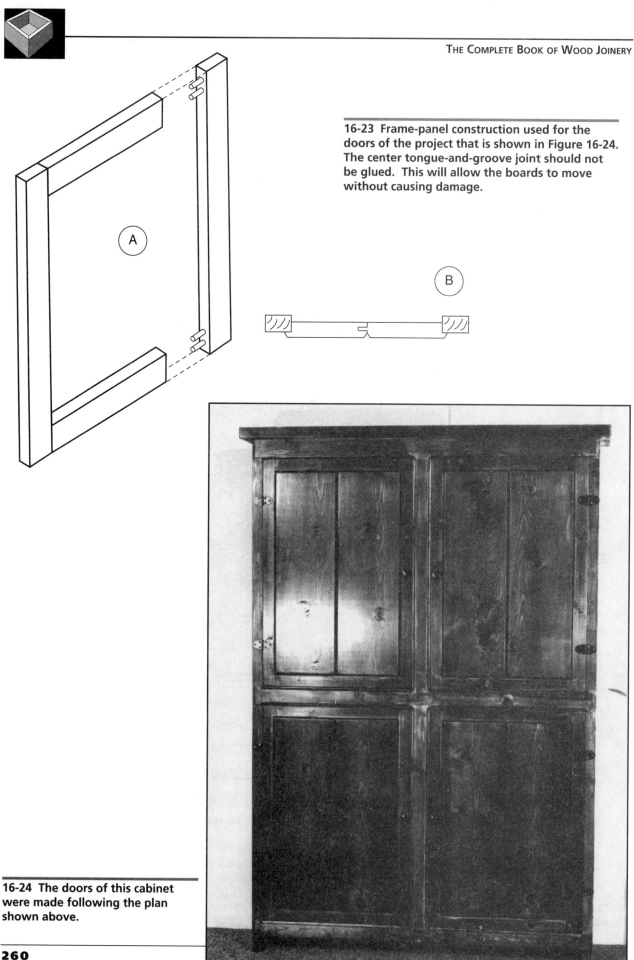

**16-23** Frame-panel construction used for the doors of the project that is shown in Figure 16-24. The center tongue-and-groove joint should not be glued. This will allow the boards to move without causing damage.

A

B

**16-24** The doors of this cabinet were made following the plan shown above.

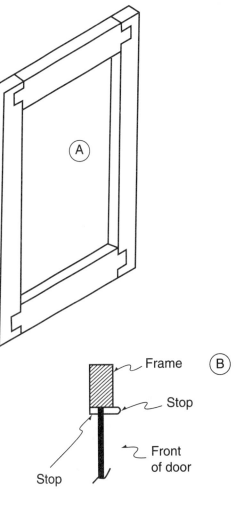

16-25 A different type of frame-panel assembly, one that was used to add some styling to the project shown in Figure 16-26. Note how the stops (B) project to add a detail. The same design was used for both the glass and the solid panel doors.

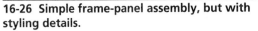

16-26 Simple frame-panel assembly, but with styling details.

## CHAIRS
Figures 16-27 through 16-28

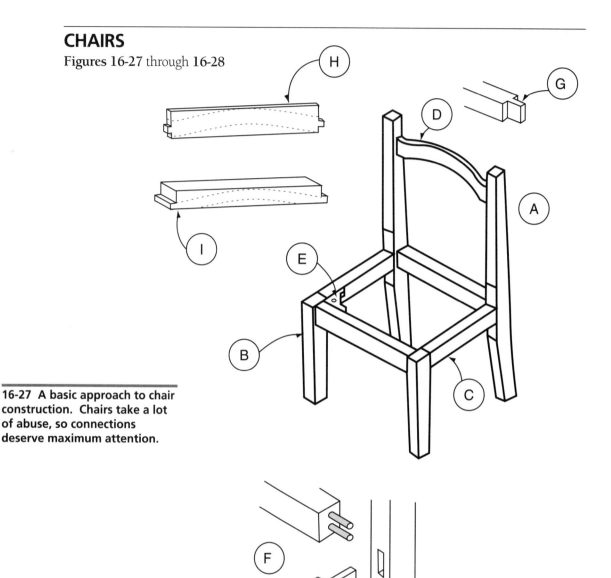

**16-27** A basic approach to chair construction. Chairs take a lot of abuse, so connections deserve maximum attention.

A    **Back legs**

B    **Front legs**

C    **Rails**

D    **Back (one or more pieces)**

E    **Corner blocks (to reinforce frame and for attachment of padded seat)**

F    **Leg to rail joint (Dowels penetrate tenon on rails. Dowels may be through leg or blind.)**

G    **Back-to-leg joint is mortise tenon (may be pegged)**

H    **How to do back if curve is vertical**

I    **How to do back if curve is horizontal**

Note that both back shapes have tenons formed before curves (dotted lines) are cut

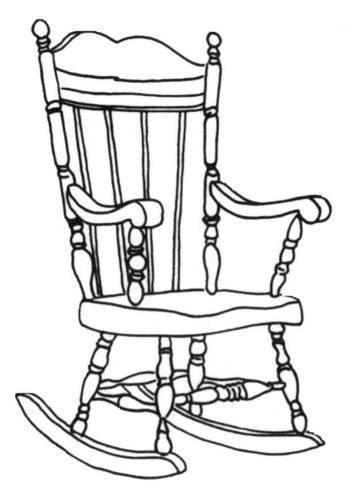

**16-28** Rocking chairs rank among the toughest projects to execute, especially when they involve the amount of turning that is shown here and the limitations imposed on joint design. All components should have integral tenons. Adding lock dowels is a plus factor.

## CHAIR SEAT-FRAMES

Figure 16-29

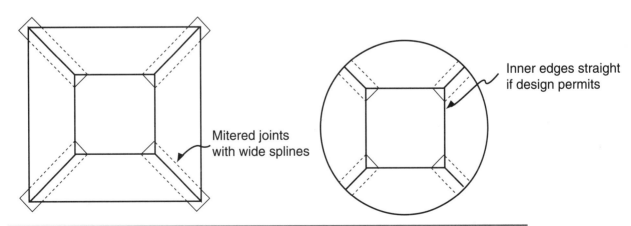

Mitered joints with wide splines

Inner edges straight if design permits

**16-29** One way to make a chair seat-frame that will support a pad. Assemblies of this type can be used for any circular component that can't be cut from a single piece of material. Assemblies like this can be stronger than a single-piece part.

## PLYWOOD EDGES

Figures 16-30 through 16-31

16-30 Plywood panels used as slab material can be framed to conceal unattractive ply lines. Here, a homemade molding was used.

**A** Plain wood strip with integral tongue; groove in plywood

**B** Molding with spline

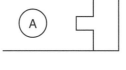

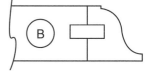

**C** Rabbet cuts in both the plywood and the banding

**D** Bulk edge with spline

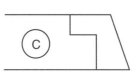

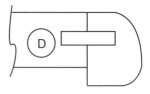

**E** Wood strip shaped to provide a lip; integral tongue; groove in plywood

**F** Strip grooved for the full thickness of the plywood (this provides bulk as well as a lip)

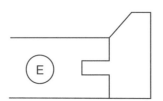

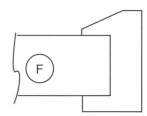

16-31 Typical methods that can be used to conceal plywood edges.

# GLUING

General Considerations • Polyvinyl Resin Glue • Animal (Liquid Hide) Glue
• Casein Glue • Plastic Resin Glue • Resorcinol Resin Glue • Aliphatic
Resin Glue • Epoxy Cement • Urea Resin • Contact Cements

well-fitted joint, correctly glued, will resist stresses that might cause adjacent areas to fail. Glue selection and application should not be approached casually. All the attention and effort used when shaping mating parts can be wasted if the final steps don't receive similar attention. Parts that go together should stay together, which is why glue is used at all.

## GENERAL CONSIDERATIONS

Glue is a liquid adhesive dispersed in a solvent, usually water, so it can be easily spread. When the joint parts are pressed and held together, the glue and the water penetrate the pores of the wood. The glue sticks to the walls of the wood fibers and gains strength as the water evaporates during the setting time.

The speed with which the glue sets and how deeply it penetrates depends on how quickly the water is removed. The strength of the joint and its resistance to outside factors, such as moisture and heat, depend entirely on the nature of the glue. That is one reason why the amount of moisture that is already in the wood can affect both the strength of the joint and the setting time of the glue. Excess moisture contributes to a weak joint. Wood that absorbs too much moisture during the gluing operation will swell and then shrink so that stresses will result along the glue line.

Most modern glues are formulated to minimize the negative effect of conditions that are difficult to control in a small shop. The individual is not likely to have sophisticated equipment for checking wood moisture content, and it's also probable that the shop's temperature and humidity are difficult to control. The best one can do under less than ideal conditions is to attempt to maintain a consistent shop temperature and, above all, to be sure that the parts being fabricated and joined are subjected to the same atmosphere. An example of how *not* to work is to make one part from lumber stored in a warm room and the mating piece from lumber taken from an outside storage shed.

Some wood species are more porous than others, but all are more absorbent at end-grain than along edges or on surfaces. A good way to handle end-grain is to apply a thinned coat of glue almost as you would a sealer and, shortly thereafter, add a second, full-strength coat. A visual check will tell whether the surface is uniformly coated.

It's possible, regardless of where the glue is used, for some areas to absorb more glue than others. Here too, a visual check will reveal if additional glue should be applied.

Much of the glue that is available today is squeezed from a plastic bottle. This tempts many workers to deposit glue in a wavy line that they feel will spread enough under clamp pressure. This not a good practice. It's better to use a stiff-bristle brush to spread the glue over all mating surfaces.

Don't be frugal with glue, but being overly generous is wasteful and useless. There should be some squeeze-out when the parts are pressed together, but it should be a minimum amount. Wipe off the excess with a lint-free cloth that is dampened, not soaked, in warm water. Glue that is not removed can cause blemishes and will act as a sealer, preventing finishing stains from penetrating in that area.

Some assemblies are more complex than others. When the job is elaborate, do a dry run first. That is, put the parts together without glue so you can set up a sequence of operations that will facilitate the final procedure. Check to be sure that a joining in one area will not interfere with adding other components.

Some glues set more quickly than others. This is not a big factor when the job is small, but on large assemblies it can be frustrating,

should the glue set in one area while it's still required elsewhere. Glue that sets before parts are clamped is no glue at all. Many glues set faster at high temperatures. Some shouldn't be used at all at low temperatures, while others are more tolerant. It's important to read and to follow the instructions that are on the container. We must assume that the manufacturer knows how to use the glue most efficiently.

Some glues will fill gaps and can be used when joint parts are less than perfect or when a less-than-tight joining is acceptable, but such a glue should not be used like plastic wood to conceal poor construction.

Don't use a *water-resistant* glue when what you need is a *waterproof* product. A picnic table, a patio bench, a dog house and a fancy mail box are examples of when to use waterproof glue. Water-resistant glues can be used when projects might be subjected to some humidity. Why make a choice? Water resistant glue is cheaper than waterproof glue.

Some glues are more heat resistant. Thermoplastic glues will soften when the temperature goes up near 160° Fahrenheit (71° Celsius). To be safe, avoid this type of glue if the project will be an enclosure for a heat-producing unit like a radiator or a TV set.

Always check components while they are under clamp pressure to be sure relationships are correct. Adjustments can be made before the glue sets, not afterwards. Use temporary braces when necessary to hold parts in alignment. Use clamps during the initial assembly, even if the parts will be secured with nails or screws. When similar assemblies are needed, take the time to organize a fixture so duplicate operations can be performed in mechanical fashion. This is especially wise when odd-angle joint assemblies are involved.

Try to do gluing in a clean, warm, dust-free area. Contact surfaces should be smooth, but not necessarily sanded. Edges that have been planed on a jointer or cut with a quality carbide-tipped saw blade are pretty close to ideal.

Remember that the chances for joint failure will increase if the parts go together in sloppy fashion or do not mesh smoothly even without clamp pressure.

There are almost as many types of glue as there are joints, but the wide variety is of more interest to the commercial producer and the provider of stock assemblies than to the individual or the small shop owner. An adequate choice can be made from the assortment of packaged products sold under various trade names. Those that follow are the most common and the most useful. Just be sure to read the label on the container. It will tell the kind of glue, how it should be mixed if necessary, how to apply it, and factors that will affect its efficiency.

## POLYVINYL RESIN GLUE

Polyvinyl resin is a white glue that is popular for general woodworking and is widely available in convenient plastic squeeze bottles. It is always ready to use but sets best and most quickly at temperatures of 60° Fahrenheit (15.6° Celsius) or higher.

Project parts should be prepared for instant clamping as soon as the glue is spread. Don't use polyvinyl resin glue if resistance to moisture or high temperature is required. Average clamping time under ideal conditions is from one to two hours, with softwoods requiring the longer periods.

## ANIMAL (LIQUID HIDE) GLUE

The glue made from animal hides and bones has always been a favorite for cabinetwork and general woodworking assemblies. It is very strong and does not become brittle, but it is not waterproof so it's a no-no for outdoor projects. It will, however, resist heat and mold, and it can supply strength even to poorly fitted joints since it has gap-filling qualities. It is available in liquid form, ready-to-use, or in flake form that must be mixed with water and heated.

Best results are obtained when the temperature of the glue is 70° Fahrenheit (21° Celsius) or higher. If the work area temperature is colder, heat the glue by placing the container in a pan of warm water.

A standard procedure is to apply a thin coat of the glue on mating surfaces and to allow it to become a bit tacky before joining the parts. It needs a longer set time than other adhesives, but this can be an asset on large assemblies and when many parts must be assembled. Average clamp time under ideal conditions runs from two to three hours for hardwoods and from three to four hours for softwoods.

## CASEIN GLUE

Casein glue is a product made from milk curds. It comes as a brownish powder that is mixed with water to a cream-like consistency. Usually, the mixture is of equal parts powder and water. A good procedure is to mix the material and then to stir it again about ten minutes before it is used. Be careful though, because it has a relatively short shelf-life after being mixed, so don't prepare more than can be used for the job on hand.

Casein glue has good gap-filling qualities, and it can be used at any temperature above freezing. But, like almost any glue, it is easier to apply at warm temperatures. It has a good degree of moisture resistance but is not waterproof.

It is *the* choice for oily species of wood like yew, teak, or lemon, but should *not* be used on redwood, oak, or maple, because it can cause stains on these species.

Clamping time is about the same as that required for animal glue.

## PLASTIC RESIN GLUE

Plastic resin is a urea-formaldehyde material that comes in powdered form that is mixed with water for use. Generally, the correct mixture is two parts of powder to one-half to one part of water. Do not prepare more than you can use in about two hours. Actually, it's better to prepare only as much as you need right now.

Plastic resin glue is not a good adhesive to use on oily woods or if the joint mesh is less than perfect. It has considerable resistance to moisture but it is not considered waterproof.

Plastic resin is good to use for general woodworking. Joints will be strong, but the glue line will be brittle if the joint parts do not fit tightly under clamp pressure.

Best results are obtained when the temperature is about 70° Fahrenheit (21° Celsius) or warmer. Clamping time for both hardwoods and softwoods can be quite long — as much as sixteen hours.

## RESORCINOL RESIN GLUE

Resorcinal resin glue is very strong and completely waterproof. It's an excellent choice for projects that will exposed to water, like patio furniture, wooden water containers, boats, and similar items.

It is a two-component product, one part being resin, the other a catalyst. When the materials are mixed in correct proportions, a chemical action occurs and the glue sets. It's important to follow the mixing instructions that are on the containers. Incorrect amounts of catalyst and resin will result in a weak joint. Bench life of the mix is quite short, so only amounts that will be used right off should be prepared.

The glue leaves a dark line and sets slowly, but it has gap-filling qualities. It will do a better job on poorly fitted joints than most other glues. Use it at temperatures of at least 70° Fahrenheit (21° Celsius); the higher the temperature, the faster the glue will set. Clamping time is long, from fourteen to sixteen hours.

## ALIPHATIC RESIN GLUE

Aliphatic resin glue is a good all-purpose adhesive for case goods and furniture assemblies, edge-to-edge joints, and face gluing. It is similar to polyvinyl resin glue but is preferred by many woodworkers. It is available in plastic squeeze bottles, ready-to-use. It has good heat resistance and fine spreadability, but it is not particularly water-resistant.

Factors in its favor are that it sets quickly and can be effective at any temperature above 50° Fahrenheit (10° Celsius), even though a temperature of about 70° Fahrenheit (21° Celsius) is preferable. It's advisable to stir it before use and to apply clamps quickly. Clamping time runs between one and two hours.

## EPOXY CEMENT

Epoxy cement has separate resin and hardener that must be mixed exactly as explained on the product's label. This is not a general woodworking adhesive, but it is a good choice for bonding dissimilar materials like metal or tile to wood. A product like this must be used carefully in well-ventilated areas. Read and obey all the safety instructions.

The epoxy can be used at most any temperature, but it will dry faster with heat. Many jobs can be done without clamping, but whether this is practical will depend on the nature of the work and the product itself. The material will not swell or shrink and is waterproof and oil-proof. Some types can be used to fill gaps and even holes.

Once the adhesive sets, it can be sanded, filed, drilled, and even machined.

## UREA RESIN

Urea resin is a resin-catalyst product that sets in seconds under high-frequency heat. This characteristic limits its use in the average, small woodworking shop. Also, the moisture content of the wood must be very low and carefully monitored and controlled.

The adhesive sets almost colorless and is highly moisture-resistant, but it is not waterproof. A common application is edge gluing in factories that have special heating equipment.

## CONTACT CEMENTS

Contact cement is a special adhesive that is ideal for doing laminations. It is commonly used to bond plastic laminates to counter tops, but it is also excellent for attaching wood veneers and applying banding to plywood edges.

The product comes ready-to-use and is applied by brush or roller to both surfaces. The word "contact" must be taken literally

since once the coated surfaces touch, they can't be separated or shifted. This calls for very careful placement of parts. A common procedure, after the adhesive is dry to the touch, is to place brown wrapping paper between the sheets to be laminated. The paper is slowly pulled away as the parts are pressed together.

Original contact cement products, some still available today, were highly volatile and extremely flammable. Some of the newer offerings are water-based and are not flammable or toxic. Whatever you use, it is critical to read and to follow the instructions on the label so the product will be used effectively and safely.

Contact cements do not require clamping and are moisture-resistant. They are easiest to use when the temperature is 70° Fahrenheit (21° Celsius) or warmer. Be especially careful about the waiting period between application of the cement and assembly of the parts. The product label will tell how long to wait and how to do a simple test to check for readiness. Most times, the test is to press a piece of wrapping paper against the coated surface. If the paper doesn't stick, the adhesive is ready.

# CLAMPS AND CLAMP USE

Handscrews • Bar Clamps • Hinged Bar Clamps • Clamp Fixtures • C-Clamps • Three-Way Edging Clamp • Band Clamps • Edge-Clamp Fixtures • Miter Clamps • Spring Clamps • Universal Clamp • Improvising

After the parts of a joint are formed, they must be held together in correct alignment until the glue has set. This is done with various types of clamps, except in those case where the joint design involves mechanical fasteners. Even then, it's often a good idea to keep parts together with clamps while screws or nails are driven.

To be prepared for a variety of gluing operations, it's necessary to have an assortment of clamps. Some types are more generally useful than others, but there is no such thing as one clamp for all work. The number of clamps needed will depend on the type and scope of the work. Some assemblies require few clamps; others are more demanding. The logical way to start a collection is to purchase the types that are needed for the job on hand. Even a beginner's needs will include designs like C-clamps and handscrews for small assemblies and a type of bar clamp for

holding together assemblies like slabs and frames. This chapter describes the clamps that are available and demonstrates some basic applications so the woodworker can make choices whether starting a collection or adding to one.

## HANDSCREWS

*Handscrews* (**Figs. 18-1** and **18-2**) are very popular because they can be easily adjusted to apply pressure over a broad surface. *Standard handscrews* can be used to clamp odd-shaped pieces of work since the jaws can be set to different angles. The jaws on *non-adjustable handscrews* are always parallel.

Handscrews can be adjusted very quickly if you adopt the habit of grasping the end spindle with the right hand and the middle spindle with the left hand. Move your hands as if they were on the pedals of a bicycle to

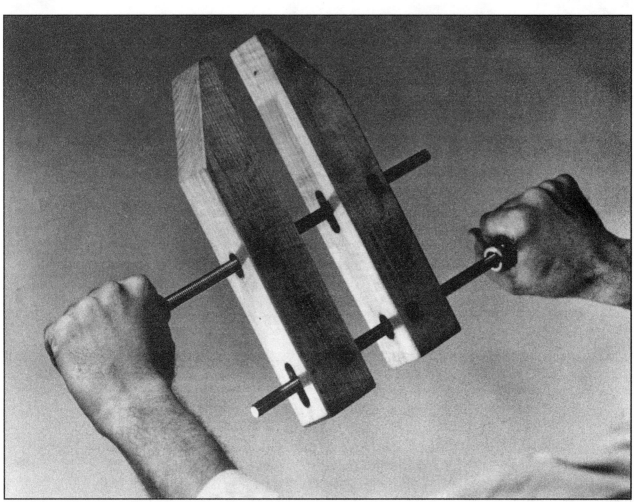

18-1 Non-adjustable handscrews have jaws that remain parallel. The jaws on standard types can be adjusted to suit angles.

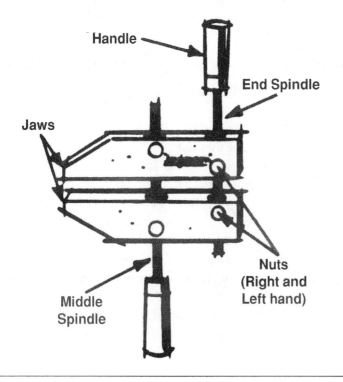

Handle

End Spindle

Jaws

Nuts
(Right and
Left hand)

Middle
Spindle

18-2 Parts of a handscrew.

| SIZES OF HANDSCREWS | | |
|---|---|---|
| OVERALL LENGTH OF JAWS inches | MAXIMUM OPENING BETWEEN JAWS inches | REACH—FROM MIDDLE SPINDLE TO END OF JAWS inches |
| 4 | 2 | 2 |
| 5 | 2$^1$/$_2$ | 2$^1$/$_2$ |
| 6 | 3 | 3 |
| 7 | 3$^1$/$_2$ | 3$^1$/$_2$ |
| 8 | 4$^1$/$_2$ | 4 |
| 10 | 6 | 5 |
| 12 | 8$^1$/$_2$ | 6 |
| 14 | 10 | 7 |
| 16 | 12 | 8 |
| 18 | 14 | 9 |
| 20 | 14 | 10 |
| 24 | 17 | 12 |

**18-3 Handscrews are available in all the sizes shown on this table.**

adjust the jaws until the opening is approximately correct. Place the handscrew on the work so the end spindle is on the left or right or in a top position, depending on the work, and with the middle spindle as close to the work as possible. Adjust one or both of the jaws until they are gripping easily but so there is a slight gap at their ends. Then turn the end spindle so the jaws will close completely and grip the work firmly.

Ideally, final pressure is applied by turning only the end spindle so the middle spindle acts as a fulcrum. Pressure must be applied evenly along the full length of the jaws, not just at one end. Since handscrews have smooth, wooden jaws, it isn't necessary to use a pad, or *caul*, to protect the work. Sizes of handscrews are listed in **Figure 18-3**.

In addition to routine clamping, handscrews can serve in many auxiliary capacities. **Figure 18-4** demonstrates how one can be used on a slab assembly so the pieces won't buckle under bar-clamp pressure. When the clamp is used this way, place wax paper between the work and the clamp to prevent excess glue from adhering to the clamp jaws.

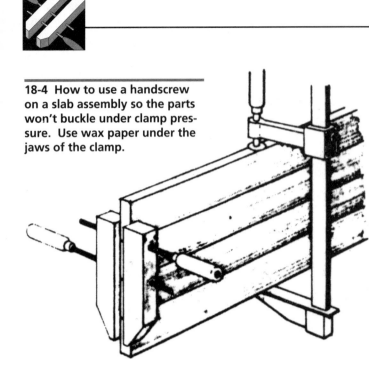

**18-4 How to use a handscrew on a slab assembly so the parts won't buckle under clamp pressure. Use wax paper under the jaws of the clamp.**

The arrangement shown in **Figure 18-5** is actually a repair job, but it does demonstrate the versatility of handscrews. A small clamp is used on each side of a crack that developed in the chair component. A larger clamp is used to put pressure on the small ones to bring the broken edges together until the glue dries.

**Figure 18-6** suggests that a handscrew can provide bearing surface for another clamp device. In this case, a leg is being glued to a round pedestal. A C-clamp is being used, but a bar clamp will work if it is required because of the size of the assembly. If the pedestal has four legs, opposite ones will be in line so a handscrew can be used on each to allow gluing two legs in a single operation.

**18-5 Here, handscrews are used to do a repair job. This application points up the flexibility of handscrews.**

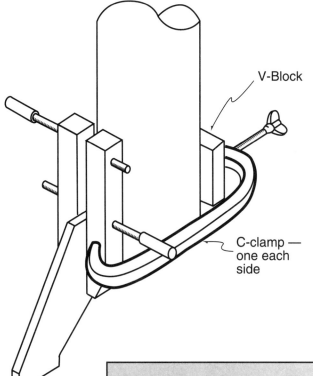

V-Block

C-clamp — one each side

**Figure 18-7** demonstrates an offbeat but practical application for the clamps that allows gripping round or square stock for, among other things, concentric drilling. The matching V-notches that are required in the jaws of the clamp will not interfere with the tools' primary function.

**18-6 How to use a handscrew to provide bearing surface for C-clamps (or bar clamps) being used to hold together a leg-pedestal assembly.**

**18-7 Cut matching V-notches in the the jaws of a handscrew and it becomes an excellent vise for jobs like concentric drilling.**

## BAR CLAMPS

Bar clamps, often called *cabinet* or *furniture clamps*, are indispensable for jobs like gluing up slabs and frames (**Figs. 18-8** and **18-9**) and similar chores that require clamping over relatively long lengths. Either the *tail stop* or the *head* of the clamp (depending on design) is movable so a quick adjustment can be made to suit the size of the work. The movable component has a built-in friction catch or clutch to keep it secure wherever it is situated.

In use, it's a good idea to unwind the screw completely and then set the clutch so the gripping length of the clamp is a bit more than the span that is required. Final pressure

is applied by turning the screw. When more than one clamp is needed, pressure should be evenly distributed by tightening each clamp a bit at a time.

Clamping finished stock calls for protecting the wood by using wooden pads between clamp jaws and work. Special non-marring pads that can be slipped on the jaws of bar clamps to protect the work are available. The pads are easily slipped on or off the clamp jaws and eliminate the need for makeshift blocks that are often a nuisance to keep in correct position.

**Figure 18-10** shows a practical bar clamp setup for a slab assembly. The cross pieces will keep the individual pieces from buckling when the main clamp pressure is

**18-8 Bar clamps are excellent tools for slab assemblies. Placing them on opposite sides of the assembly will equalize the clamp pressure. (Adjustable Clamp Co.)**

18-9 Using bar clamps to secure a frame assembly. Check the corners of the frame with a square as the clamp pressure is applied. (Adjustable Clamp Co.)

18-10 A good way to organize a slab-clamping operation. The cross pieces will keep the slab parts from buckling. Use wax paper under the cross pieces. (Adjustable Clamp Co.)

| CLAMP | NAME | DEPTH (or reach) | OPENING |
|---|---|---|---|
|  | *I*-bar | Jaws are 2" high | 2'–8' |
|  | Light pattern | 2 1/2" | 6"–36" |
|  | Deep reach | 5" | 6"–36" |

18-11 Types and sizes of bar clamps. These are typical; other designs are available.

applied. Use wax paper between surfaces that must not become attached. **Figure 18-11** lists typical bar clamps and sizes.

## HINGED BAR CLAMPS

*Hinged bar clamps* (**Fig. 18-12**), when attached to a bench, will swing to a clamping position when needed and out of the way when not in use. A typical application is suggested in **Figure 18-13**. The setup is ideal as a jig or fixture for repeat operations. The clamp's swivel plate can be mounted on any flat surface so use is not limited to bench work. Actually, the clamp can be used like any bar clamp and, because of the swivel plate, it is especially useful when a project component has an angular shape.

Special steel tracks are available for mounting the hinged bar clamps, as shown in **Figure 18-14**. The tracks do not interfere with the swivel action and make it possible to easily remove the clamps for use elsewhere.

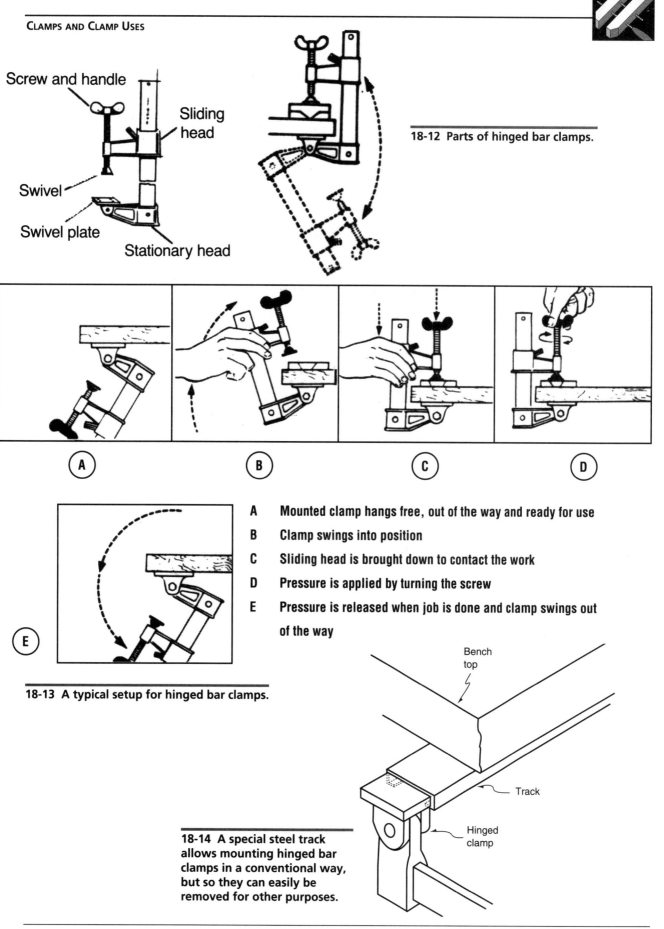

Screw and handle

Sliding head

Swivel

Swivel plate

Stationary head

18-12 Parts of hinged bar clamps.

A

B

C

D

E

A    Mounted clamp hangs free, out of the way and ready for use

B    Clamp swings into position

C    Sliding head is brought down to contact the work

D    Pressure is applied by turning the screw

E    Pressure is released when job is done and clamp swings out
of the way

18-13 A typical setup for hinged bar clamps.

Bench top

Track

Hinged clamp

18-14 A special steel track allows mounting hinged bar clamps in a conventional way, but so they can easily be removed for other purposes.

## CLAMP FIXTURES

Clamp fixtures are actually a kit that includes an unmounted tail stop and clamp head that can be mounted on any length of readily available pipe. Thus, a single set of fixtures can be used to provide any number of different length bar clamps merely by stocking different lengths of pipe.

Clamp fixtures are available in all the styles shown in **Figure 18-15**. The double bar design is a unique concept that exerts pressure equally on both sides of the assembly. It's an especially useful clamp for multi-piece slabs.

Other types of clamp fixtures, like the one shown in **Figure 18-16**, are designed for use on wood bars that the buyer supplies.

**18-15 Clamp fixtures are made for use on easily available pipe so clamps can be designed in whatever length is needed.**

| CLAMP FIXTURE | DESCRIPTION |
|---|---|
|  | Designed for mounting on 3/4" standard or extra heavy pipe; it has fixed head and sliding tail |
|  | Similar to above but mounts on 1/2" standard or extra heavy pipe |
|  | Mounts on 3/4" pipe but has fixed tail and sliding head (tail and head may be reversed to push instead of pull) |
|  | Double bar mounts on 1/2" pipe; it will pull evenly on both sides of the work |

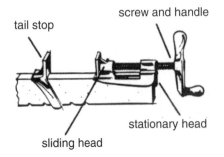

tail stop
screw and handle
stationary head
sliding head

**18-16 A type of clamp fixture that is mounted on a wooden bar.**

**18-17 Clamp fixtures that are designed for use on wooden bars can be used in other ways — here, as a bench-mounted assembly jig.**

The sliding head on the one that is illustrated is supported by guides so the screw is relieved from bending strain that might throw it out of line. Several types of these fixtures are available for mounting on wood bars of any length that have a cross-section measuring 1-1/4-inch X 2-1/2-inch. Others are designed for mounting on a standard 2X4. The latter type are made with a head assembly that can be mounted on any flat surface or bench top, as shown in **Figure 18-17**, so they can be used as special clamping fixtures for similar assemblies.

## C-CLAMPS

*C-clamps* (**Fig. 18-18**) are available in an endless variety of shapes and sizes, allowing applications to vary from straightforward clamping jobs to limitless other uses. Always use a pad, at least under the swivel, regardless of the style of the clamp. This is suggested for two reasons. First, the swivel will mar the work if it makes direct contact (**Fig. 18-19**). Second, a pad will distribute clamp pressure over a broader area.

*Carriage clamps* (**Fig. 18-20**) are usually classified as C-clamps but are made to industrial standards with ribbed cross-sections that will resist considerable strain. The general design and the bulk of the clamps puts them in the heavy-duty category.

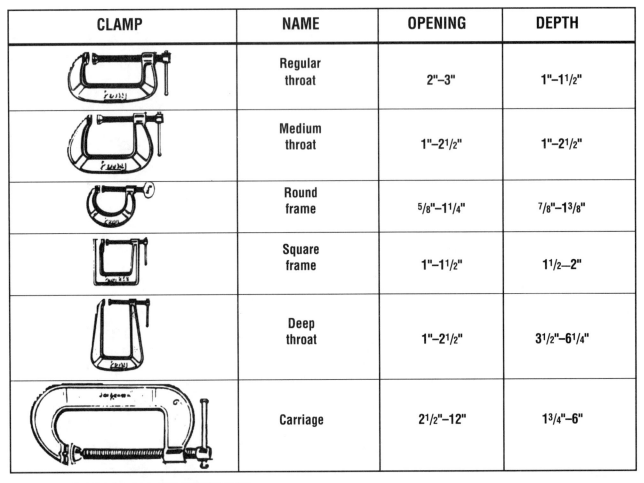

| CLAMP | NAME | OPENING | DEPTH |
|---|---|---|---|
| | Regular throat | 2"–3" | 1"–1½" |
| | Medium throat | 1"–2½" | 1"–2½" |
| | Round frame | ⅝"–1¼" | ⅞"–1⅜" |
| | Square frame | 1"–1½" | 1½–2" |
| | Deep throat | 1"–2½" | 3½"–6¼" |
| | Carriage | 2½"–12" | 1¾"–6" |

**18-18** Sizes and styles of the most common C-clamps.

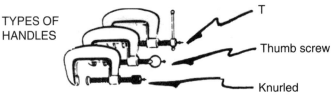

TYPES OF HANDLES — T, Thumb screw, Knurled

**18-19** C-clamps will mar the work (arrow) unless a pad is used under the swivel. The pad also helps to distribute the clamp pressure.

**18-20** Carriage clamps are a type of C-clamp but husky enough for the kind of heavy-duty work being done here. (Adjustable Clamp Co.)

## THREE-WAY EDGING CLAMP

A *three-way edging clamp* looks like a C-clamp but is designed so it can apply right-angle pressure against the side or edge of a workpiece (**Fig. 18-21**). The design makes the clamp especially useful for installing or repairing edge trim or moldings. Because of the three-screw configuration, the centered or right-angle screw can be used on or off center. The tool may also be used as a conventional C-clamp.

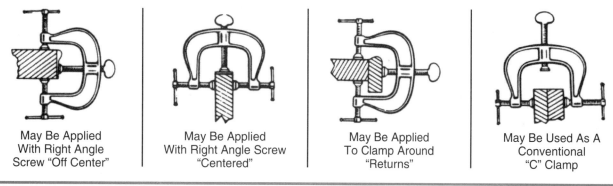

May Be Applied With Right Angle Screw "Off Center"

May Be Applied With Right Angle Screw "Centered"

May Be Applied To Clamp Around "Returns"

May Be Used As A Conventional "C" Clamp

**18-21** Some practical uses for a three-way edging clamp.

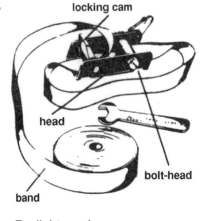
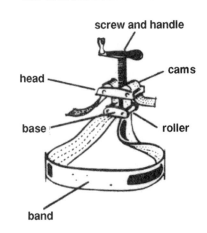

**18-22 The two basic types of band clamps.**

For light service;
1" x 15' nylon band

For heavy duty service;
available with canvas or
steel band; bands are 2" wide
with 10', 15', 20', 30' lengths

**18-23 A typical application for a light-duty band clamp — attaching banding to a circular table top. (Adjustable Clamp Co.)**

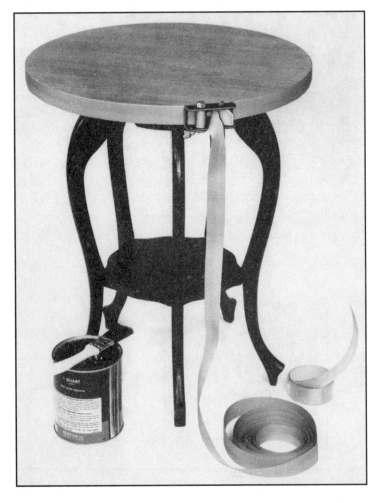

## BAND CLAMPS

*Band clamps* (**Fig. 18-22**) solve the problem of clamping the round or irregular shapes that are often encountered in furniture constructions, pedestals, and segmented forms. With both light-duty and heavy-duty types, the band is placed about the work and pulled as snug as possible by hand. The final tightening is done by turning the screw or the bolt of the clamp, whichever applies.

A heavy-duty type with a 2-inch wide, prestretched canvas band is recommended for most of the applications likely to be encountered in a woodworking shop. Types with steel bands are also available, but they are difficult to handle and can kink. They are recommended only for curved and round shapes.

Light-duty band clamps are easier to handle and are ideal for jobs like the one in **Figure 18-23**. Some of the units are furnished with specially shaped steel corners for use when clamping picture frames and the like. The steel corners make it easier to provide clamping action, and they serve to protect the band as well as corners of the assembly.

## EDGE-CLAMP FIXTURES

*Edge-clamp fixtures* (**Fig. 18-24**) are accessories designed to apply pressure at right angles to the axis of a bar clamp. A typical application is demonstrated in **Figure 18-25**. In this case, the fixtures are used to apply mid-point pressure to keep the assembly flat as it is glued. Some edge-clamp fixtures can't be used on bars that are more than 5/16-inch thick, so this factor should be checked before any are purchased.

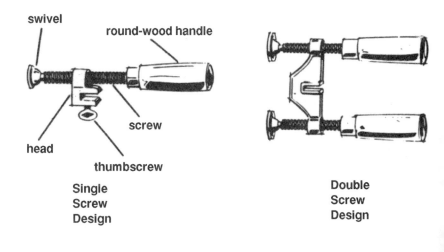

18-24 Two types of edge-clamp fixtures.

18-25 The assembly shown here demonstrates two ways to use edge-clamp fixtures. (Adjustable Clamp Co.)

## MITER CLAMPS

The clamp shown in **Figure 18-26** is especially designed for mitered, flat casings that are thick enough to take a 5/8-inch blind hole. The clamp pulls the mating edges tightly together no matter what the miter angle is. There is little tendency for the parts to creep out of alignment.

A more common type of miter clamp is shown in **Figure 18-27**. A feature of the design is that the joint, if necessary, can be touched up with a backsaw or dovetail saw while the parts are clamped. Then, after loosening the screws, glue is applied and the sawed edges are butted together before the clamps are tightened again. Since the corner is accessible, it's easy to drive a screw or a nail to reinforce the joint. Once the fastener is installed, the assembled pieces can be removed from the clamp. Thus, work can be done on other corners, or parts, without delay.

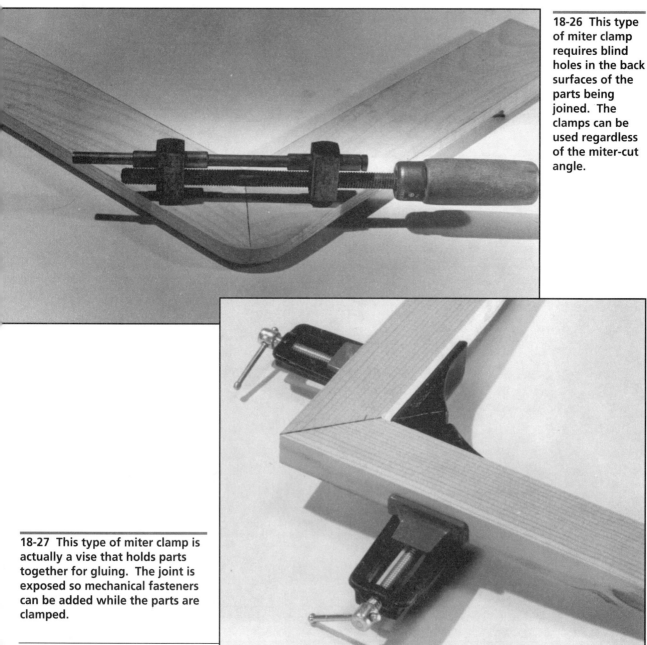

18-26 This type of miter clamp requires blind holes in the back surfaces of the parts being joined. The clamps can be used regardless of the miter-cut angle.

18-27 This type of miter clamp is actually a vise that holds parts together for gluing. The joint is exposed so mechanical fasteners can be added while the parts are clamped.

## SPRING CLAMPS

Spring clamps (**Fig. 18-28**) are like extra, strong fingers that can be used to hold parts together or to keep a piece being worked on positioned. The clamp pressure is always at the end of the jaws so the grip can be localized anywhere within the tool's reach. Often, a wooden pad is used under the jaws so pressure is distributed over a wider area.

Some types are equipped with specially shaped jaws to grip round objects; others have pivoting jaws with serrated edges so they can actually grip around a corner as in a miter joint. Most types are available with protective sleeves over the jaws or the handles, or in both areas, to provide protection for the work and to make handling easier.

Spring clamps come in various sizes — so you have a choice in relation to the work to be held and the amount of pressure that is needed (**Fig. 18-29**). The springs on some of the larger ones are powerful enough so that two hands are needed to spread the jaws.

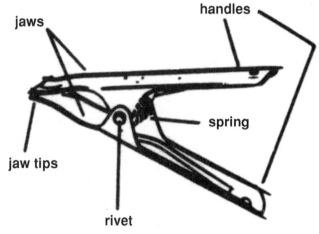

**18-28 Parts of a spring clamp.**

| SPECIFICATION OF TYPICAL SPRING CLAMPS | | |
|:---:|:---:|:---:|
| **CAPACITY BETWEEN JAWS** | **LENGTH OF JAWS** | **REACH ONTO WORK** |
| 1" | 4" | 1 1/4 " |
| 2" | 6" | 2" |
| 3" | 9" | 3" |
| 4" | 12" | 4" |

**18-29  Sizes of spring clamps.  Larger ones have very strong springs and can exert a lot of pressure.**

## UNIVERSAL CLAMP

The *universal clamp* is a relative newcomer in the clamp world and is actually a kit of parts (**Fig. 18-30**) that are assembled in various ways to do a multitude of assembly and gluing work. The tool can do a bar clamp's work without having to span the assembly, which is one of its major features. Thus it can be used as shown in **Figures 18-31** and **18-32** to secure T-joints as well as end joints.

The key to the clamp's versatility is the interchangeable U-shaped jaws that will grip stock from 3/4-inch to 1-5/8-inches thick and that can be inserted on either side of the clamp. Each U-shaped component has a toothed leg that grips the wood. Since the leg can leave a mark, the clamp is placed so the mar will be on a hidden side of the work, or a protective shim can be placed between the jaw and the wood.

**Figure 18-33** shows how the clamp is organized for a miter joint. The miter attachment hooks over serrations in the arm and is adjustable to accommodate materials of various widths. The openings in the jaws of the clamp allow driving a nail or a screw while the parts are held firmly together. Because of the special mount that is part of the kit, the clamp can be used on a bench like a vise. It slips easily out of the mount for portable applications.

**18-30 The parts of a universal clamp**

**18-31 A universal clamp being used to hold the parts of a T-joint. The serrated leg of the U-jaw should be placed on the side of the stock that won't be visible.**

**18-32** Using the universal clamp to secure an end joint. The clamp slips easily in or out of the base which, here, is screwed to a bench top.

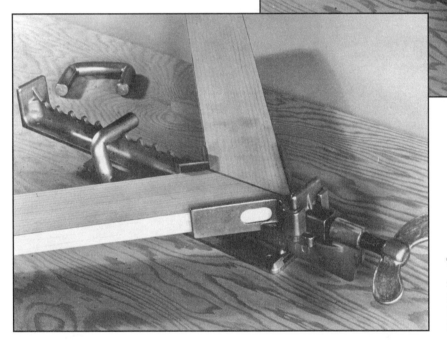

**18-33** The universal clamp has special attachments for securing miter joints. Nails or screws can be driven through the openings in the V-jaws.

## IMPROVISING

There are times when the right clamp for the job is not available or when the job is unique enough so that a standard clamp won't do. Then the woodworker has no choice but to be creative and imaginative, inventing a clamp device that will solve the problem. Often, the jig or fixture becomes a permanent tool. Other times, it is a quick, makeshift setup that is justified simply because its one-time use solves the problem on hand.

A clamp must apply point or area pressure to keep parts correctly aligned while other work is being done, or to keep mating points in firm contact until the glue dries. The ideas and procedures that are shown in **Figures 18-34** through **18-43** have been tested and proven adequate for the jobs being done. They can be used as shown but, more important, they should serve as examples of how to improvise when you lack a specific clamp, or how to succeed when the assembly problem is unusual.

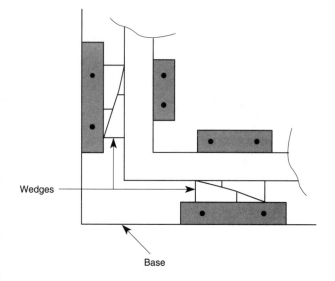

Wedges

Base

**18-34** A type of homemade miter assembly jig. Twin wedges hold the parts in place until the glue dries or until nails or screws have been installed.

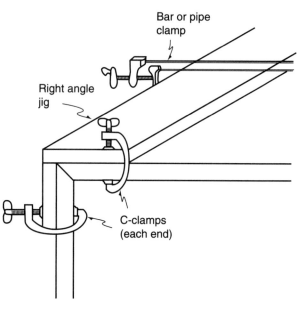

Bar or pipe clamp

Right angle jig

C-clamps (each end)

**18-36** This is another way to set up for clamping cross or rip miters. The right-angle jig is just two boards put together to form a 90 degree turn. Use wax paper between the jig and the work.

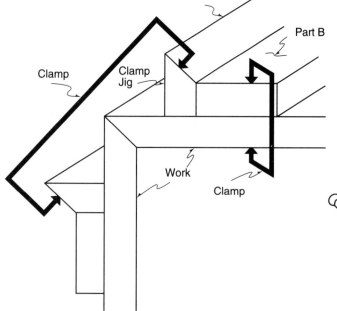

Part A

Part B

Clamp

Clamp Jig

Work

Clamp

**18-35** Cross and rip miters are difficult to assemble with routine clamping procedures. The idea shown here makes it possible for clamps to span the corners so parts will pull tightly together. Parts (A) and (B) must be joined strongly with glue and screws.

Stop

Vise

Work

**18-37** How to improvise clamping for a slab assembly. The stop is tack-nailed to the workbench; the bench vise supplies the clamp pressure.

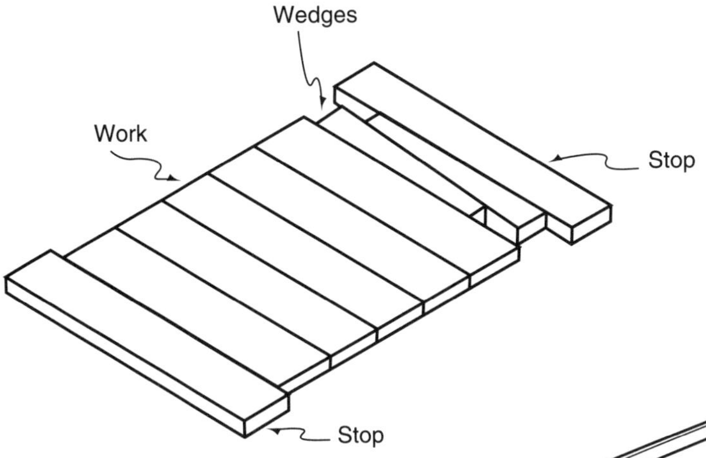

Wedges

Work

Stop

Stop

**18-38** Another way to handle a slab assembly. Two stops are used, each one tack-nailed to the workbench. Twin wedges supply the clamp pressure.

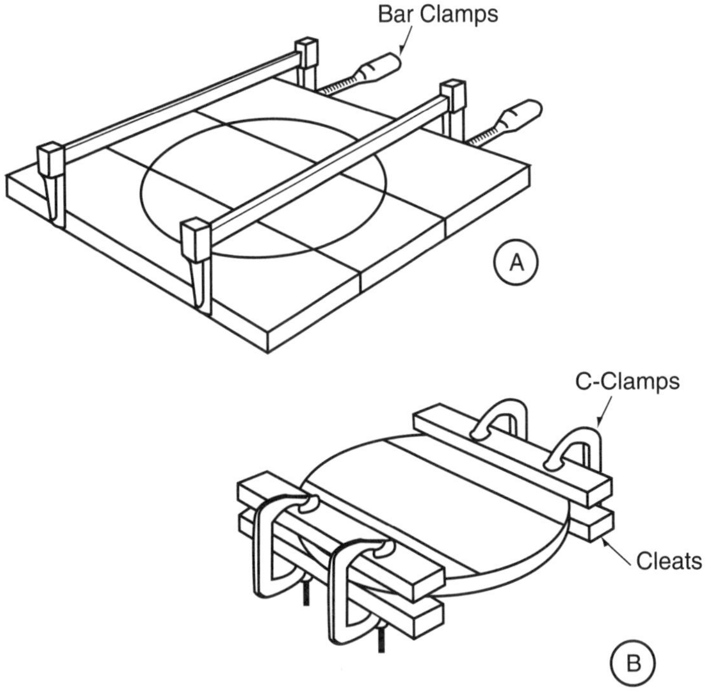

Bar Clamps

(A)

Sash Cord

1/4" Bolts

Nut

Washer

Hardwood Blocks

C-Clamps

Cleats

(B)

**18-39** Two methods that can be used to clamp circular assemblies. Assemble the boards and then cut out the part as in (A), or cut the parts first and then assemble as in (B). Use bar clamps across the cleats that are held in place with C-clamps.

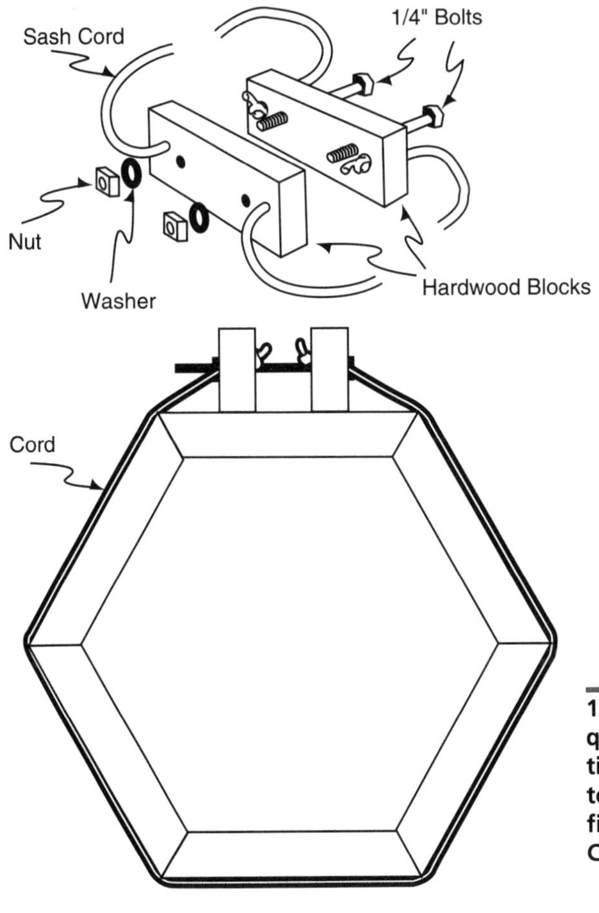

Cord

**18-40** An example of the classic tourniquet rope clamp. Here, the rope is pulled tight and knotted. The blocks are pulled together with the bolts to provide the final clamp pressure. A handscrew or a C-clamp can be used instead of the bolts.

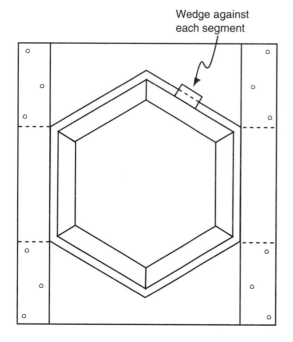

Wedge against
each segment

**18-41** A special form made to suit the shape of a segmented assembly. Wedges are used against each side of the project to force the corners tightly together.

**18-42** Using a one-piece holding device as a clamp for an assembly with compound angle joints. Slim wedges are used between each side of the project and the jig.

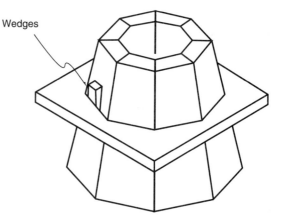

Wedges

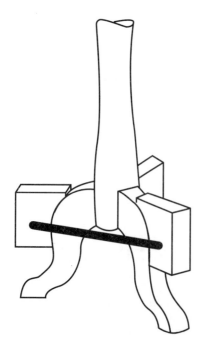

**18-43** The rope trick again — this time to clamp legs against a pedestal. The bearing blocks can be the pieces of stock that were removed when the legs were formed. Always work with sash cord or something similar when rope plays a role in a clamp. Other types of rope, like clothesline, may stretch too much.

# ILLUSTRATED GLOSSARY

**Bare-Faced Tenon**
*(page142)*

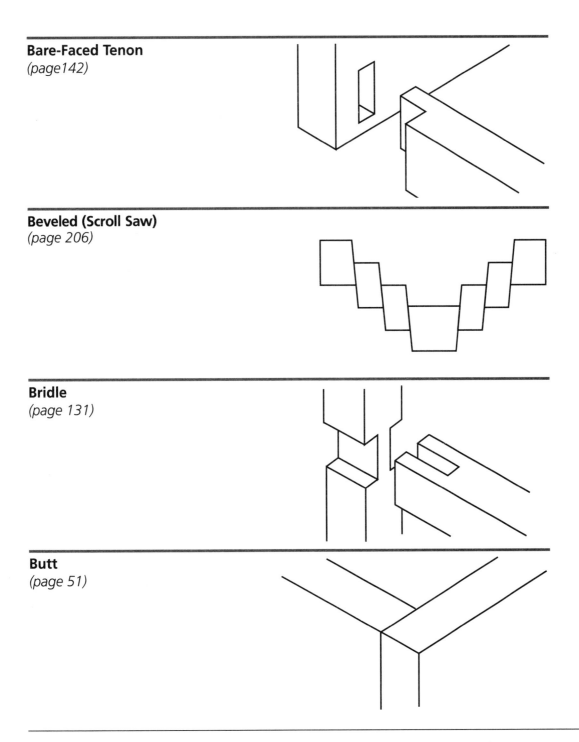

**Beveled (Scroll Saw)**
*(page 206)*

**Bridle**
*(page 131)*

**Butt**
*(page 51)*

**Cogged**
*(page 228)*

**Compound Miter**
*page 101, 292)*

**Coped (Frames)**
*(page 227)*

**Coped (Molding)**
*(page 202)*

**Corner Blocks**
*(page 44)*

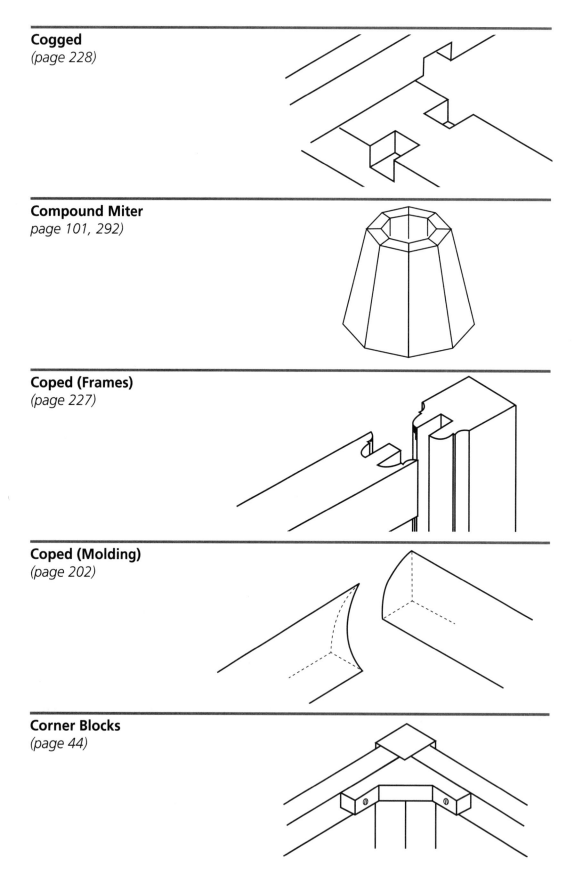

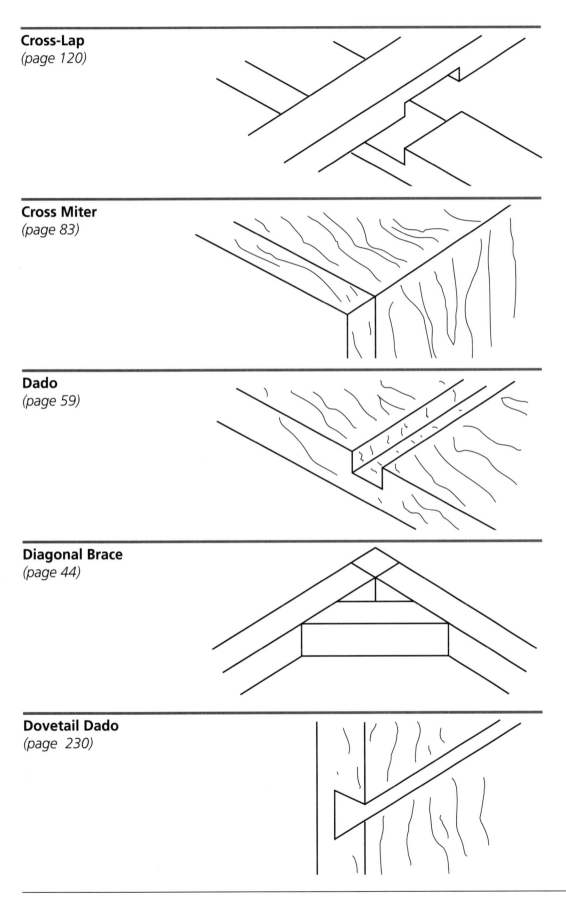

## Cross-Lap
*(page 120)*

## Cross Miter
*(page 83)*

## Dado
*(page 59)*

## Diagonal Brace
*(page 44)*

## Dovetail Dado
*(page 230)*

## Dovetail Groove
*(page 181, 183)*

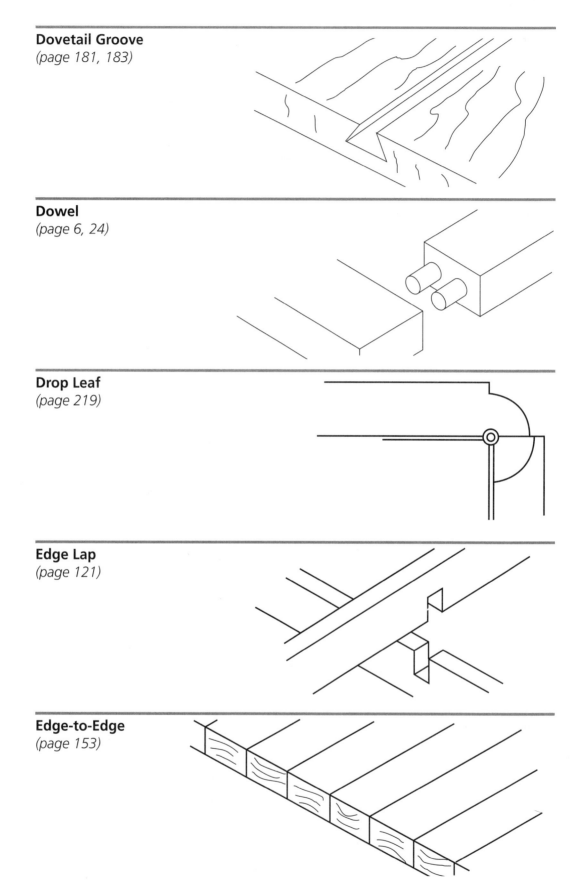

## Dowel
*(page 6, 24)*

## Drop Leaf
*(page 219)*

## Edge Lap
*(page 121)*

## Edge-to-Edge
*(page 153)*

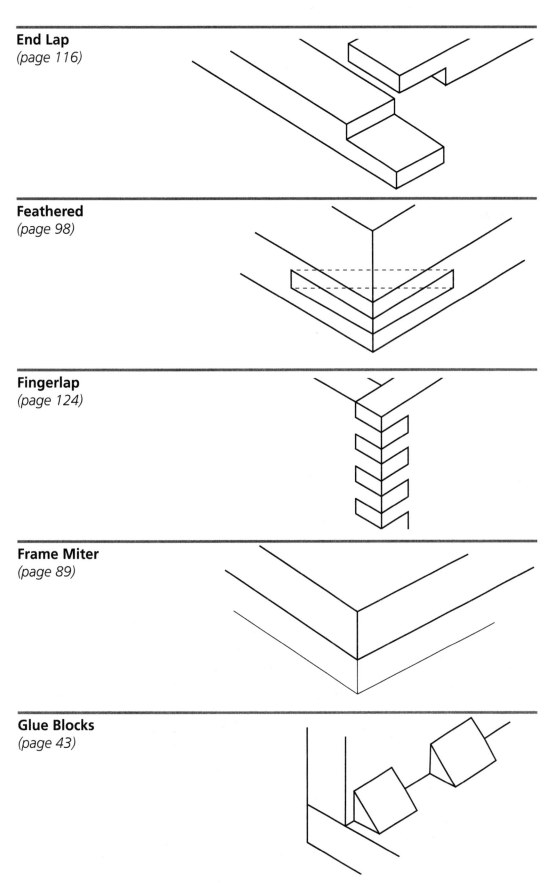

**End Lap**
*(page 116)*

**Feathered**
*(page 98)*

**Fingerlap**
*(page 124)*

**Frame Miter**
*(page 89)*

**Glue Blocks**
*(page 43)*

## Grooves
*(page 59)*

## Gusseted
*(page 54, 57)*

## Half-Lap Splice
*(page 119)*

## Haunched Tenon
*(page 151)*

## Lap Dovetail
*(page 181)*

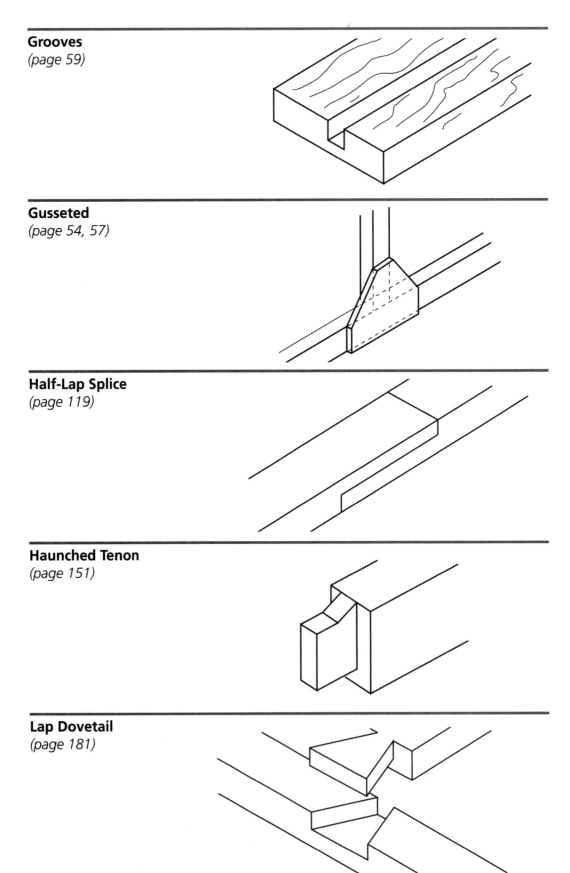

**Lap Miter**
*(page 118)*

**Lock Corner**
*(page 220)*

**Lock Miter**
*(page 114)*

**Middle Lap**
*(page 119)*

**Mitered Tenon**
*(page 150)*

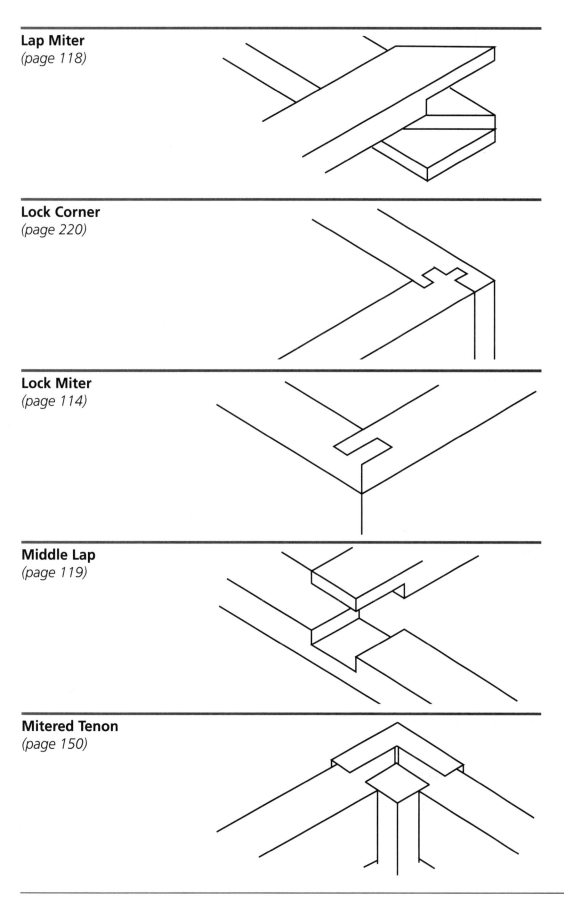

**Mortise Tenon**
*(page 132)*

**Multiple Dovetail**
*(page 170)*

**Open Mortise Tenon**
*(page 141)*

**Pegged**
*(page 6)*

**Plate Joinery**
*(page 215)*

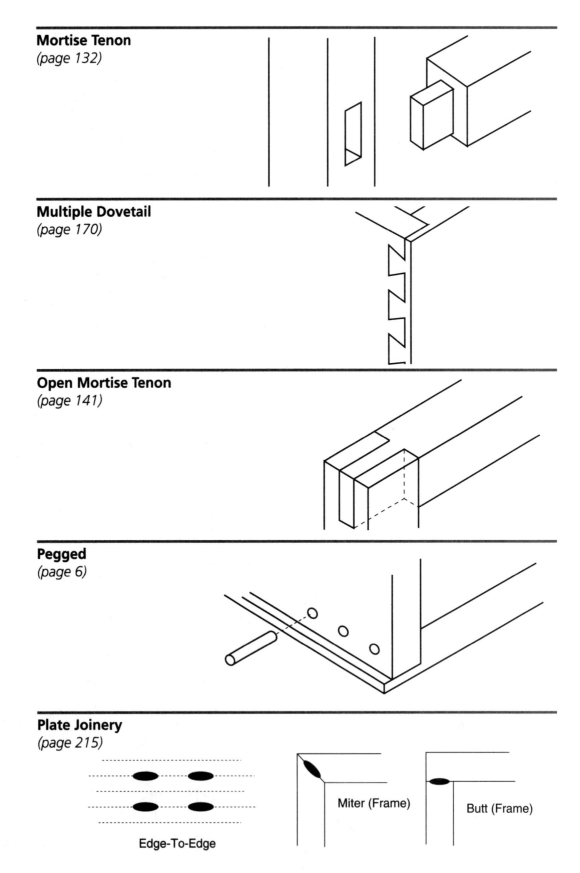

Edge-To-Edge

Miter (Frame)

Butt (Frame)

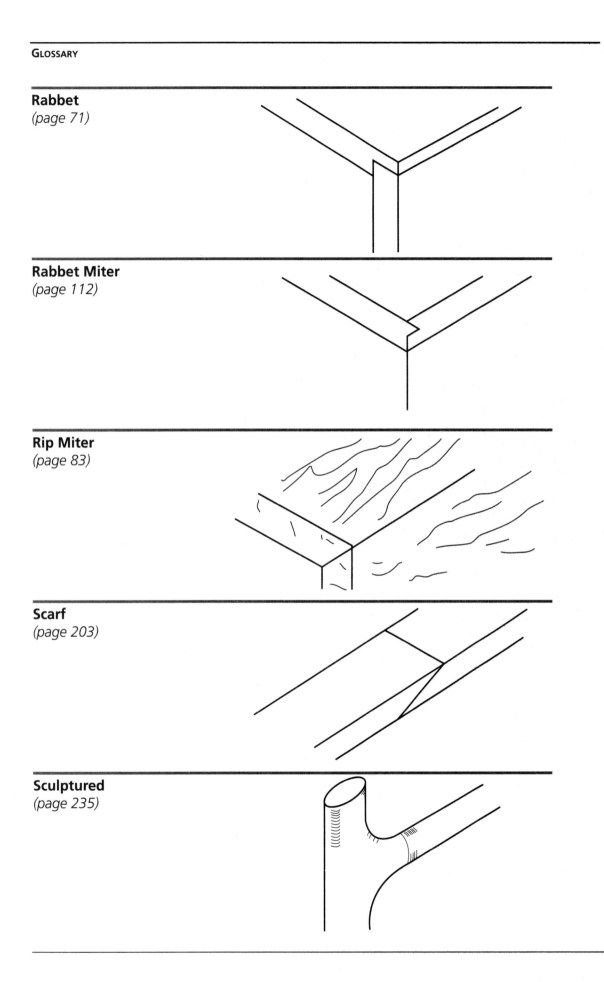

**Rabbet**
*(page 71)*

**Rabbet Miter**
*(page 112)*

**Rip Miter**
*(page 83)*

**Scarf**
*(page 203)*

**Sculptured**
*(page 235)*

**Segmented**
*(page 189)*

**Shaped**
*(page 165)*

**Shouldered Angle Lap**
*(page 120)*

**Single Dovetail**
*(page 187)*

**Splayed Lap**
*(page 118)*

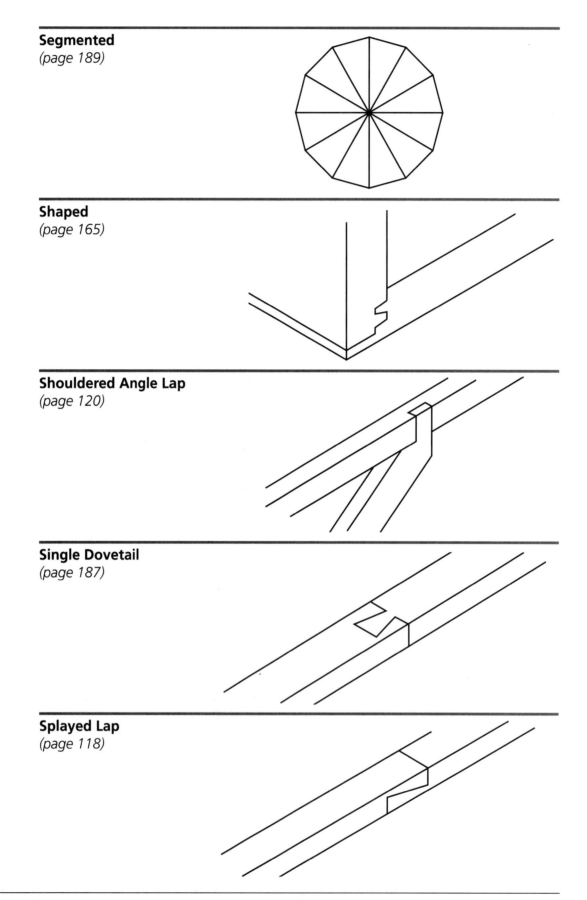

## Splined
*(page 160)*

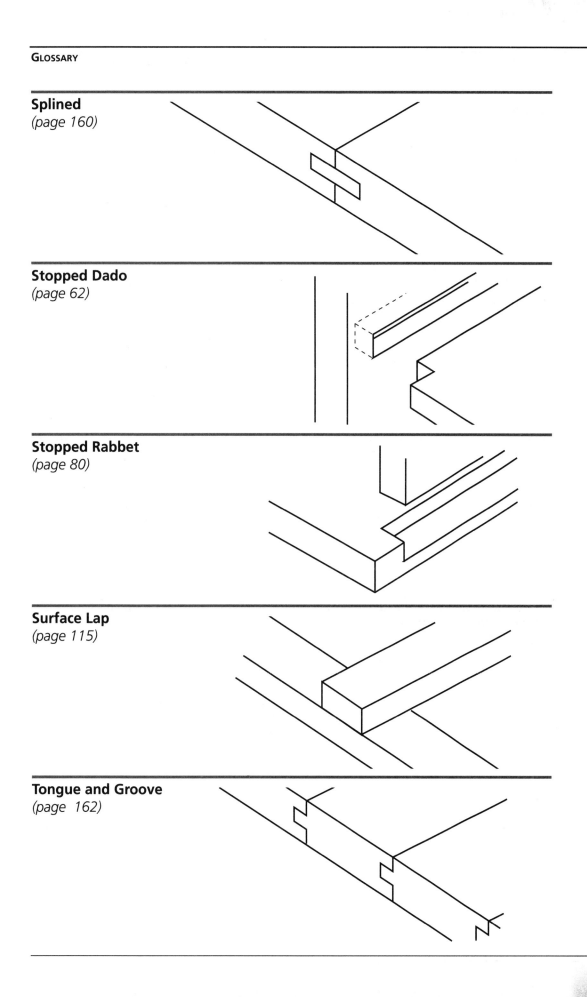

## Stopped Dado
*(page 62)*

## Stopped Rabbet
*(page 80)*

## Surface Lap
*(page 115)*

## Tongue and Groove
*(page 162)*

**Trestle Lap**
*(page 4)*

**Tusked Tenon**
*(page 149)*

**Waterfall**
*(page 222)*

**Wedged Mortise Tenon**
*(page 148)*

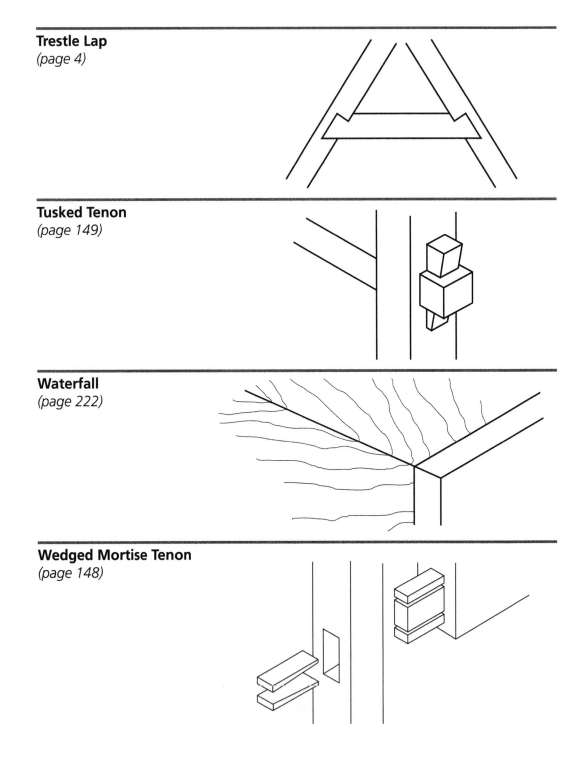

# INDEX

Crown molding, 198, 199, 200
Cut-angle factor, 193

**D**

Dado set, 69, 76-77, 111, 141, 144
Dado, *See also* Grooves, 59-70, 119-21
  back-to-back, 66
  corner, 68
  for cross half-lap, 120-21
  for edge half-laps, 121
  with electric saw, 67-69
  for lock corner joint, 220
  rabbet-dado joint, 221-22
  stopped, 66-68
Decorative spline, 166-67
Depth gauge, 117
Diagonal stretcher, 121
Divider, 14
  for spacing, 157
Door joint, 224-27
Dovetail, 169-88
  in drawers, 5
  face, 186
  half-blind dovetail, 176-79
  half dovetail design, 4
  keys, 188
  pocket, 186
  rabbeting, as substitute, 6
  for round parts, 186
  slots, 181-86
  splices, 186
  splines, 188
  T-joint, 179-81
Dovetail saw, 23, 95, 125, 173, 203
Dovetail slot, 181-86
Dovetail splices, 186-88
Dowling jig, 28-29
Dowels, 24, 26-27, 52-53, 99-100,
    129-30, 147-48, 156-60
  butt joints, 52-53
  for fingerlap joints, 129-30
  for frame miters, 99-100
  for leg and rail assembly, 253
  lock, 230, 254
  for reinforcement, 52-53
Drawer, 5, 72, 73, 251-52
  assembly, 251-52
  construction, 251-52
  front joints, 252
  guides, 247, 251
  rabbets, 73
Drilling, 18, 27-28, 99
  bit gauge, 28
  blade insertion hole, 208
  dovetail slots, 181-82, 184, 185
  dowel holes, 155-60
  drill press, 136-37
  in mortising, 136

Drop leaf table joint, 219
Drum sander, 203, 229

**E**

Edge-band, 47
Edge-clamp fixture, 285
Edge guide, 182
Edge half-lap, 121-23
Edge-to-edge joint, 153-68
  splined, 160-62
Egg crate pattern, 122-23
Electric saw, dado set, 69
End board, 168
End grain, concealment,118, 128-29,
    222, 264
End lap. *See* Frame half-lap
End strips, 161
End-to-end half lap, 119
Epoxy cement, 268

**F**

Face dovetail, 186, 187
Faceplate trim. *See* Front frame
Fasteners, mechanical, 45-46, 94, 286
Feathering, 98-99, 135, 173
Feed-block, 138
Fence, for drill press, 136
Filler block, 228
Fingerlap joint, 1, 124-29
Fingers
  and grooves, 126-28
  sanding, 129
Finishing nail, 40-41
Fixture, clamp, 280-81
Flat corner iron, 53
Flat segments, 193
Flathead screw, 35
Flat square. *See* Square
Flex tape. *See* Pull-push rule
Folding wood rule, 8-9
Frame butt, 51, 56
Frame construction, 151-52
Frame half-lap, 116-18
Frame joint, 46
Frame miter, 83, 89, 95-96, 97
Frame-panel construction, 258-61
Front frame, 61
Full lap joint, 115, 116
Furniture clamp. *See* Bar clamp

**G**

Glass panel insert, 152
Glue block, 43
Glue joint, 164, 222
Gluing, 43, 47, 54-56, 111, 115, 124,
    131, 150, 191, 194, 212, 265-69,
    271

Grain, 47, 52, 59, 71, 83, 191, 222
  direction, 47-48, 52
  end grain, 51, 222, 266
  pattern, 83, 190, 222, 237
Grid construction, 130
Grooves, *See also* Dadoes, 59-70
  centering, 159-60
  cutting of, 127-28
  in dovetails, 181-86
  for paneling, 226-27
  for splines, 160-62
  for tongue and groove, 162-63
Guide
  block, 96, 126
  clamped-on, 88
  line, 85-86
  slots, 86-87
Gusset plate, 53-54

**H**

Half-blind dovetail, 170, 176-79, 186
Half-lap joint, 115
Half-pin, 170
Half-round molding, 203
Handscrew, 271-75
  non-adjustable, 271
  standard, 271
Hanger bolt, 44
Hasp hinge, 220
Haunched tenon, 151-52
Heartwood, 154
Heavy duty clamp, 281, 282, 283, 284
Height block, 110
Height table, 125, 141
Hinge, 132
  back flap, 220
  hasp, 220
Hinge mortise, 133-34
Hinged bar clamp, 278-80
Hold-down, 137, 160
  for drill press, 138
Housed rabbet-miter joint, 112
Husked joint, 1

**I**

Inlay effect, 166-67
Interlock, 58

**J**

Jig, 94, 97
  doweling, 28-29, 158
  for egg crate patterns, 122-23
  for fingerlap joints, 126-28
  hole centering, 158-60
  mitering, 288
  for molding, 204
  for radial mortises, 138-39
  right angle, 290